SO-AIF-754

PADRE!

A PLACE WHOSE RULES REARRANGE YOUR OWN

Dear Angel,
Great meeting you!
Please enjoy!

Raven Moore

Love,
Rav
05/25/2014

BOOKS
by
RAVEN

Padre!
Raven Moore
Books By Raven

Copyright © 2013 by Raven Moore
All Rights Reserved

Copyeditor: Nicole, Owner of Ford Editing
Cover Design: Bethany Forcello
Interior Design: Tracy Atkins of Book Design Templates
Front Cover Photo: Amy Moore
Back Cover (print) and Last Page (e-book) Photos: Victor Shoup

All rights reserved. This book was independently published by Raven Moore under Books By Raven. No part of this book may be reproduced in any form by any means without the express permission of the author. This includes reprints, excerpts, photocopying, recording, or any future means of reproducing text.

If you would like to do any of the above, please seek permission first by contacting Raven at http://booksbyraven.com

Published in the United States by Books By Raven
ISBN 978-0-9897266-0-3 (print version)

Contents

To my sister,

AMY:

The funniest person in the world.

Books By Raven is Raven's own publishing company where she publishes her works and the work of others.

Acknowledgements

My Parents

Dr. Valerie Lundy-Wagner, the motivator

Dr. Fumiko Sakashita, the genius

Sayali Ketkar, the dependable

Solange Jorge, the visionary

Paul Sack, the compassionate

Antoinette Campbell, the go-getter

Sylita Thomas, the Internet master

Randall Martin, the kindred spirit

Kortni Lane, the best cousin ever

PREFACE

This is a true story, but most of the names of places and individuals have been changed for privacy. This story does, however, occur in Cote d'Ivoire, West Africa. Most of the people in this story are Ivoirien except for us Peace Corps Volunteers and some Peace Corps staff. I switch from formal to informal English in an effort to sound more natural as often as possible. It's the voice of Generation X. A few languages are used sporadically throughout this story, but enough context is given for you to figure out what you may not know. Don't worry. Any parts you don't understand will be clear by the end—that's the Peace Corps.

1   Les Ivoiriens

"If you don't help me, I'll be stuck here forever like this . . . No good, worth nothing. You're worthless, too. All of you . . . motherfuckers. Bogo too. I told you. You are the only one who can help me," Céline insists.

"What? What did you say?" Do I hear her right? She insults me somewhere between her Bèté and her French.

"The passport? I should do my passport, right?" she paraphrases. I find it hard to reply in a way that satisfies and I can't be angry. It is, after all, my fault she is like this.

Céline is dead now. Bogo is too. I think about this phone call from America to Céline in Cote d'Ivoire while reading the news from Antoine in an e-mail that says, "Not any good news to be had here in Cote d'Ivoire. Céline is dead."

White people, Europeans, or Westerners are not devils by design, nor am I sharing this story with you to perpetuate the stereotype that Africans are inherently poor. There is nothing special about the treatment of Africans in the history of time. Every region in the world has had its taste of power over other peoples and has also been devastated itself. The power structures we see today are not what the world has always experienced but, in fact, a new world order in a long list of world orders. We don't know if the civilization we call ourselves today will last any longer than previous ones.

The Ivoirien children who you see me living with on the cover of this book are poor, but poverty is not a permanent condition, nor does it have a recognizable face. Color was and is not often the reason for our mistreatment of one another. The Egyptians, the Moors, the Mongolians, the Romans, the Jews, the British, the Ottomans, the Dutch, the Americans, the Mandinka, the Mayans, and more; the list of conquerors is as diverse as those conquered. Ivoiriens in the Ivory Coast—La Cote d'Ivoire as it is called in West Africa—have it badly, but I'm not here to make you feel sorry for Ivoiriens. Feel sorry for me that it took me so long to figure out why I came here in the first place.

Shit. It forms in front of me without shame. Dark green and brown, the little baby chick dumps its load without thought of how its addition alters my view. It doesn't bother me like I thought it would, but it does throw me off. Where am I? I often find myself sitting here on this plastic prayer mat that doesn't belong to me, calculating how long I've been here and when I might go home. I am definitely no longer the same person as the one I was on the plane. Chickens and baby chicks. Goats and rabbits, too. It's a zoo, but it isn't. Peaceful and not so purposefully designed other than to keep the outside out and the inside in. I am at a house surrounded by high walls and thick trees that block out every part of my view except for the sky directly over me. As I squint in the blinding sun, I marvel at the evolution of things. Basic things have stayed the same like the hot of the sun, the red of the dirt, the green of the grass, and the taste of the food. I have found a way to change over these months, but the same conversations persist. The journey doesn't start here, but you get a warning first . . .

I am not White.

I am not White!

I am Black.

No. I am Black.

Why are you laughing?

What's so funny?

Do you know me?

If you knew me, you would know I am Black.

You've never seen anyone who looked like me before who called themselves Black?

I am Black.

No! I am Black!

I know that I am not black, but I AM Black.

Do you know what it means to be Black?

Passengers sitting next to me on the bus to the Ivoirien capital, Abidjan, start up in their refreshingly colloquial French I find to be so familiar in energy to that of Black English. "Il fait chaud, eh."

"Yes, it's quite hot," I reply back in French.

"I got some peanuts. You want?"

"Oh, yes. Thank you."

"Where you goin'?"

"Oh, to Abidjan."

"Me too. You live 'roun here?"

"Yes, in Zragbi. In Daloa." To this, she gives a pause and warm but wary smile. Then, the question I have been waiting for hits.

"Where you from?" Ah hah. There it is. The moment I learn to anticipate. I can hear that first, lonely drop of rain hitting a still lake off in the distance somewhere. The record player is screeching to a halt. Has the bus chatter stopped? Is it just my imagination or is everyone suddenly in on the conversation, leaning in for my answer?

"Je suis americaine," a response to which, while slowly leaning back, her mouth finally closes and her eyes set into an even deeper frown of confusion than when she began. She shows resigning dissatisfaction. The bus still has not resumed its barrage of noise. Maybe I don't fully understand the question? So, I stumble to add "noire . . . americaine noire" and with this the singer Alpha Blondy starts playing again, sounds of crickets in the distance disappear, and the bus party resumes. I have suddenly become the James Bond of Cote d'Ivoire.

'Black . . . American Black' that is. Unless I say 'americaine noire,' I get a disappointed and dissatisfied look signifying that I am not answering their real question. Ivoiriens wonder why my hips and lips are like theirs but have whiter skin and call myself American.

I am much happier with an invasion of questions than by naysayers who indiscriminately yell out, 'Eh, La Blanche!' I hoped this just happened to mean something else in some Ivoirien language and not the meaning of the French words I know . . .

People seldom ask me my name before applying their own, and if they do I then hear, 'Raven? Quoi?' After spelling it out, I get an 'Ahhh, Raaahvn' in a phonetically French pronunciation.

Depending on the ethnicity of my friends, my name is accorded with such in mind. I am "Acua" to the Abé, jokingly "Aishya Koné" after the Ivoirien singer to the Jula, and "Pahdré" to the Bèté. The latter ethnicity is one with which I spend most of my time.

In all, there are approximately sixty ethnicities in Cote d'Ivoire. I also have the names "Gomana Ngono" and "Toubabou Muso"; the first from the Bèté ethnicity and the second from the Jula one. Gomana Ngono and Toubabou Muso mean the same as the La Blanche mentioned before—'White woman.'

It is quite out of the ordinary indeed to find an Ivoirien who acknowledges me as Black right away. On one such occasion, I was going to renew my carte d'identité in the capital Abidjan. City Halls always being difficult to navigate, I can't depend on signs but rather my social ability. How to, while feeling and looking like or probably more so acting like an alien, approach a stranger and make them comfortable enough to speak to me so that I can get directions?

Ivoirien government buildings are grave at best. Austerely colored walls and shadow-filled hallways leave no signs that allow me to comfortably navigate the passageways alone. I approach an Ivoirien, female guard in a dark blue and yellow jumper by the gate. "Madame? Où est-ce que jeee . . . je . . . je peux aaaah trouve aaaaahhh le . . . le bureau aaaahh de faire aaaah la carte d'idente . . . d'identité?" I struggle.

"Carte d'identité? Oui. C'est là, là. Tout droit là." Just straight is all it is? Just straight is a wall. Where does she expect me to go? "Où ça?" I seek more clarification.

"C'est là. Là bas. Tout droit là. Et puis tu prends un droit." Straight and then I take a right? Okay, but then what? Getting directions is a riddle on its own. I have to learn to think that as long as I am going in the right general direction, I am home free. Okay. Straight. To the right. It will appear.

I am beginning to see that what she really means is go straight, turn right, and ask the next person who will in turn get me as far as the next person and so on. People here will at least put you in the right direction. In America, a person is usually expected to either know all of the directions or not to give any at all. It might be they that get you lost and potential blame for bad directions is to be avoided. In Cote d'Ivoire, the opposite is true. You get yourself lost and if you can't get yourself out of the situation, you aren't meant to be where you are trying to go.

On reaching a third person just coming out of an office, I ask again.

"It's here," they say in disbelief that I do not realize my point of destination is right in front of me. Forget about not having any obvious or existent office signs—I'm the crazy one.

It is a very small office; the back of the office is just steps away but separated by a semi-transparent glass window with a wooden frame. There is light behind it and shadows of people sitting there. I step forward as there is no door shutting off the partition from the waiting room. The Ivoirien man sitting at the desk reminds me of a relative as soon as I see his face.

"I can wait," I say, but he rushes me on in.

"Pas de problème," he insists. I do not, however, want to hurry anyone before me just because I am here so I shake my head 'no' back into the waiting area.

"No, no, no. Viens, viens, viens," he insists. Pleasant enough he is, but I still reluctantly sit down at his desk with the people who entered before me. They don't really seem to mind, and I'm learning that such a thing as private business in public facilities does not really exist in Cote d'Ivoire. In village hospitals, nurses see three or four patients at a time. Short of staff, not enough space, and limited time to help many people all demand this. As a result, everyone knows everyone else's business. The other guests in the office soon know mine.

"Yes?" The conversation switches between French and English as I obviously am not very good at one.

"Oh, I just want to renew my foreigner's ID card."

"Americaine?"

"Americaine noire," I emphasize.

"Je sais," he replies just as quickly without looking up. Did he just say 'I know?' You know? What do you mean you know?

"Peace Corps?" he pushes out with a French accent.

"Oui, Corps de la Paix," I affirm. I go on to tell him at which village site I am stationed and how the people there call me 'La Blanche' everyday.

"They know you are Black," he professes. I can't understand why they would not. It would not go over well if I ever tried to pass for White in the States.

"We did you a favor," he peeps out. What? Has the topic changed? Who did whom a favor for what? "You guys have so much there now. We have nothing over here 'en Afrique' but disease, war, and starvation." I am dumbfounded. This Ivoirien sees the African-American misfortune of slavery as a blessing in disguise?

But, how can I correct him when I know that had I been born a member of the Bèté, Baoulé, or Jula tribes with whom I now live, the reality for women here would force me to accept quite a different life. This is a country that was decolonized only recently—in my parents' lifetime. Many disparities remain.

'We did you a favor' keeps echoing in my mind. I wonder if my ancestors, who survived or succumbed to the months of horridness across the Atlantic Ocean, would want me to accept this point of view. I wonder if my ancestors were mostly angry with the Europeans who took them away into slavery or with the Africans who sold them to those Europeans in exchange for jewelry and other odds and ends.

Focusing on his tone and the fact that he uses the word 'we' the Africans instead of 'they' the Europeans, it becomes clear to me that my ancestors would be most angry for the latter. If indeed we African-Americans were given and not taken, in fact, then it makes perfect sense that I am now again being rejected as the man here is displaying with his rude comments.

There are so many things I never knew that I needed to know and that I never experienced but had to. And, all of that, in turn, even if obtained, would never make me African as they knew and know it to be. And, my proclaiming that I am 'Black' in Africa makes my existence no clearer for most of the Africans that I meet while in Cote d'Ivoire. What an African-American, so used to sticking out in the States, will find here is that in Cote d'Ivoire there is no need to say one is Black because everyone is so.

A Jolly Rancher doesn't walk into a candy store and say, 'I'm a piece of candy,' does it? Well, it doesn't walk or talk either, but you get the point. Such a statement just makes that Jolly Rancher stick out more and makes the other pieces of candy then ask themselves if that Jolly Rancher really is a piece of candy given its superfluous statement.

To the villagers, it's as if I am trying to create a new identity by calling myself Black. Their identities are not shaped by the differences in skin color amongst them, as in the States, but by their strong cultural differences. An observation of a characteristic that is more or less a meaningless commonality for them is too simple to state. Ivoiriens still have the languages and cultures, which we lost in coming to America as slaves, and so these types of diversity have naturally become the basis of African identities.

Gee, if only I could tell them the ethnicities of the Black people, the Africans, from which I originally come. That might do me some justice. Nonetheless, I don't even strongly have their single commonality so what am I really to do to convince them? Granted, I see a variety of colors here, but my color is rare in Cote d'Ivoire and therefore, the hardest with which to identify.

There are sixty ethnicities/languages in Cote d'Ivoire. What ethnicity could they even place me in if they wanted to? I still have commonly West African features in spite of my skin color, but I talk with a funny French accent and I don't speak any Ivoirien language from any of the towns or villages here. The fact that I need to say it and that they need to ask it and that even after I explain, it still does not place me in any ethnic category that they use to refer to themselves on a daily basis, shows true the fact of the matter.

For these people I meet in Cote d'Ivoire, Black is black—nothing more than color. There is no Black-White revolution going on here, as periodically happens in the States—the French do not walk around in the villages, or even in the cities, parading the economic and political stronghold they still have over Ivoiriens. They know they don't need to be seen to run the show. Why reinvent the wheel like those crazy Americans?—is what they know. Throw them all together, make them speak one language, and see how they fare? No. The French approach of control is different and, therefore, partially continues and partially creates a different sense of unity than I am familiar with—me coming from a history of ethnicities so forcibly clumped and then, later, necessarily united under one single nomenclature in the States—just Black.

Black American similarities are based on imposed reasons to be similar: curly hair, darker skin, shape of features, being slaves in a new environment . . . the Black American reference point began externally. We did not define ourselves but were stripped down and redefined. Black in the States is truly an identity in America, although it's not one here, and not self-explanatory because the spectrum is so wide—to the extent that it's not even in the same category as American 'White.' So many shades are made to fit inside of 'Black' that you have to ask yourself, 'What is Black in America?'

The physical diversity you find among Blacks in the States is not due to their obvious mixture with Whites only but also to their original diversity as separate ethnicities who were made to forget each of their separate ethnic cultures and languages before getting there. Slaves were ethnically intermingled upon collection at slave castles on West African ports to prevent rebellion among those who could communicate in the same language.

My claiming that I am 'Black' does little more for Ivoiriens than make them think I'm crazy. But, slinging the words White, Yellow, Red, or any other color than Black against a Black person in the States would be a just cause for an argument. Doing so means the assaulter is trying to break that Black person's historical connection, which they hold onto no matter the quantity of African ancestry in their DNA. Slinging the same words would be simply just in Cote d'Ivoire where color doesn't weigh as much as ethnicity and where those colors can naturally occur due to a diverse gene pool.

Africa is the gene pool. All humans started here. In fact, more than ninety percent of all human genetic diversity resides in Africa alone, even now after humans have already spread out all over the damn place. So, what is race? Is it real? Am I getting upset with this man because he might be right? Or, should I really be upset with myself because after all of this time I now realize that Black people in America have used slavery and color as their only historical imprints, with nothing else to show for their connection to one another except the culture they've had to piece together and innovate anew in order to survive?

Eventually, I recognize the truth. The images of slavery are still here. It really isn't the 'they' who have done something but we, Africans, who have done this to ourselves.

Promenading through my village site as I often do, to see all of the ethnicities and the sights with my still very National Geographic–impressed mind, I pass a house full of Jula women who share a surprise. So lively. So beautiful. Wrapped in multicolored cloths, boo-boos, and head cloths. I have to stop. With this action on my part, everything around me stops as well, of course. They stare at me and I stare back. What is that word I have learned in Jula for good morning? Shoot. Knowing the first impression will be the last, as I might be too scared to come this way again if I mess up, I give the biggest smile I can as I sing the phrase that finally bounces back into my head, "Ani Sogoman!"

Before I can play back and check in my mind whether I speak correctly or use the correct pronunciation, there comes forth the voices of more than fifteen women at once—"HÉRÉ SIRA!" A siiiiiiigh of relief dear friends, for the difference between three seconds earlier and now is scary. With the look they gave, I was gonna' get a beatdown and it would be in tomorrow's paper. How far a simple greeting in another person's language will get you! All fifteen of them beam bright with their beautiful smiles and I sense they are relieved, too.

Everyone goes back to work as if nothing has even occurred—except for one woman. She must be the head wife. She gets up from where she has been sitting, watching two younger women take turns, one downward thrust at a time, beating manioc with two long, large wooden objects into a mortar. Speaking Jula, she calls me over with her hands. Momentarily disappointed that I cannot converse with her, she starts to speak in French—the official European language of Cote d'Ivoire. Her ethnicity's tongue is as widely used in Cote d'Ivoire as French, if not more so, but no one bothers to stamp the word 'official' on it.

Speaking no more French than I do and not needing to in order to survive economically, she soon returns back to Jula with a few French words here and there as she can see it isn't really gonna' make a big difference which language she uses with my brand-new state.

The other women simply look up from time to time. She ushers me to the door of her house. Whisking the long door cloth aside, I see a teenage girl sitting in the dark in a corner by the bed with a black cloth over her head. The front of her shirt is soaked with sweat. There is no light in the room except the light from the doorway that forces its way in and onto her frame. She is shaking, but the woman insists that I look. She pulls the cloth off and the girl's hair, somewhat straightened, is pulled straight up on top of her head from the force with which the woman snatches off the cloth.

The moment reveals a girl so frightened that she looks at me as wildly as I am looking in clear disbelief at her. I can see her heart beating fast and her chest heaving in and out. In her severely psychologically damaged state, she stares at me the way slaves must have looked at their new American masters after being on a boat for months of disorientation and darkness. The woman switches back to broken French to explain that she has bought and brought her from the north. Another wife for her husband. Another servant for the house.

This and still more to be considered, weighted with the sudden feeling of infinite unknowns about where I am, given the frightened girl in the corner and the cavalier comment on the blessing of slavery, you might be able to form some idea of the pending two-year challenge. How will I for the next two years as a young person, as a female, as a self-identified Black person, as a single gal, as a middle-class American, and as a fresh-out-of-college potential brat, present and defend myself in this new milieu? All of those identities I hold have stigmas attached. All of them compete daily inside this one little body to be the dominant lens through which I see the world and subsequently make decisions as I duck, jump, and hide my way through this amazing thing called the Peace Corps Volunteer experience.

AFRICA THE COUNTRY

The journey starts here. Everything is happening in the 20's. On the 29th of December, in the last month of the year, in the last year of the 20th century, 23 of us all in our lower to upper 20's, coming from about 20 different states, get on a plane to depart at 22 o'clock, and I sit in seat 28B. I myself am 22 years old and we wait exactly 20 minutes before the airplane departs. Except for the 23 and some odd seats we occupy, the plane is empty. It seems like a prank, getting on a plane with 22 other volunteers I'd never known existed until nearly 20 hours earlier. The scenario does not differ much from that of going to prison. We have to wait for a decision about where we are being sent, seemingly up to the last minute, not really understanding what will happen to us until we get here, bunched with a group of people we don't know as if part of some sort of experiment. And, despite the terms and time frame set, never really knowing when we will come back home, if we will, and how. Maybe it is an experiment—taking preventive malaria medicine without knowing what long-term effects they will have on us. A doctor, who accepts the volunteer challenge, decides last minute not to even show up for the plane.

The plane ride is uneventful. Snuggling back into my seat under the covers, it is so cold in here and I am imagining how hot it really is outside as I stare at the clouds and the sun at eye level. The moment I step off the plane, the once cool atmosphere of our eight-hour plane ride disintegrates with the rest of my short-term memory. The air seals around my frame, completely and without a way out. The heat is searing me. My heart is starting to beat very strongly to pass the big waves of heat that will soon melt my brain if I do not get under shelter soon.

Blinded by the sun sitting on the grass in front of us, I don't know whether to continue the descent from the white stairs attached to the airplane or sit down and pray to the Sun God who is staring me so blankly in the face. The heat here is real. It is what makes everything exist. It pours over everything and there is no place in which you can hide from it.

I went to the prestigious Georgetown University, where I was surrounded by wealth that I couldn't understand—of Black, White, and Yellow, under the illusion that things were so easily attainable in spite of having none of the necessary things to attain them. I lack real knowledge of self and it isn't until graduation that I decide I need to know myself better if I am going to survive in the mostly White American corporate world I believe I want to enter at some point.

So, yes, this is why I think I am in Africa right now. Not the country, the continent. And, in spite of my education, I don't even know that Cote d'Ivoire exists until my interviewing Peace Corps Officer tells me that that is where I will be sent.

"Now I see what this is all about," Jason says and slips on his shades. Why is this the first and only thing that anyone dares to say as we step off the plane?

I descend the steps. I don't exactly know where I am, although I supposedly know. I have no idea what to expect. Before coming, people were feeding my fears with stories of endless war and starvation, animals running wild everywhere, monkeys swinging from trees, villagers running around in loin cloths, kidnappers waiting to take me and throw me back into slavery, eating all kinds of bugs for food everyday, wiping my butt with leaves, catching horrible diseases, and dying some mysterious death. Depending on what site a volunteer ends up in, one or two of those things do turn out to be not so far from the truth.

As we walk into the airport terminal to the baggage claim, a strange smell washes over me. If this is what the baggage terminal smells like, what new odor is going to be on my things? People are bringing animals for cooking, not the domestic kind, and other kinds of food on the planes. The customs officials start to check our passports so quickly that I don't even think I show mine. There is a cage to the left separating the customs area, where I am, from the baggage claim on the other side of it. I must now be entering either a bag terminal or a prison. Inside the cage are people of all nationalities waiting in despair as if no one cares that they are there and they don't know when they will be released. I see some Africans, including a lot of Arabs, and mostly Asians from Indian to Chinese. A woman appears suddenly flashing credentials that enable us to pass through quickly.

"Eeewwww, there is some sticky something on my bag . . ." I look around and all the other volunteers picking up their things have my same look on their faces, too. Yes, my bag has definitely been compromised. The wheels of my romantic journey come to a halt.

The smiles of several current volunteers waiting to greet us starkly contrast the faces of the many Ivoiriens standing around for what seems a very long time; waiting for their loved ones to appear at the same gate that we have just so expeditiously passed through.

"Welcome," a woman says in English while walking toward me, credentials still in hand. Who is this African woman who knows my name and speaks English? It doesn't occur to me for several hours that not only is she the head of the welcoming committee, but she is the Peace Corps Cote d'Ivoire, Country Director and most of all, American.

We are swept away on the bus where I suspect the truth of this experience we are about to embark on is somewhere deeply hidden behind the smiles of all the volunteers who seem cheerful in a place that, so far, seems to have nothing to be cheerful about.

It's kind of beautiful. The airport isn't surrounded by much. Passing humungous palm tree after palm tree, we fly down the road with the windows wide open and a few of us stare out the window in a trance. Everyone is nervous. No one is talking. We have just gotten off a plane that shows us an hour after hour display of the plane's image inching itself on the computer screen over the Atlantic Ocean toward Africa. No one imagines that we would actually land.

We are in a new place where few foreigners go. We have to understand what we see for ourselves on our own—Cote d'Ivoire country, West African region, on the continent of Africa. The hundreds of millions of people here get one mono-cultural, mono-linguistic, mono-everything identity fashioned from the likes of National Geographic, CNN, and Save the Children telling us 'this is Africa' or 'here' without any description of where exactly they are filming. The media feeds us most of our daily images of African countries as just one country where bad stuff happens, and we come away with 'naaah, that won't be much of a vacation spot.' Europe. Asia. South America. The Caribbean. Now, that's the ticket.

"There is war and fighting all of the time? Why do you want to go there? People get their arms chopped off. There is A.I.D.S. Don't go there," my friend insists in his Salvadoran accent.

"Isn't that a problem in one main area? Africa is pretty big you know?"

"No, it's everywhere. Watch out. I wouldn't be going there if I were you."

"What about San Salvador? Isn't it dangerous there?"

"Yes."

"Do you love your country?"

"Yes," he contradicts. What is the truth? What happened to the part that people love about these 'dangerous' countries that we don't get to see on the news? I get all kinds of mixed comments from family and Black friends.

"You can't make any money in Africa. You just graduated from college and a top one at that. You should be makin' money, girl! You'll die in Africa!" Doesn't anyone have anything nice to say about Africa? Here we are, Black folks, calling ourselves African-Americans every day and we don't know for what.

"It's a wonderful experience. How many people can say they have been to Africa?" sings the cheery voice of one White friend.

"You think so?" my mouth stays on the 'o' in 'so' and my brows raise.

"You will learn so much. So many languages. Different food. A new world. Plus, you are going through Peace Corps. Peace Corps wouldn't send you anywhere that is not safe." This makes sense. He has travelled a lot. Or, maybe his experiences were only great because he has never travelled as a Black, or as a woman. Either way, I'm going to take the risk and find out.

'Is this the Ivory Coast or the Ivory None?' sparks my brain as I stare out the window of the bus we take through Abidjan. I have a moment of temporary insanity and naivety in which I am surprised to find that Abidjan is actually a city. Where are all the elephants that give the country its name? Where are all the lions and tigers and bears oh my? There aren't even any trees out here other than the palm trees that line the highway. Where are all the huts and spear throwers? Where are all the beating drums? The only way I know I am in Cote d'Ivoire, is from the Ivoiriens walking along the streets, the Ivoirien drivers in every car, the Ivoirien-faced advertising boards along the streets, and the Ivoirien clothes that half the people are wearing while the other half wear Western-looking clothing. Many young kids wear beat-up Tommy Hilfiger shirts, Keds with holes, and worn-down baseball caps on their heads . . . Anyway girl, snap out of it! I don't know why you thought the sky didn't exist until you saw it with your own two eyes!

After an hour drive that feels like five minutes from all of the eye scanning I do waiting for a tribal warrior to jump out of the bushes, we arrive at a place. Some place. No one has any idea where we are and when we are going to get to see Africa. All of it. All at once!

We get to a mission along the beach in a place called Bonoua.

It's camp. They want to break us in. We are lodged in two large, separate male and female rooms. Half of us are in one room and half of us in another. When are we going to get to see Cote d'Ivoire? But, there is no when. Here it is. One-storied buildings create our rectangular space of stomping grounds. No one rests.

"I don't know 'bout y'all, but I just wanna' know how I'm gonna' get a coconut down from one of these trees? Do you shake it?"

"Shake what?"

"The tree."

"Ummmm," is the only answer that comes out of Steve's mouth.

"Shoot, I want a coconut."

"Maybe we shouldn't eat anything yet," Kaylin offers.

"Why not? It's surrounded in a hard shell. What can penetrate?" I walk off and come across a man sitting at a small shack on the outer edge of our grounds. He is surprised at first but smiles. My French isn't coming quickly, but I manage.

"Bonjour," comes out weakly. Before I can complete the phrase, I hear the kind response from not just one but three different directions at once.

"Bonjour!" Someone greets as they walk behind the shack in the distance, another man greets as he carves something in front of the shack, and a woman speaks while she cooks on a stool at a small black pot. We all stand or sit there staring at each other. The first man puts down his carving and walks up.

"Coconut," I add after pointing up. Only the first two syllables of 'coconut' mean coconut in French, but in a flash this forty-year-old man catches it and is now shooting up a tree. Excited. My first coconut straight from a coconut tree. The outer shell is green and oblong. He finds his machete and carefully hacks away at the top with his right hand as he turns the coconut with his left.

"Merci beaucoup," I thank him. He nods graciously and walks away.

A few buildings down, there are a bunch of women standing outside. I take on the task of hurriedly gulping down the sixteen ounces of water from my humungous coconut and rush over. Beautiful. Eight ladies draped over and around each other like sisters.

They are sisters. The religious type. They wear short afros and gray-colored skirts with clean white collars. Mahogany skin and ivory smiles. Each one rushes forward with these smiles, greets me in handshake, and shares their name one after the other.

Leaves from an invisible tree suddenly fallen to meet me. But, it isn't me. They are just naturally happy. So pleasant and merciful that I feel instantly welcomed without any pretentious threshold to cross over and be welcomed into—just into their smiles and hearts. They motion for me to wait. They are looking for something. One woman pulls out a piece of paper and every single section of it is used to fit each of their names and numbers. I do not know what I did with that piece of paper. Everything is a movie right now, not real.

Every day is full of activities and there is always lots of food. Umhm. They are fattening us up for the kill. I know it. There is no food in Africa. Everyone who watches TV knows that. They must have stolen this food to trick us into some fine hospitality we know cannot exist.

We have plenty of workshops. "Today, we would like to teach you about Ivoirien customs and greetings."

Two of our Ivoirien formateurs, our trainers of Ivoirien languages and cultures for the next three months, walk toward each other. The handshake. It is complicated and long but fun. It reminds me of how many Black men in America have a multitude of handshakes to meet, greet, and even say goodbye. The two formateurs then grab the top of each other's heads and knock the sides of them against the other's, one knock for each side! Ow! Such monumental ways to greet.

"Black folk do the same stuff at home," I state to no one and everyone.

"You're just trying to make something out of it," Bridget retorts.

Stunned. I mean, we aren't knocking heads, but we do invent many a cryptic handshake as they just did. We have certainly maintained some African customs; I just didn't really know it until seeing it with my own eyes.

"Do you have any Black friends?"

"No," Bridget answers after looking skyward to jog her memory. Uhm, uhm, uhm. I've come all the way to Cote d'Ivoire for this? To be told I am hallucinating? But, then again, how can I expect someone to understand who has not regularly been surrounded by people of African descent until now?

The customs role-play continues with two female formateurs who rush to greet each other. They have not seen each other in a long time. Making circles around each other, they take in big breaths and heavy sighs, joyful screams. They grab each other around the shoulders, the waists, and the arms and X-ray one another's figures, faces, and outfits and tell each other how great the other one looks.

With a sexy 'um hmm' strongly accented on the 'u' and a 'whaaaaa' having no relation to the word 'what,' this must be the same 'whaaaaa' that I use thinking it was 'what' all along. Cool. The expressions are certainly similar although deviating due to linguistic differences.

Screams and then "Girrrrrrl. I haven't seen you in such a long time. You look so good. Look at that dress. Gimme' dat. Oooh, your hair, girl. Oooh your figure, child. You look so gooood. Uhm, uhm, uhm," interrupting with many hugs and pleased stares at each part of the other person's frame. I am happy so far. Right at home. I have always been seen as loud and too energetic in the context of my majority White university or in my majority White high school AP classes. Here, I am not enough.

Many Americans, Black and White, get their education on what it is to be Black and White from TV since, to this day, we still live in largely segregated communities in America. So, how can we know what another group does? Good traits like watermelon somehow become bad traits and Black people stop eating it in front of White people. Being poor is no longer something that White people can be so some pretend they have money or dye their hair blond to fit the stereotype of real Whiteness. We grow up with these images fed to us of who we are instead of being allowed to just be.

3 AGBOVILLE

The drive away from Bonoua is long as we move further inland. Again, they don't exactly tell us where we are going. We pass many small villages along the side of what is sometimes a cemented road and sometimes breaks off onto a cleared and bumpy dirt road. Just when I think we will pass the next village after a long stretch of nothing but tall grass and gigantic trees, we stop. We are getting off? This is where we are going to spend our next three months of training? There is a large market with at least fifteen taxis on the side of it, mounds of garbage in the middle, and a restaurant shack close to where we stop.

"Just a break. This is Agboville, one of our smaller cities. The village is up ahead," says one of our formateurs.

No concrete. Just dirt and mud and pockets of dirty water that aren't only mixed with dirt. It smells badly and we are hopping and skipping from one dry patch to the next. It rained really hard and then dried up everything except for these pits of water everywhere. The merchants are so surprised and don't even rush out to get our attention or ask us to buy anything. We can't be real.

If every market is like this, I am determined to starve to death. I can see why they need Waste Management Volunteers. I am a Health Volunteer so what's that going to be like if this is the way things are? Cote d'Ivoire had been developing at the same rate and time as other countries back in the 1960s and then for some reason it stopped. Why? Why is it like this? There are no sewers to drain the water from the market, and every time it rains the market turns into a mud pool.

Up the way, past the market along a hill, there are other stores, but in structurally sound buildings not owned by Ivoiriens. Mostly Lebanese. The French had colonized Lebanon as well. Why don't more Ivoiriens own buildings?

I am ready to get out of there. No sense in us walking around just staring if we aren't going to buy anything. The outdoor merchants are probably wondering, 'did they just come to look down on us and leave?' Sarah is feeling a bit more adventurous than me.

"Oh, look. That store is nice. Let's go in there." Inside are a range of products and supplies, all French and very Western to our Western eyes, so not what we came to see.

"Let's get out of here." The familiarity inside suddenly alarms me that I must be missing out on something on the outside.

People line the streets. They sell all sorts of things. Some things we recognize and some things we have never seen before. Odd fruits. Gigantic root vegetables. We weave in and out of their goods set-ups.

"La Chinoise!" What on earth are they yelling now? I know they aren't referring to me because when I am alone I always hear 'La Blanche!'

"They're calling me Chinese. I don't really care. I'm not even Chinese. I'm Malaysian. They can call me whatever they want. Sometimes, they even call me White just because of my skin color," Sarah replies.

"You've heard them call you that, too?" Is everyone with light skin seen as White to Ivoiriens?

"But, I was raised by White parents and my culture is White. I think like a White person. I've never known any Malaysian culture.

So, I actually think of myself as White." I keep walking. What can I say to something like that?

"We're gonna' eat," our formateurs yell as we approach the van.

Gonna' eat? What we gonna' eat out here 'cept somethin' we might find in one a' those mounds of garbage over there? Two veteran volunteers lead us all to a restaurant shack that we first saw on the side of the road when we arrived.

"Chicken, beef, or fish?" is the only question the formateurs ask each of us. What comes is another mound—albeit a much smaller one—of something yellow called Futu. Futu banane. It is covered in sauce and meat and the sauce falls down around the sides of the mound.

"C'est le plantain," a formateur responds to my question-marked forehead.

"Leplantain?" hearing only one word as I sit mesmerized by the soft, yellow, mound. Is this candid camera? Why am I eating yellow silly puddy? Leplantain, leplantain . . . Let's sound it out. Leeeplaaan . . . Oh! Plantains! Wait. Plantains? How'd they make it look like this?

I look up to see if anyone else has dug in yet and off in the distance I see several little eyes from the outside poking in between the spaces that the shack's slightly bent pieces of wood offer. They are waiting for us to eat. Something is wrong with the food and we will soon provide these little children peeping in on us with plenty of entertainment as we fall down on the floor, writhing in pain. The only thing to tell me this isn't so is our formateurs who plunge in.

One formateur is foot stompin', elbows stretched out on both sides of his shiny metal plate. The oil from the food moisturizes his lips. He grabs a piece of meat with his right hand, sucks the meat completely off the bone, save a few tugs at the actual bone, and then tosses it to the floor! This reminds me of that place people go to watch knights fight on horses and eat large amounts of food on the sidelines with only their hands and drink wine in huge glasses.

"Eat," he says, and it shocks me because I don't expect him to start speaking. I'm still in a movie. This cannot be real. He continues to toss, place on the table, or sometimes spit bone after bone out of his mouth and onto the floor. Isn't he a formateur? I watch his every move and every munch.

"Once you finish the bone, don't put it back onto your plate." I start to mimic him and amazingly I cannot stop. I even start to crack the bone in between my teeth at the side of my jaw and suck the marrow out with my tongue while the edge of my lips lock around the head of the bone. The more I imitate the way the formateurs eat, the more relaxed I become. I feel more free and any bit of pretentiousness that tries to creep in, as often happens to people while eating, is now impossible.

If you eat like this, then you will show etiquette. If you eat like that, people will think you are high class. None of that applies here. Stereotypes or formalities do not get attached to food. I don't have to eat like a woman or a man or a person schooled in the world of fine dining manners. I just have to eat like a person who is hungry and happy to have something good to eat.

"I'm not eating this," one volunteer says as she secretly pushes her plate forward after moving the food around on it for several minutes.

"It doesn't look or smell bad. It tastes great. It just looks and feels different plus we are eating with our hands on top of that," I chat up a volunteer sitting next to me who slowly eases into eating as I do.

"I don't eat this kind of fish . . . What kind is it?" Ann spurns confusedly.

"I don't eat beef really," Kaylin joins in, as if she had forgotten this fact when the formateurs asked her what she wanted initially.

What am I gonna' do? Starve myself until April 2002? I'll just have to get over this fear of the unknown. I'll learn what to eat and what not to and how to prepare it—washing fruits and vegetables with water I purify myself. First boiling it, then straining it with a cloth, or filtering it in our big blue bulky filters later provided. Soaking fresh food in water with drops of chlorine helps too. All food has micro-germs on it, but if you are not used to those germs, they can make you sick.

4 OPEN SPACES

I n every part of my view is the color white. I see an immense circle of women in white shirts, dresses, and head wraps just standing in the middle of the street. Isn't white the color of death? Even their faces are smeared with white paint or chalk. But, as we approach, they start dancing and twirling white cloth in the air. The closer we come, the more beautiful.

The van carrying us slows so that we catch a glimpse of every bit of the crowd—stares but mostly smiles and arms waiving in the air. Hordes of children behind these women jump up so high in the air with big, bright smiles. People are cheering all along the sides of the street behind the women in white. This is our welcome to Grand Noyaré—our host village for the next three months of training.

We descend the bus one by one carrying our heavy luggage. There is a long canopy for us prepared and a large, rustic stage outside. Several token people are extremely dressed up, sitting in the front row of the rows of chairs set up underneath the canopy. Round hats have pieces of gold affixed to them. My unblinking eyes take in finely embroidered, long, thick blankets of cloth in dark blues and browns wrapped around male bodies with one shoulder out. These are our host family members. One woman wears a large, pink, silk booboo robe with a plunging circular neck line embroidered in gold and matching cloth wrapped up in archs and sharp points over and around her head.

An old woman comes up smiling energetically. The language she speaks is fierce. It runs smoothly from her tongue and at the same time full of n's, and ng's and m's with sudden k's. An 'o' for emphasis appears at the end of each song-filled sentence, like the 'yo' in Japanese. How sweet, but then instead of the greeting I expect, her smile fades and she grabs my bags and gives them to several children who quickly run away and she runs behind them. I don't know any older woman that can move that fast. In her 70s at least, she is short and with a honey-coated undertone in her autumn brown complexion.

My host dad is regal. He sits at the front of the canopy. He shows surprise on his face only for .008 seconds and then looks away. The same skin as my Grandfather—charcoal brown. His white whiskery mustache and saturated medium lips are the same, too. He is in his 80s. The same woman who took my bags is already back telling me several times what I imagine means 'sit down next to' who I assume to be her husband.

Us volunteers sit there for a long time on the other side of the great space in front of the stage. I look at my new grandpop secretively, pretending to look off beyond him. I admire the baby gap in his teeth. I like his cane, his clothes, his leather sandals. Everything on him is grand and made by hand.

A woman and a man in their twenties appear before us in the huge empty space below the stage. They have ankle bracelets on that have strings hanging from them that stretch down, gently touching the ground. The two dancers have little on up top or bottom, but everything that is important is covered. Dancing around and around each other. It is more of a competition than anything sexual.

Everyone is an observer and the observed from all points of

view. The crowd lines around the back of the canopy, along the sides, and up by the stage. They are staring back at all of us and it is a show for them on top of the actual show before us. No one has ever seen so many Americans before and none of us have seen so many Ivoiriens before in one place and with such eagerness to know each other.

The couple finishes their acrobatic, ballet-esque welcoming dance. Nice. Oh, but what is this? The host mothers are going to dance for us, too? After that running I saw my host mom do, I pay extra attention.

"I think they want us to get up," I say to Laura sitting nearby since I can't take any cues from my host dad. He sits as stone. Each mother comes out to greet their hosted child and each child has to get up to greet their new mother in return.

Each mother starts from a point at the stage across from us. I shouldn't diminish it to a gigantic soul train line, but that's what it is. Large crowds at both sides of the great open space cheer each mother on as the drums beat ferociously for them. One Abé comes from the left and another from the right. They dance with each other between the two crowds until the one out-dances the other. A pat on the back for a dance well done is apparently a tilt. Then, each host mom waves her respective host child up and over one by one. Steve gets up and does the funky chicken. Then, Laura does the 'what do I do now.' Everyone is incorporating any kind of movement that involves bent knees and flailing arms.

Finally, my host mom waves me up and over. Great. I'm last. Now you know me being the only American Negro and all, I have to represent. I stand up.

"Wooooooh, aaaaaaaah!" the crowd goes crazy before I can even get out there. It is a roar that they have not made for any of the other volunteers. Shoot, well I guess I can just sit down now since I've already gotten the applause? No doin'. So, I walk out there slowly to build back up some sort of suspense. I push and I pull. I stomp and I jump. I switch my body quickly from left to right, up and down. I am doing the best I cannot to do the Cabbage Patch or any other Black American dance. I hope this is okay. I hope I don't look stupid out here trying to do some imitation Abé dance! My host mom suddenly rushes toward me nimbly. Gee, am I that bad? Is she about to chase me out of Grand Noyaré? Should I run? Without a moment to think, and without yet seeing the subtle smile on her face, my host mother quickly whips out a white cloth from nowhere and pats the imaginary sweat off my forehead. Before I know it, tilt! Wow, this little old lady of 5 foot 4 inches just handled it. I'm not so heavy, but I'm not a new baby girl either. Tilt! Twice. The sky is suddenly down and then up again and the welcoming party has officially ended with a bang.

"Come, come, come," she must be beckoning in her Abé language. Apparently, our host families receive pictures of us beforehand, study them in minute detail, and by the time we get here they know us better than we know ourselves. People are coming from everywhere, under rocks, behind trees, dropping down from the sky, rushing toward us, and swooping the new children they've long awaited back to their homes.

Some volunteers get spirited off to one side of the long main road back to Agboville town and the rest off to the other. Boy, am I anxious. Nothing much is explained about what will happen from one event to the next.

The house now on my right is unfinished. Tons of bricks lay piled up beside it. To the left is another unfinished house with the basic structure done but no windows and no roof. We slide between these two structures to get to what will be the first of many places I will stay during my time in this country. Chickens run in and out of these tiny passageways and host mom abruptly shuffles forward shooing them off, bent over, clapping her hands together, rushing back and forth in this tiny little space to get the chickens out of my way. One chicken pauses at me and clucks, "Lady, who arrrre you?"

The courtyard opens up from the tiny passageway. There, I find even more chickens. Are these chickens running around screaming to get away from me? They are certainly more scared than I am. No doubt, the increase in head count means a more rapid decrease in theirs.

The central part of the courtyard has small blocks of trees

stacked up in a little pile. There are miniature hand plows leaned against the back of the building to my left—the unfinished building across from the only house done. Three iron poles support an overhang and underneath it are three large bricks to the left of the front door that serve as the stove. They cook outside all of the time? Dirty rags lay up against the windowsill behind the brick-laid stove. Let's just call the stove the Bricks. My host mom makes way for me to enter the house. Or, so I think. She suddenly jumps back in front of me, squeezing past me. I step in soon after and stand there. The walls are all light green including the high ceiling.

"Come, come, come," she says hurriedly in Abé and runs back up to me to pull me along by the arm. She is half my size or so it seems because she is always leaning forward and over in preparation to do whatever. I scurry forward at her quick pace. Off to the left and down the two-foot, light-green-painted, narrow hall is my bedroom.

Host Mom throws my door wide open. She smiles and talks the entire time and I have no idea what she says. Okay. I can get that hand gesture there. Oh, you want me to go here? Sit here? Be here? Her smiles reassure my actions.

Of course, the first thing that my American self notices is the humungous roach off in the corner making a home for itself.

"That thing, that thing," I say and point. "A roach, a roach," I announce only a few seconds from panic and kill-the-roach mode. Wait a minute. What's wrong with me? Do I think that somehow my words are going to miraculously morph into Abé? Well, at least she can see my gestures. I point some more and look back and forth between Host Mom and the roach. She looks at me and looks at the roach and then looks back at me with a confused face.

"Aaa, eh, eh, aa," Host Mom speaks to the roach as she proceeds to shoo its gargantuan body down the corridor with a small, straw broom the same way she shooed off the chickens. This is a bad sign. Will I have to pet it, too? Man. I follow her. I know she can't be serious. I know she is going to kill this cockroach, but no. Host Mom simply persuades it out of the door, throws the broom down, and on about her business.

I rush back. I duck down swiftly underneath the bed and do an eye scan from left to right. I look in all eight corners, ceiling to floor. I stick my head out the window to see if any friends are bringing up the rear. Nothing. I finally sit down on my bed. My bed. No volunteers on other beds in the same space with me. I'm in my host family house, in my room, on my bed, and maybe I'll have a few little four-legged roommates but oh well.

Right before my head can hit the bed, four kids step in and sit down on the bed as well. I precipitously sit back up. Nice. All the little brothers and sisters I never had. My body is still tense with disbelief that there isn't another roach hiding in the room, but I manage to squeeze out some French to my new little sister poised beside me.

"What do you think of roaches?"

"I think they're beautiful."

"Roaches are beautiful?" Maybe she didn't understand my poor French. Still, she blankly nods an affirmative "yes." What else, at which my American mind has been trained to repulse, will suddenly become inspiringly beautiful?

But, my new little sister is certainly beautiful and no one anywhere can refute that. She is very calm and controlled and, no doubt, a young scholar. Her posture is elegant, her sudden smiles full of a trillion sun-beamed mornings, and her skin is a deep, bittersweet chocolate. Her hair is half an inch of the tightest, microscopic black curls. Real curls. You have to get close to see. They do not refract light in the same way as straight hair so their true shape is not easy to perceive.

Her naked eyes hold the answers to all questions in the universe. She stares. Maybe it's because I'm staring. Maybe she wants to hang with her new big sister. After the roach commentary, however, I'm sure I'll be her apprentice.

"Eeoeonmngrarraaa . . ." Host Mom's yell breaks our trance. I step out and walk down the narrow hall followed by the children. Host Mom runs toward me. The kids file out the front door into the sunshine.

"Eeoeonmngrarraaa," she says again. That's what I hear at least. I can't parse that. The sounds are a bunch of e's, o's, ng's, m's, r's, a's, and y's. No hard sounds anywhere. The illusive vowels and soft consonants are jellyfishes lightly swirling around my head.

When that doesn't work, she begins to show me as she speaks; taking both hands to her face as in prayer, opening them up toward her only, and moving them up and down very quickly in front of her face.

"Eeeongngngmrrraaa," it comes again in another version.

She takes her right hand and puts it over her left arm as if she is frantically wiping something off of it. Oh, I don't smell that badly, do I? Just as I figure out what she means, she runs outside again and comes dashing back in with a purple and yellow striped bucket filled with water. She places it by the door, gives me a cut of soap, and ushers me out the small, back bathroom door. This must be extra water just in case. Time to take a shower. My mother knows that I am stinkin' and it must be true. Our travel started early this morning. We had been on that bus for hours.

I don't think I want to know how it is when it really gets dark. There are two street lamps in the entire village and the light that comes from some houses. And, they are houses. They are not shacks or mud huts or straw-roofed circles.

I run back to gather my things—a tube of toothpaste, a hairbrush, and a washcloth—and run back to the door where I take up the bucket and crouch down out the tiny back door. Not too many African-Americans could have originated from this ethnicity because everything they have here is narrow and short as hell.

Peeping over the wall on the left side, I see the toilet and that's all it is—a toilet. No seat cover. No water tank that flushes away the water. There is only the toilet bowl itself right smack dab in the middle. I don't need to go now and I am glad. Walking back over to the shower side, I open the door and discover that there is no shower. No showerhead. No shower hook. No shower cord. No soap holder. There is nothing at all in here except space and a wire along the back wall where clothes are hung.

What is that in the corner? A curly, wiry clump of yellowish-white hair sits in the corner. It's too coarse to be human hair. What, are they washing their sheep in here, too? A light draft smooths over my shoulder and when I turn around still with the shower door in hand, I see my host mom with the back door cracked open. How long has she been standing there? A smile suddenly breaks across her face. Just then, some tall young man with nothing more than dirty slacks on and muscles, comes in from the outside. He is returning from the farm fields, but my mother shoos him away the same way she shooed away the cockroach and the chickens. Is that my fine, new host brother? Ow.

A bucket. Some soap. My washcloth. I place my toothbrush and toothpaste on a tiny, tiny stool and then begin. The only time I ever used a bucket of water, it was to throw it at someone. There had been showers at Bonoua. Not anymore. Okay. Dip the rag in the bucket. Soap it up. Lather. Oh. That worked. Okay now, lather some more. I dipped the rag in and oh, shoot. My only bucket of water was getting cloudy from the soap. Shoot. Okay. Put the soap down.

Crash! A sudden thunderous noise comes rolling down the aluminum roof. Aaaaaah! What the hell is that! My eyes widen and dart. Silence. Okay. Let's start again. Scoop some water into my hand and rinse the rag away from the bucket of water. Oh. That worked. Okay. Take soap and lather again. Do this several times.

Crash! Roll! I crouch down in fear again, looking up and around slowly. It is a sudden tumultuous noise of three bodies that have been thrown on top of the bathroom roof and are currently rolling down it. No, no, no. Somebody has got to come out here and get me. What the hell is this?! Crash! Roll! Thunder!!! Now coming more rapidly again! And, again! Maybe it's raining, but the sun is still out and I don't see any rain when I stand on my tiptoes to look over the shower door to the outside. Crash! I crouch down more, so afraid that the roof will cave in and several dead bodies will crash through the roof and onto my head.

I am crouched just low enough to see underneath the door and on the next crash and boom, a little lizard jumps down from the roof, stares back at me for a second with its wrinkly neck, sticks its tail back at me, and scurries away. Aw shit, man. Those damn lizards crash-boom through my entire 'shower.' I throw on my old shirt and a towel around my waist to step into the house.

My host mother steps in the front door just as I'm running down the hall and her head turns as I fly by her. She's gotta' think I'm crazy. Finally, the stereotypical, booty-tight American manifests itself. Relax, Raven. I throw some powder on to slow the sweat from forming that always ultimately does in this heat, no matter what time of the day, and stroll back on down the hallway. Grandpa is sitting in his chair. The mother steps in and encourages me to sit with him.

The rain. Clouds quickly grow dark as each drizzle commences to turn into a rain shower. Everyone has disappeared off somewhere. It is a temperature-less rain. It doesn't blow cold, only interrupting our sense of sound as we are sheltered from it. Out of the silence, an unspoken friendship forms.

"The Abé believe it's good luck when a visitor comes with the rain," says fine Host Brother, peeping in the front door, unfortunately with a shirt on this time.

The next morning, through some more good old, bootleg sign language, we figure out that I need to wash clothes. They have an indoor washer machine? Awesome. My new mother, little sister, and all of her little cousins, brothers, and sisters follow me over to the washing area—a stool, a basin, and some water. No washer machine . . . No toilet . . . No shower.

It takes seven people to wash clothes—mother as the managing director, little sister as the instructor, an audience of four children wondering why the hell this grown-ass woman needs them to figure out how to wash her own clothes, and me the apprentice.

I sit down on the tiny stool with a large, round, silver basin on the ground in front of it. I throw all of my clothes in the water and watch them sink into the water. My mother brings a big slab of white soap and then stands to watch. Does she want me to wash myself again outside, right here and now, using my soap and clothes as a rag? What I do now? Where's the Tide? My little instructor grabs the soap out of my hands.

Standing on the other side of the basin, she plunges one hand into the water, and comes out with one of my shirts. Little instructor takes one end of the shirt with her left hand and quickly bends down to take up the soap with her right. She throws a moment's bit of a glance my way and crosses the soap back and forth over the end of the shirt once. She is now in the position she began in, with shirt held out in one hand draping into the basin and soap up in the air in the other. She looks at me again. Throwing the shirt up slightly, she grabs a bit farther down the shirt and crosses the soap over the new section. She looks at me a third time, goes farther down the shirt crossing soap over it again. She gradually reaches the end, and then flips over to the other side and does the same.

Little instructor hands over the shirt thinking that I will know what to do next. Momentary confusion passes across her face upon realizing that she has to give me a full demonstration. She works at the shirt until she is satisfied she has gotten all of the dirt off.

You can see the brown, sandy earth that had floated up from the ground and plaqued itself to my clothes, coming off in the water with every smack of one part of the shirt to another, the soap gliding down into the water. She throws it into a second empty basin, reaches back into the first, and then thrusts the next item toward me. I'm sure if I could have understood, 'I'm not washing your clothes lady,' in Abé, she would say this.

I finish and Host Mom pours buckets full of new water in the second basin. As I rinse each piece of clothing, my instructor hangs them. Her little brothers, sisters, and cousins crouch down by the basin still watching me but looking up every now and again to see what fine piece of clothing I hang up next. They are clean, they smell good, and I did them—the human washing machine. A new sense of independence creeps up on me as I can now literally wash my own clothes. No more dryer either—only the heat from hanging in the sun for the next 2.25 years.

The volunteers seem to drink more than talk about what is odd in their new situation. I came to Cote d'Ivoire to get away from being the minority, to see how it feels to be in the majority. I doubt the White volunteers came for the reverse reason. They now, however, have my old affliction. Do they ever think about why they are getting together so often? Not even French people are in sight. Do they form the thought in their mind that they are now a minority or do they just think, 'Man, everyone is Black here'—the emphasis on the larger numbers of Ivoiriens as the oddity instead of themselves as what's out of place?

Grand Noyaré is empty. All of the Abés have long since gone off to the fields to work. I don't want to go to the village juke joint where the other volunteers are sure to be on a day off from training. The owner doesn't sell nearly as much beer as he does with us around. I'm not compelled to participate, however, not even after seeing the 1950s-shaped soda pop bottles. When did that shipment come in?

Instead, I take a stroll down the path that draws from the back of my host house. When I get to the edge of our backyard and the beginning of someone else's, I see some kids running my very happily to see me . . . Oh, all of my new little brothers and sisters. The happiness is mutual. It is a relief to be around kids. They have not yet lost the ability to express emotion and fun through their eyes and actions. Language barrier? No problem.

They reach me and stand excited. Some with basins completely balanced on their heads full of some spoil of the fields that I have never seen before. Others have whole parts of trees on their heads to fuel the pots that feed all of our bellies. Umh, are those machetes? But, I look down at all of them smiling up at me and realize that there is no TV or any other type of outward influence to make them aware that machetes could be used for anything other than cutting through thick forest, cutting down trees, or anything that goes in a cooking pot.

Long, brown, chiseled calves and sinewy, strong arms from sweeping large objects off the ground and onto their heads; they have stomachs cut unlike any five-, seven-, or ten-year-olds I know. The little Olympians walk barefoot on anything and their strong feet tell the tale. When they smile, all of the muscles in their necks stand up and smile with them. I'm happy and they're happy, but how long can we stand staring at each other?

"Tu aimes les photos?" I ask all six of them. They start to bounce up and down in the air. Some put their basins down and quickly pull the basin-stabilizing cloths and rags around their heads off as if the camera will magically appear in my hands next. A whole chatter begins.

"Attends," I say while giving the signal to wait, raising my hand up in the air. I run back in the house and come dashing back out as excited as they are. It becomes their gift after a long day at work in the fields and they are so ready to throw down all of their fieldware to strike up a pose.

I take one shot. Some are not ready yet and frown after they realize I have already snapped one. Others can smell the shot coming and throw their arms around each other, smiling and beaming for the shot. They need a background. Off in the distance I see a wall of wood, with branches and chunks of wood shooting up and off in all directions, creating spaces in unpredictable places.

"Come," I say in English not caring. They get it. They take pictures in front of it. It draws out the warm red and brown tones in their skin. The straight lines of the wood enhance the perfect curliness of their hair, millions of ringlets per square inch. They clobber over each other, stand apart facing each other slightly tilted toward me, or stand straight up proclaiming in body language, 'here I am!'

"Here. You here. Over here," I say to each of them positioning them. They don't understand, of course, and do their own thing once behind the wood. Of course, they stick their precious faces, eyes, lips, noses, and hands through whatever spaces they can find and what results is a maze of eyes and hands that blend in with the wood. The longer I look at the scene the more beautiful, brown eyes I find. Life is everywhere and weaves itself through everything.

Malaria is also something that weaves itself into everything in Cote d'Ivoire and around which Ivoiriens must live. For Ivoiriens, malaria is as common as the common cold and deadly. Each and every one of these little kids has had to battle with malaria from the day they were born. If us volunteers didn't have our anti-malarial medicine, most of us would be dead by now. Our immune systems are not familiar with it. I don't know why Ivoiriens aren't given the same medicine we, as volunteers, are. The preventive medicine we take is not a cure, but it sure does make life more productive when you're not struggling with a deadly disease your entire life! Supporting Ivoiriens to get rid of the mosquitoes that spread malaria, as most countries around the world have long since done, would be the best idea.

Malaria used to exist all over the world. Now, it is mainly in Africa. Don't walk around in Cote d'Ivoire at night with short sleeves and shorts on for too long. And, make sure you sleep with a mosquito net. No mosquito can get through those tiny, open spaces. Oh, and don't forget to take your malaria medicine. And, don't forget which day you usually take it if you aren't taking the daily type. There is no cure for malaria although there is preventive medicine to keep it at bay in your system. And, make no mistake about it. If you go to a country with malarial mosquitoes and you are bitten, then you have malaria in your blood even if you never actually get sick and you won't be allowed to give blood upon return to the United States for some years after that.

Eighty percent of all malarial-related death cases are under the age of five. In other words, these happy children before me have me beat on any day of the week. Their immune systems have already had five years of preparation. I haven't even been here a year yet. My first few months in Cote d'Ivoire are equal to that of a newborn.

I'm in health training class when something begins to squeeze my heart. Mysterious chest pain it is. Am I having a heart attack? A little while after I take my malaria medicine each day, I have this same pain not too long after. Clock work. I particularly notice that if I take the medicine in the morning on an empty stomach, then the pain is even stronger for the next couple of hours. My remedy, in any health crisis, is usually more water and exercise. The stronger my heart is, the better it can do whatever it needs to do to get these meds through my bloodstream, is my theory. I can't just stop taking the medicine, right?

I get up early the next morning to go for a run, sneaking down the hallway in the dark. Host Mom and Dad only have a curtain for a door so I tiptoe by, sliding along the opposite wall so that not even my feet are noticed from the space underneath their dark purple curtain. I stealthily squeeze in and out of the bathroom and then I'm off to the paved road dividing the two sides of the village. If Agboville is in one direction then the other direction can't be so much different. I usually see Grand Noyareans taking this paved road in the opposite direction of Agboville when they leave to the farm fields each morning. I'll go this way.

I start walking first until the road winds out of Grand Noyaré's view. My eyes dart. What will attack me first? The formateurs say there are no lions or gorillas out here, at least not in this area anyway, but I can't be sure. Shoot. If I were a gorilla, this looks like where I would be.

This is a good pace. Nice and easy. The earth here is made up of a smooth, reddish-light brown, sandy dirt. There are humps here and bumps there and the sides of the road fall off into high grass so green, thick, and plush that it can no longer be considered grass. It is pretty much a forest to your right and a forest to your left and what lay ahead is indeterminable because the road winds every five hundred feet. Maybe this isn't a good idea. But, I can still see most of the sky. Trees aren't obstructing my overhead view, but if a gorilla decides to cross the road I am shit out of luck. I hope I don't come across an agouti—those possum-sized, long-snouted, fierce-fanged, heavier-than-a-small-child, hairy, gray-bodied, long-tailed animals that Ivoiriens often eat . . . Okay. I've had enough. It has been ten minutes.

I run every day at 6:00 a.m. and usually no one has been up, but lately I've been noticing that the bathroom is cleaned to perfection before I even slip in there, the grounds around the houses in our courtyard have already been swept smooth, and my breakfast is brewing on the Bricks. But, I haven't seen anyone yet.

"Good morning Baya-Gey!" 'Yet' I said! Gosh damn! And, she can't take that smile off her face at no time of day. My host mother catches me as I'm walking out the front door on her way in.

"Baya-Gey?"

"Baya-Geeeey," she repeats warmly and smiles even more as she is bent over looking up at me, head switched to the side. I continue to look down at her and she keeps her posture smiling up at me. It's conveying a question this time, however. I can see now that her smile means something different every time she does it.

How am I going to explain that I'm having heart palpitations and have prescribed myself with running? She looks down at my shorts as if I am in my underwear since every woman in Grand Noyaré and everywhere else we go, wears pagne wrap dresses.

'Where are you going?' are the words that spring into my head as her eyes peer deep into mine, the eerie smile still on her face.

I step out the door and begin to jog in place to show her. This takes her head aback for a second or two, she glances up at me, scans me up and down, nods her head a few times, mumbles something which resembles a 'well okay' shrugging her shoulders, and then walks inside with her normal bent over, hurried walk.

I was not out of shape coming here, I get a good sweat every part of the day in this omnipresent heat, we walk everywhere, there is no refrigerator for me to wake up to in the middle of the night and snack, and my body is still learning how not to reject, on an every-couple-of-hours basis, the new things I introduce to it. However, weight loss, something all of the volunteers now have in common, does not equal a strong heart. The only way I know my heart is strong is by getting out here every morning and dealing with whatever comes on a run. Agouti, gorillas, Tarzan, Atila the Hun, and all of that.

Ten minutes down the road does not get me far since I'm too scared to break out fast . . . out here . . . like that. My fears and the looks from a few passersby always get the best of me. More than a week goes by when I wake up one morning to find my host mother and brother waiting at the front door. Did she ask her grandson to run with me? He is tall, in his late 20s, and extremely polite.

He attempts to say some things to me but mostly just pleasantly smiles and looks away. Awkward. With his fine, strong ass. Umh. We start running. He gauges my speed and follows suit. I run a little faster this time, more confident being with someone from here.

No words are exchanged, although I would prefer not understanding to listening to nothing at all. We pass one or two people along the way, but they are few and far between. They don't even look at us. Before I know it, we are very far out. A lake or a river emerges. I can't tell because it disappears into the immense trees and foliage that hang down and over it. A mist hovers here and that combined with the autumn colors make it immensely beautiful. We reach it and my brother automatically stops. He has either had enough or knew from the beginning this was as far as he was going to go.

We run a few more times in the morning, but after a while the lake becomes limiting. This lake is not that far from Grand Noyaré. I want more.

One evening, my host mother throws a mat down in the courtyard for me and light brown dust flies gently up into the air and settles down around it. She is smiling as usual and strongly encourages me to lie down. The moon is big and instead of being a half-moon standing up, it is a half-moon lying down. From my new position on the earth in Cote d'Ivoire the moon fills up in a different direction. Is that the same moon? Is there more than one?

The moon I am used to has become another moon. The stars I am used to have become some other stars. These stars are large and brilliant and so many that they fight with each other just to reserve their spots up in the sky.

"One, two, three . . ." I count them with my finger, but before I can even finish pronouncing the 'f' in four, everyone starts screaming.

"Stop!" Host Mom yells in Abé as she rushes toward me, grabs my hands, and pleads. Counting the uncountable is bad luck. I'm embarrassed and I go to bed.

Host Mom has been proudly walking me to church every Sunday morning and keeping her own church to herself. She simply smiles in that eerie way and pushes me off. I figure this out early one morning when impending diarrhea from something I shouldn't have eaten forces me up earlier than usual. The faint sounds of drums off in the distance cannot go unnoticed any longer. It's time to see some real Abé music, culture, and get . . . on . . . doooown.

The ears lead me all the way to a circle of women. Aaaaah. There is nothing in the middle of the circle itself, but the women crowd around this small space as if something is trying to get out and they are pressing it down—letting it out slowly. So many tricky interplays of beat and song, hand claps, and drum strikes with my host mom almost unseen right at the edge of the middle nothingness as I stand on my toes and stick my chin out to see.

Strong Black female bodies of maple leaf, chestnut, mahogany, and dark amber colors, undulating forcefully but tightly to the rhythm, swirl into vision. The greater intensity that wants to materialize is held back, creating such a tumultuous, stir that I suspend in air surrounded by sound. I ease up not wanting to interfere, but as soon as Host Mom catches me she yells "Baya-Gey!," which I discover means 'Baya's baby.'

All of the women turn to me and encourage me to dance at different points but are truly more taken with the energy that rises from their music. All of them are instruments whether they have one or not. They each contribute sounds and laughter that vibrate with the music. It is a power that speaks to my soul more than any American music has—Abé soul music.

This musical revelry greatly contrasts with the setting of church where I am led every Sunday morning. The image of a stark White idol with long, flowing hair hanging up center stage behind the pulpit in a holy house full of Ivoiriens is not what you would expect after witnessing an early morning of stomach-pulsing drums. It's even stranger seeing myself in a blue, yellow, and white wrap dress and wrap scarf around my head with these thick-rimmed glasses I've worn since age seven.

Those who are normally jumping for joy at every single opportunity, on every single occasion, laughing with intense emotion, are all of the sudden quiet and still in their seats in church? No. This cannot be their religion. They look like outsiders in it. When I enter, they frequently stare back at me as if I can assure that their behavior here is the way to act in church . . . like I'm the church auditor sent from Jesus Christ after facsimile.

Don't the Abé have their own version of God to worship? Religions either make God in their own image or present no image at all—believing it sacrilegious to be so vain as to create God in one's own image. Jesus wasn't born in Europe. Do the Abé know that their hair more so resembles the 'hair like wool' described of Jesus in the Bible than the straight-haired images displayed here?

The Abé church looks like a church, has rows like a church, has many people sitting in these rows like a church, has a pew and choir, and even stained glass windows, but the energy is completely different. People are waiting for something to happen immediately. Anxious. Energy high. Sitting up so anxiously, they float in their seats. They are waiting for something, anything, to happen.

5 SPEAK ENGLISH

Walking back to Baya's house from class this morning, I see three women on a porch.

"Bonjour," I exchange greetings with one of them while cutting through someone's backyard to get to my host house.

"Oh, tu as un joli teint," the same woman replies with this compliment from the almost one-hundred-foot distance, admiring what she perceives to be a pretty skin color.

"Doesn't she?" she then turns to the two other women for confirmation. I stop to admire as well—these other two are engaged in the all-too-known-for putting-you-in-a-trance world of hair braiding. The one sitting has probably been sitting there for the last two hours as her head is half-done and she has less than a few inches of thickness. The one standing may have been there a while and several hours in the fields before this, but doesn't mind doing what her friend will surely reciprocate in the near future. They both nod a silent yes, but their eyes throw a glance of stone.

"She is light just like you." Well, you know what this gets started. The woman getting her hair coiffed is lighter than the other two women and no doubt has been the lightest one in this village until my yellow frame came.

"Mmmm," she lightly acknowledges from her braiding trance. Maybe she gets these comments on her skin often. But, then two seconds later, she snaps back into reality and pulls her head back in horror.

"She ain't the same light as me. I ain't light like that!" she quips. That's fine. If she prefers to be aligned with them rather than me that's cool. I don't feel alienated. It makes complete sense. She is Abé after all and, from what I can see, color might be the only thing she and I have in common, besides being women and loving to get our hair braided. My dilemma is currently the same as hers although less justifiable. She culturally aligns herself with the predominantly darker Abé. I superficially align myself with the darker Abé. Looking at it this way, I can now fully comprehend why Sarah says she feels more White than Malaysian.

But in my case—no. That is not my experience. Americans do not generally grow up in a society where culture is stronger than color. I, in fact, never referred to myself as American and had never really thought about it until I got my first passport at age fifteen. 'I'm American?' I thought. I don't even think I would have blinked if instead of the American bald eagle, my passport came back with an eagle in an afro on the front.

Of course, I am contradicting myself. On the one hand I am saying that color separates Blacks and Whites from identifying with one same American culture. But, on the other hand, I'm saying that color doesn't separate people of a variety of colors in the States from grouping themselves into one subculture identified as Black.

No, I'm not Abé, and maybe, we are all just a bunch of kids out here, none of us even born when Cote d'Ivoire got its independence from France, but if the Ivoirien association with White or light is colonial and that's the reason why Baya keeps bending over obsequiously to me with that eerie smile, then I must insist on something that quite frankly makes no sense—I'm light, but I'm Black.

Maybe in the future, when there is complete equality in the

States and around the world, it won't matter to me so much what I call myself or what I am mistakenly called because it won't be any indicator of where I fit in some color hierarchy. But, for now, I resist this hierarchy.

"Do you see what I mean?" I ask Kaylin later.

"It's not that big of a deal. It's not the same," she says. "You are more accepted than us."

But, the truth is there is pretty much no way any of us volunteers can win, no matter which volunteers seem to have it a little better than others. Race relations and tensions here are akin to the civil rights period in the States. It is possibly even more morose and psychologically disturbing here because Ivoiriens feel the pressures of an invisible French presence that only tangibly metamorphosizes into the shape of their limitations: their limitations of trade rights, their limitations to globalize with their own materials and resources on their own terms, and their limitations to own property on their own land. Most corporations here are not Ivoirien owned.

We receive lessons throughout the day that have us walking all around Grand Noyaré. We take the classes at different host family houses when the families aren't there. We receive personal survival training and Health Volunteer project training, but it's our French lessons that are pressed upon us the most. Learning French in our Abé context makes no sense to me, but it is necessary as that is one of the languages many Ivoiriens have had to understand.

It may not seem like it, but countries like Cote d'Ivoire that have managed to keep an identity separate from the language of their colonizers due to the fact that they also speak the languages of their own ethnicities are in a better fundamental position than countries that have no language other than the official language of their country.

People in England speak English. People in Japan speak Japanese. People in Germany speak German. People in Sweden speak Swedish. These countries don't have to use a linguistic identity outside of their country. When your language matches who you are, it's easier for you to retain your culture. When it doesn't, you are retaining someone else's culture and you lose yourself in it.

I come off amorphous to Ivoiriens when I say I'm African-American, but I don't speak any African language, speak English although America is not England, and am dark relative to White Americans but light relative to Ivoiriens. I become a more or less, 'what is it?'

Language ownership is a form of power and the name of your first language in Cote d'Ivoire is 99.9 percent of the time the name of your ethnicity . . . except for the Jula. Jula is the name of an Ivoirien ethnicity, but it is actually a single word taken from the language Bambara. The Jula traveled down from the North— Mali, Burkina Faso, and so on—as merchants and being merchants is how they got their name. Jula means 'commércante' and the Jula are indeed the merchants of Cote d'Ivoire. They dominate the transportation system, produce a wide variety of foods sold in the market while most other ethnicities can barely get by on subsistence farming (farming only to eat and not to sell), own cotton manufacturing, thrive in avriculture (raising of animals), and don't rely on the government to financially back all of their schools.

Maybe you would like to argue that although England forced English on America, language cannot be a deciding factor of power because America is wealthy, independent of England today. However, in terms of culture, we are much devoid compared to other countries that are poorer, as there are many poor countries that have a greater sense of community and family than Americans do. And, the American obsession with color differences instead of linguistic sameness never ends. Long-term, who will be better off?

America's lack of cohesiveness culturally, the lack of a 'we are all American' stance, is certainly a reflection of having been colonized under English only and not understanding how to—as in Cote d'Ivoire for example—retain all of those cultures we initially started out with two-hundred-plus years ago. Americans give surveys to kids asking them to choose either a color, a linguistic affiliation, a region, or a continent to identify themselves all within one question, as one category, as if one cannot simultaneously be the other—'Are you Black, Latino, Middle Eastern, or European?'

Baya, my host mom, always speaks to me in Abé even though our Ivoirien language classes are either in French or Jula, and I love her for it, but I'm sorry that she must take care of such a grown baby. You need a tutorial for these chores. Everything is done from scratch. The water has to be fetched. The wood for the fire has to be chopped from a tree and carried back home. No machines here. Baya is the machine.

Baya takes care of everyone except herself. She is strong from all of her responsibilities that she regularly takes on, but she still gets tired like everyone else. Later in the day, back from language and training classes taught outside in the shade but still under the hot, hot sun, I find Baya lying down on the floor in her room with one of her grandchildren. Paulette is around my age. Tall, jet black complexion, cheeks full of love, a smile that makes you trust her, and eyes always wondering what will happen next.

"Acua!" Paulette calls me by the new name Baya gave.

I step to the door and see that Paulette is giving her grandmother a massage. Paulette ushers me in. Baya lies out with just a thin wrap cloth separating her from the floor. When I kneel down closer, I see that Baya has a shiner. As soon as Baya looks me in the eye, I know that Host Dad hit her.

The Color Purple movie comes to mind. It's the scene where Celie is still being hit by her forced husband, Mister, late into old age. Do people really continue to do that for that long? That's crazy. To be that old and have another old person hitting you like that . . . Umh. Seeing her without a smile today disorients me.

Baya and I look at each other for a moment, Baya looks at Paulette, I look at Paulette, and Paulette looks at me then she looks back down at her grandmother and sadly frowns. The man, who seems to not be able to easily get around on his cane, can still muster up enough energy to put the smack down on Grandma.

It is a bit of a strange massage because Baya is lying on her back and Paulette is rubbing her chest. All of it. No shirt on. Between a grandmother and a grandchild, I can take nothing negative from it in this environment where there aren't so many layers of meaning to actions of touch and a chest. Breasts are often displayed outside and a chest is a chest in the same way a man has one. No one conjures up porno images from it. There's no TV to watch a porno on. Breasts are mammary glands. That's it.

"You do it," Paulette says in Abé, taking my hands and pulling them over Baya's exhausted body.

Look, the massage was fine until you asked me to do it. Am I supposed to do it the same way? This is a little strange rubbing on Host Mom's chest. So, I rub around them—the breasts on top of her chest. They are saggy and long, hanging off to the sides, so I can't go in circles and end up doing a massage in parts.

I can't get past my American idea of intimacy and borders. Baya's chest is sore from being hit, but I can't bring myself to do it completely. Both of them look at each other and then look at me and laugh. Baya just barely gets her laugh out—too tired and in pain to forget long enough to laugh at me fully.

With Paulette's expression, they both have gotta' be thinking, 'what is wrong with this woman afraid of roaches, can't wash her own clothes, goes running in her underwear in the morning, and is afraid to touch breasts?' So, I stop. They aren't offended, thank goodness. I'm happy to at least make them laugh.

"Tonight," Paulette starts in very stilted French, "we go out."

A live Ivoirien band is invited to the village. The drummer hits the drums in such an absolute blur of motion that my mind can't keep up with the sounds that come out. The Abé and Americans mixed in the crowd give a roar at the music and dancing begins in a joyful frenzy, but we stop to stare once we see how the Abé move.

Abé dancing is one style I eventually come to learn how to imitate and even today I have no problem looking a little off getting down Abé style in the club. It is a style that I do now no matter what country I'm in, but it is very jerky. On your tiptoes and your knees pointed out as you are slightly squatting, 1-2-3-4 forward, 1-2-3-4 backward, and you pop your chest out and body up before changing direction each time. Everyone is creative with it, but it is a scene as everyone is doing some variation of this tiptoe, boogey man, pop, and undulate dance.

Paulette never speaks to me but dances with me the whole time. Well, she can't. I wouldn't understand. Now, it's near the end of the party and the slow songs start to play. She shrugs her shoulders, sticks her head up in the air, and grabs me to her as if we are a couple. One of her hands goes around my waist and the other hand holds my hand out to our side. Some people are jiding her from what I can tell, and I know at the very least that Paulette has told somebody off in between deciding to continue to dance with me, regardless of the intruding slow song, and grabbing me next to her. She sticks up her nose at those around us. As weird as it might look for one reason to an American or another to the Abés, who tease her throughout, I cannot deny the energy from her. The greatest interactions must certainly go beyond language. The actions that require no explanation. No creepiness. No awkwardness. I am accepted. That single energy being recycled between us. That energy that we all transmit. How can I cultivate that to feel more free to be me?

I instinctively know it cannot be the woman thing that makes everyone make fun of Paulette for dancing with me. Public displays of affection are the norm here. I never see anyone kissing in the middle of the street, but I always know when two people are good friends and have grown up together. Little girls hold hands. Little boys hold hands. Teenage girls hold hands. Teenage boys hold hands. Buddies hold hands. If a woman here cradles my arm, leans up against me, pats me on the backside, or jokingly taps my breast, it does not mean that they are a weirdo and that I am a weirdo for allowing it. It means there is an element of trust already established.

Female-to-female contact and male-to-male contact needs no attention. Contact across the lines of male and female—now that is what attracts attention. It is the other way around in the States. Here, I feel accepted rather than a victim of some random homosexual act because here, when a woman touches you, you can always be sure that you aren't being taken advantage of.

The most startling situation to be in, however, isn't even being touched by the opposite sex but rather having no one to touch or not being touched at all. Being touched means that the Abé I meet no longer think of me as alien and feel that I am possibly a part of their life and even well-being.

6 JESUS AND GRAND TYPES

The bus ride to my tentative village is packed full of people. I am either on a Black university field trip, going to the Million Man March, or in Cote d'Ivoire. Everyone on the bus is Black, or I should say African, or I should say Ivoirien. I don't know these people. They might not all be Ivoirien.

"You ready, Raven? Here we go!" Oh! Steve! Even as loud and White as he is, he fits in the crowd.

"Yeh," I say less enthusiastically. I do not know what to expect. I am glad, however, that there is a White volunteer on the bus as well. It keeps all eyes off of me. My homologue can't make it to accompany me to my potential village, so Steve's homologue escorts the both of us.

A homologue is your community project partner in the village. He or she is usually a Grand Type in the sense of being a doctor, nurse, midwife, or whichever public servant, depending on what kind of volunteer service you perform. We are Health Volunteers so ours are such.

The first and only stop is Yamoussoukro. It takes about three

hours to get here from Abidjan. It is the past, historical capital of
Cote d'Ivoire and half-finished. So much land has been cleared off
and nothing constructed in its place. There are well-manicured,
long stretches of lawn, wide sidewalks lining the major avenue, and
stores or at least many empty buildings where stores used to be or
were supposed to have been.

Actually, all of the volunteers were brought here before. This
was one of our volunteer trips away from Grand Noyaré. On that
trip, our private bus headed straight for the main attraction—the
Basilica. A lot of us would not otherwise have a reason to come
through here, as each of our future sites will be spread out
throughout the country. What is a Basilica? I can see what it is,
but what it is in Yamoussoukro is something else.

Never any street signs, so I can only say that the main road is
what we drove along for a long time before reaching our destination. On the left side along the way is a very long, high, white wall.
The only things I can make out beyond the wall are purposefully
lined trees along a well-manicured hill that ascends up to the height
of the tall trees and then suddenly drops. What is beyond there?
The formateurs say it is the presidential palace. The house is not
visible, but however it is, it must be huge. The long, tall, white wall
stays to the side of us for a good three minutes as we pass by at
about eighty kilometers or fifty miles an hour (the metric system is
what is used here).

The Basilica is up next, surrounded by acres and acres of land.
We pull up to it along a long, curvy driveway to the security gate.
We park, get out, and although no one says it, everyone must be
wondering what all this has got to do with Cote d'Ivoire given our
faces of confusion. There is no one around save for its guardians
and the grounds are mysteriously well kept as if they are always
expecting someone. Church definitely is not in session and has not
been in a while. As we get closer, the sheer massiveness and height
of the dome engulfs us. The roof is round at the top of the wall
where it slowly reaches upward toward the apex. There are pillars
in the front and an expansive front walkway. I start spinning
around to see how long it will take before I bang into a pillar on

the small island walkway, but I never do.

Simply put, it is fantastic but odd in its environment—an ostentatious display of wealth that stops at the corner. Houphouët-Boigny, the first Ivoirien president after liberation from France, commanded that it be built in the 1960s. The Basilica is finished but wide, marble walkways stretch out in every direction off into the distance and end in nothing more than grass. The addendum constructions you would expect to be at all of those end points were abandoned.

We walk inside cautiously. It is so big, so white, and so majestic on the outside. There is deep red crimson on the inside, plush carpet everywhere, beautifully carved wooden pews, golden lining along the altar and the stage, velvety drapes, and colorful, stained glass windows that reach up toward the dome. Many pictures from the Bible are depicted in the stained glass windows, but one in particular catches our eye.

Jesus is painted with twelve disciples kneeling down around him. There are eleven White disciples and only one Black one. Jesus spoke Aramaic and was from a region today known as the Middle East, so if anything, the White disciples look out of place. But, according to our guide, President Houphouët-Boigny's intention when he commissioned the artist was to make an addition—of himself—as if Houphouët-Boigny had lived at that time, as if he was a disciple. Race claims of ancient religious figures are continually disputed, but what was Boigny trying to say by putting his own self up in there . . . and a blatant anachronism at that?

What Boigny did is nothing short of what many presidents continue to do around the world with their country's wealth—waste it. The non-existent sewers at the mud pool of a market in Agboville would have been at least one better, and far less expensive, choice to materialize. Ivoiriens must be as upset with Boigny as I am with the companies responsible for the half a billion-dollar eyesore called the SkiDome (ski dome) on the New Jersey highway, left undone since 2009. That money could have put at least five thousand homeless, American teenagers through college instead.

Cote d'Ivoire is obviously a country that at one point had great

economic potential, being the world's number one producer of cocoa, and at points when the price of cocoa had actually done them
some good. Why has all of this mass-scale potential disappeared?

So, yes. I can only look around at Yamoussoukro confused as
Steve and I pass through it and see the Basilica again—only this
time on our way to test-visit our individual sites.

We have a volunteer house in each of the five major cities—
Daloa, Bouaké, Korhogo, Odienné, and Abidjan, the current capital. Our village visit takes us straight into Daloa City first. This
five-hour, bus ride sandwich of hot bodies is underrated. The wind
hitting me in the face, at the 120-plus kilometers an hour this bus
is going, leaves me dry-eyed and the right side of my face plasters
to the seat as I turn my head to get away from it. My painful belly
is barely holding on after holding it in so long. There is no bathroom on this bus or any pit stop the driver will take besides Yamoussoukro, as sticking to his schedule and being able to make as
many trips back and forth as possible in one day means more money.

"There!"

"What there?"

"Your village!"

"What?! Where?! Right here along the road?!" I stand up peering out my open window as the people, walking along and across
the street, look back up at me.

"No, there," I whirl my head around for a fifth time to look at
where his finger points and all I see is a very long road that leads
off into oblivion. Trying to look damn near twists my head off. My
village? . . . My village! Enthusiasm returns.

"This is my stop. I have to get off now."

"No," Steve's homologue pats my shoulder.

"What? Why?"

"We go ahead first."

The long road to my village heads off into nowhere, ending in a
big opaque mist. Oooo, spooky. A few shacks or makeshift stores
stand at the very entrance to my road, and there is a village on the
opposite side of that road but the area hardly seems populated,

nowhere to go and nothing to do.

The fields are burning along the wide Abidjan highway road into Daloa. Just two lanes with no line dividing them down the middle and nothing to the sides but fields, fields, more fields, maybe the entrance to a village every five miles, and gigantic trees here, there, and off in the distance. Farmers take their waste and create mysteriously controlled fires that carry smoke twirling, swirling, and spreading up into the air. Most Ivoiriens are farmers. The only Ivoiriens I've met that aren't farmers, are Grand Types or those raised in Abidjan where there is no farm to cultivate anything except on the very outskirts of the city.

The Daloa Volunteer House is surrounded by high walls and open sky. There is a thick metal door that keeps us in and others out. The whole neighborhood is full of Ivoirien Grand Types. They have all built walls up around their houses. The front porch is made of old black and white marble that wraps around one side of the house. The other side on the left faces the guard's quarters attached to a front garage with no garage door. Plastic prayer mats are everywhere to lounge on as well as a hammock. The house is big but not decked out in any way—just a regular house where a bunch of twenty-somethings visit and third-year volunteers can opt to live as the House Leader.

The kitchen has a cabinet full of food that volunteers buy at local Daloa City stores selling Western treats. Macaroni & cheese and Pop-Tarts are the main items in stock. The sink is not in the kitchen. It's on the left side of the house outside of the kitchen door facing the guard's quarters and is more of a deep, cement faucet that gets all kinds of use. The stove inside is a little gas stove that you have to light with a match every time you turn it on.

"Everyone always thinks they're going to blow up, but they never do," laughs a spunky female volunteer walking around the kitchen.

All in all, the house is what it is and is far better than any house that any volunteer is living in, out on site, except for a few who get the former house of a Grand Type or whose villagers decide to finish a house they are already building so that we can live in it. I assume the Peace Corps gives the money for that. Otherwise, that is asking a lot when they don't even know what kind of volunteer they are going to receive and what projects, if any, will actually be done.

We meet our homologues for the first time at a Homologue and Volunteer conference, staying at a quasi-hotel in another small town on a previous break from Grand Noyaré. The landscaping is more than adequate with thriving flowers and the likelihood of being the grand, former house of a Frenchie.

The hotel is by no means the Ritz Carlton, but let's call it that. It is the first time in two out of three months of training that we get the chance to clean ourselves with water that shoots out from a showerhead. I've been using a tiny make-up mirror as my mirror. That's it. The first morning of being at the Ritz breathes life into me; stepping into the bathroom area, being amazed at shower curtains, seeing showerheads for the first time in weeks, and spinning around to see mirrors over actual sinks. Seeing my body in full length after so long turned me into a creature— an elbow, a knee, and a back are such interesting things.

"Oh my God! A shower! Hey guys, we can take showers in here!" Kaylin runs out of the bathroom as soon as she steps in it, knocks on all the doors, and gets her roommate out of bed to witness and experience the miracle of us ladies being able to take the first Western shower in months. Ivoirien-style body cleaning is not so bad. It allows you to suds up and scrub more with just the bucket, not to mention the fact that it saves a whole lot of water. Ivoiriens usually bathe twice a day and conceivably use less water in a week than in one American shower. But, still, I am excited and strip down as fast I can, shove my feet into plastic sandals, throw my clothes over the shower rod, and snatch the curtain back.

In rushing, I am not so thorough with closing the curtain, but being naked in front of others is the last thing on my mind. The showerhead and dial are the focus. I inspect them. Could that be hot and cold? Would warm water, better yet hot water, actually come out of the showerhead if I put it all the way to one side?!

"It's hot, y'all!" another volunteer yells out, quicker than me at the draw. This causes a stir in everyone's feet and the scurry begins.

"It's hot? No, it's probably just lukewarm. It can't possibly be hot," Bridget yells into the shower area.

"How would they get hot water out here anyway?" Denise disputes.

"I think you're hallucinating. They would have told us if we were going to get hot water," Bridget's voice echoes into the stalls.

"Why don't you get in and try it?" responds Kaylin the shower pioneer.

"It's hot!" A male volunteer runs by the door and sticks his head in the bathroom long enough to scream out his joy. This finally confirms it. Clothes fly off. Some throw clothes on shower rods and others throw clothes on the floor. Some step in the shower with their clothes still on anxious to give the fingertip test before they waste any time stripping and being let down by the wrong temperature.

"This ain't hot!" I yell just before the impending, piping hot water scalds my doubt. "Aaaaah!" I scream stuck in the shower curtain trying to get away from the water. "Oh, thank God! It is hot!" Then, panic sets in. I better hurry up before it turns cold. But, miraculously it stays hot for what must be a while because when I finally step out of there, there is a line of volunteers with their towels and arms folded over those towels with scowls on their faces.

"I smell different. Any of you notice that?" Kaylin asks.

"What do you mean?" I remark as no one else knows how to respond.

"I don't know, but since we got here my scent has changed," Kaylin shrugs.

Hmmm, it is true. My feet in America normally would have stunk up the whole room on a hot day like this in sandals, but now

I can't remember the last time I noticed.

"You're right." But, I can't say why. People say that smell is connected to the food you eat. We haven't eaten anything artificially flavored, out of a can, or shipped from afar in months. Everything is fresh and chemical-free.

"It's probably because we're eating differently."

"I don't know," Kaylin says with frown on brow ready to call forensics.

We shower, get dressed, and head to breakfast. Will we also be able to brag that we have American-style breakfasts to go along with our American-style showers? It is a nice thought. Honestly, I forget what we eat. I just remember Denzel.

He is a Denzel wanna-be, my homologue, the person with whom I am to set up projects, the name you saw on page one—Bogo. His eyes freeze at the sight of me only a moment before he jerks himself straight up in his suit and magic-tricks a smile on his face. Meet your first Ivoirien mack.

"Oh, this is your volunteer," the other homologues standing around quickly inform him. I am his volunteer, his teammate, his partner in crime. He tries to force a solemn look on his face to suppress a smirk.

"Nice to meet you," he says after a pause then extends his right hand. He is handsome but too old for me. Bogo has to be in his forties and just knows he is the Grand Type of all Grand Types (pronounced 'Grahnd Teep' in French). He is an accomplished Head Nurse and as head of the hospital in my village site, he is treated as a doctor. Something tells me, however, that I have just gotten the short end of the stick. All of the other volunteers are getting along well. Bogo doesn't have much to say and he doesn't ask much either. Say something man, damn. He is here and gone in a matter of minutes.

A cab screech from outside the Daloa House walls jolts us, followed by obnoxious thumps on our huge metal door. I jump to open it and Bogo smears into view.

"Raven, ça va?" He greets me nicely enough. Although Bogo didn't accompany me to Daloa with Steve and Steve's homologue, he does finally come to meet me at the Daloa House to take me for my first visit to my potential site.

"Yes, I'm okay. Thank you. Please come in."

"No, the cab is here and ready to go," I guess is what he just said. Bogo's mouth moves faster than a belly dancer's stomach and eye contact will surely happen once this door turns into a golf club. He gestures me to the cab so I get my things.

Bogo and I reach our gare in two minutes. Four baidjans are parked in front of the gare and around the right. Right near the street, my gare is a little cottage put together with slabs of dark brown wood slanting in all directions. It is a wonder it stays up on its incline. There are two more long slabs of wood for benches right up against the wall of the cabin. I booty surf until one adjusts to my weight.

"Waaah!" A woman yells as she crashes to the ground. My eyes widening is the only reaction from anyone. She gets up, dusts herself off, and this time sits from the center of the other seesaw bench.

Inside the gare is the cook who, although missing a tooth on the top right side of his mouth, has an always joyous, peek-a-boo smile that you are lucky to get a glimpse of and it cheers up your next two days at least. Smiling is simply dropping his mouth open. You can see his head moving around through a tiny, cut-out window without a frame that sits above the outside bench where I sit.

There are the two owners of the gare—one the color of bitter-sweet chocolate whose smile is extremely bright and a face of numerous expressions from minute to minute. The other owner is always looking around with a stern face, intently waiting for someone or something to come along. He folds the money that he receives from all the customers long-ways down the middle and sticks it in between his fingers. No one ever jumps him. He is the owner and the accountant and he moves through people like cars going the wrong way on his side of the highway. Bogo informs me of their names and assures me that I can depend on them not just for a ride to my village but to protect me whenever I am in town if needed.

Man, I thought the NTT bus to Daloa was rickety. My gare's baidjans take the cake. These vans used to be white, but red rust forms near every edge that gets action—around the window frames, on the metal over the wheels, and on the door linings. Oh . . . no . . . they . . . didn't punch holes in my window and sew the two pieces of glass together! That right there, is what you call using what you have.

Someone's bag is half in my lap and half in hers. The other half of her lap has her child on it. Much more than squished up in the back of the chair in front of me, I have to raise my legs up off the ground, feet dangling where my knees should have been. Of course, in this position, I can't even sit up straight.

As we approach the Ivoirien Gendarmerie blockade, we see other baidjans that have been stopped, and still others automatically waved through. One Gendarme officer makes a woman with a baby get out and stand there while he chastises her about the ID book she gives him, flapping it up and down in front of her face. It is not laminated but faded and torn. He is dressed in green army fatigues and big black boots with a green hat on.

Every stopped baidjan has a Gendarme walking around the bus, peering in the windows, asking questions to passengers in some and quickly passing on others. My green army man comes up from behind. He walks around to the driver's side and asks the driver a few questions. The driver looks straight ahead the entire time and keeps his responses tight-lipped and brief. I don't understand the exchange, but the Gendarme almost waves us off until he peeks back in the baidjan and sights my light, bright ass. He asks the driver a few more questions while looking in my direction, and then yells at me to get out.

Me? I point to myself in disbelief. I motion to climb over everyone after untangling myself out from the pretzel that I have worked myself into.

"She's with me," Bogo comes alive. Shoot, I forgot he was here. His rapid fire French busts out to which Mr. Green nods up in the air every few seconds and off we go. Phew! No ID check or twenty odd questions this time.

"Ah, oh, oh, ugh, mmm, ee," I try to muffle myself, but when we finally get to the road, or I should say the dirt, that leads off to my site, all of these sounds come out. Far from smooth, there are bumps everywhere. Up and down and up and down and to the sides.

"Ahuuuuh," I catch my breath every time the baidjan tilts to the side or veers toward the edge of the dirt road that takes a sudden, deep, two-foot decline off into the grass. All of our luggage non-strategically strapped on top of the baidjan, doesn't make me any surer that we won't tip over. And, isn't that grown young man hanging out the side door, using just his left hand to hold onto the car frame and his right foot dangling in the air, going to make us fall over even sooner?

My long body scrunches up and I deal with each bumpity bump by grabbing at the window to hold myself steady, getting my fingers caught in the holes punched in the windows when I use them to brace myself. Everyone is ooohing and aaaahing just the same. Yes, comfortable is not what transportation is about. Getting around alive in one piece is the goal.

My new village is called Zragbi—'Zrahgbee.' When we finally arrive in Zragbi, Bogo and I go straight to the hospital where Bogo runs things. With nothing immediately around the hospital except land, it is the focal point of the entire village. Bogo stops here and salutes people, gets clued in on the goings-on and then remembers me still standing here and takes me to a second building without a word.

"Je vais dormir ici?" is what I can muster out. Is this where I am going to stay? Don't they have a house for me? Why am I sleeping at the hospital? Bogo beckons a girl to take my bags from me and into a back room.

"This is my house," he says.

"Oh." With all the people lounging around, I thought it was just another extension of the hospital. There is a straw thatched canopy where a woman is cooking and Bogo introduces her.

"This is Céline." She rushes up from what she is doing, anxious to greet. Bogo's wife is 5'4", reddish-brown toned, and has a gorgeous smile with teeth strong enough to cut a board. They aren't disproportionately big to her face, but they are so white you wonder where her milk farm is. She is demure yet strong.

"She is the Fille de Salle." The girl of the room? That is French for maid, right? No, no, no. That means Nurse's Assistant. Wait a minute. If she is the assistant then why is she at Bogo's house making his lunch? She follows us back to the hospital.

The hospital is packed. No introductions again. A hallway splits one section of the hospital from the other. No hallway entrance doors—just a roof overhead in the hallway protecting patients from the roaring sun and giving them a place to stay while they sit on benches lining the walls waiting to get in to see the Head Nurse—Bogo. There is a side for men and a side for women. The women are called into the back wing section closest to Bogo's house while the men are called into the front side of the hospital facing the market. It is the same market we wade through earlier after getting off the baidjan.

The women take up the benches and the men mostly stand and wait, crowded around Bogo's office door. His office is a light, aqua blue as is the rest of the hospital, aged by the dust that swirls up around it slightly, staining the walls at the bottom, and aged by the stains of sweaty hands in from the fields or some other hard day's work. The windows have no glass—only brown wooden shutters that hang onto their nuts and bolts for dear life, propped up with a slab of wood or hanging off to the side. Bogo finally looks between the open shutters and calls us in.

"Viens, viens." Quickly forward, Céline goes to his command. I rush in after her yanked by invisible rope. Bogo is sitting at his desk surrounded by men standing there for one reason or another. There is no such thing as private consultation.

"This is Raven," pronounced as 'Rahvehn.' He mutters a few more phrases, the end of which he punctuates with hearty laughter.

Some men laugh back with him. Some men glance quickly in my direction and then away with no expression. Céline glances up at me demurely and shows a smile, meant to either pity or comfort me. This cannot be good. Is this supposed to be my homologue? Cracking jokes on me and laughing in my face? No, Raven. Don't worry. You don't know the language. Laugh along with them. But, all I can manage is a Kermit the Frog smile.

"Céline viens," Bogo calls, reaching into his pocket to give Céline 10,000 CFA Francs. "Take care of her." Céline's eyes burst and her mouth drops open momentarily as she looks at the 10,000 CFA now in hand. She smiles.

"You are her homologue," he then adds. What? He is the one who applied for a volunteer to come to the village. He is the one who had been invited to Peace Corps training sessions on how to work with volunteers as a homologue. Céline is not trained to work with a Peace Corps Volunteer. Maybe it is a great day for Céline who only sees that kind of money pass between any other hands but her own. But, for me, it is a slap in the face. Back we go toward Bogo's house under the thatched canopy where she gets back to work in front of her big, black iron pot.

Céline has chosen a colorful cloth to wear while cooking. The top has a round neck that goes up into extremely puffy shoulders, making her head look even smaller and cuter. The bottom half is a pagne—not sewn but simply wraps around her, outlining her strong yet curvaceous body. I love Ivoirien wrap skirts. Keeping that long cloth around the body with no pins, buttons, or zippers is a science, looks great, and can be fitted and styled in many ways.

To sit down she quickly bends forward, scooping the back of her pagne up between her legs and sits down with this part of the fabric sticking up from in between her lap. This allows her to sit on the eight-inch-high stool without exposing anything. I do the same with my twelve-inch one and watch her sit in steam and smoke rising up from the pot. She is used to it, but I have to put my head off to the right. The heat smothers my face and my nose searches for pockets of air.

Different vegetables and spices plop into the pot. The water is blood red from the unsaturated, red palm oil she brews. Just looking at it makes my mouth grow hot and I am scared a bite may make my tongue fall out. She finally leaves the pot alone to do its thing and drags over a huge mortar. This mortar has the shape of a large drum with no skin on top. From a small silver pot, Céline grabs one boiled plantain at a time and throws it to the bottom of the mortar. With her right hand, she grabs a long, dark, cedar-colored wooden stick three inches thick and three feet long. It is rounded at both ends from use.

Less sound comes from me in these first couple of months in Cote d'Ivoire than in my first couple of months of life. All I can do is watch and learn. Still sitting on the tiny bench, squeezing her legs together to keep the back of her dress from falling down and exposing anything, Céline continues to throw plantains into the mortar with her left hand and starts to smash them with the wooden stick in her right. Céline breaks off a plantain piece and pops it into her mouth then breaks off another piece and hands it to me.

"C'est doux," Céline remarks. It really is sweet, but this phrase is also used for anything that simply tastes good. If it's really good, a 'dey' is added on the end of it. 'C'est doux, dey!' Aaaah, the language of food. The boiled plantains are firmer than a regular banana but tender to the taste. Boiling plantains preserves much more sweetness than fried.

After Céline finishes throwing all the plantains into the mortar, she raises the wooden stick higher to come down harder. Each time she does, she sticks her left hand in to fold over the mushy mass that is quickly forming into a playdoughy substance.

The girl who takes my bags earlier runs up and a true sport begins. Jijina grabs the stick with both hands, lifts the stick straight up into the air until her back arches, then comes smashing down into the bottom of the mortar. Up and down, quickly she makes this motion and each time with the rhythm of a heart beating. Jijina raises the stick and Céline puts her hand down inside to scoop around the base and pushes everything back into the center of the mass that is quickly forming into a cohesive substance. I squint every time the stick comes down. Is Céline getting her hands smashed?

The stick definitely makes contact with Céline's hands on the way down, but she lets it smack her hands only a little. They are on perfect pace.

Céline says something to Jijina and Jijina quickly hands me the stick. I raise the stick up in the air and all of its weight is suddenly straining me. I place my left hand on my left knee to keep it up. This then causes my dress to fall down from between my legs and I re-group. I lift the twenty-pound stick again, but my legs have to work just to stabilize myself and keep me from falling over or exposing myself. I'm finally able to smash down one time, proud of myself, but when I go to raise it, it does not happen. The bottom of the stick gets stuck in the mass. Ain't this some shit? The more you hit the plantains, the stickier they become as they start to fuse together and I have to raise the stick with equal if not more force then I come down with just to dislodge myself from the mass every time. Oh, that's why Céline is throwing splashes of water on it in between each lift.

Céline smirks at me, the cute act gone. It is harder than it appears. I try twice more and give up. I struggle to pass the stick back to Céline with one hand and Jijina takes it, commencing to wail down again as she stands. Standing would have made more sense, but Céline was sitting when she started at the beginning!

I notice Jijina's arms now. Their arms . . . I don't expect muscle on women, but the muscle on Céline and thin, twelve-year-old Jijina cannot be denied. Céline's muscle starts at her neck, shapes her shoulders, glides down her red-undertoned, maple syrup complexioned biceps and forearms. It is hard for fingers to be muscular, but Céline passes this test, too. The most amazing thing of all is that as strong as she is, she is all woman from the way she talks and carries on to the way she switches when she walks. Seeing women here gives a new sense of femininity.

"Ça va devenir quoi?" What is this going to become, I struggle in French to ask. What is so important that Céline has to get a Jane Fonda workout every time she makes it?

"C'est le Futu." Ooooh, we ate this in Agboville but a similar one called 'Fufu' a few times in Grand Noyaré. What is the difference? Céline sees me frown.

"On mets le manioc aussi," and with that said, she begins to add what looks like a potato, only longer. So, the difference between Fufu and Futu is that Fufu uses plantain only. A cultural difference between the Abé and Bèté—using cassava. Now, I see why Céline's food sits on the pot so long. If cassava is not boiled enough, it produces cyanide. Either the Abé don't play that or they're not worried about a plantain shortage.

Zragbi is mainly the Bèté ethnicity and there are a lot of things that differentiate them from the Abé in Grand Noyaré five hours southeast of here. Wow, so different ethnicities not only mean different languages but different customs as well? Different style of dress and music, too? Hmm, sixty languages in Cote d'Ivoire. I have none down and sixty to go.

Bogo walks into the courtyard right as Céline scoops the Futu up onto a clean, white, shiny plate. She turns to the pot with a big metal spoon, dips in and pulls out chunks of chicken and steaming hot, blood red sauce with rich brown, miso-looking broth that swirls around the spoon when the sauce is stirred up. She pours it all over the Futu, which has now formed into a large and firm, oblong yellow mound. Pieces of chicken slide down the sides. It's 1:00 p.m. and I did not eat breakfast because Bogo rushed me out of the Daloa House.

After Bogo's plate, is mine. Céline fixes my plate, heads toward the door, and turns around just long enough to command "viens." I understand that. I get up from the stool and quickly walk after her. 'Come.' It's lunchtime.

Bogo sits in front of the wall that faces the TV. I can't say that I don't like Ivoirien food, but there is no guarantee that every person you meet can cook. The textures of the foods are different and Futu used to create a gag reflex since only playdough would come to mind. I sit down in front of my plate near the back bedrooms. My things should be back there somewhere. I haven't seen them all morning.

On the wall by the long couch is a mug shot of a woman who must have been walking through the desert for five days without water right before she took the picture. Bogo catches me staring at the picture and in between hand licks shares, "C'est ma mère." Just a picture of his mother on the walls and nothing else.

"Elle est jolie," I try to compliment in what is sure to be an awkward moment.

"Elle est villain," he returns. How can you call your own mother ugly and if she is so ugly then why would you put her up on the wall just so that you can tell everyone how ugly your mother is?

"Non. Elle est jolie," I insist again. Bogo stops and stares a little longer at the picture. As if about to say something, he opens his mouth but then closes it, shakes his head, and looks away. He says a few other words that Céline translates into slower French. It takes three times, said in three different ways. It is more the oddity of eating alone with Bogo than not understanding—Céline has after all been pointing to the chair the entire time she addresses me.

"You want her to understand. I want her to understand me!" Bogo snaps.

Perhaps, I have selective comprehension because this last statement goes in my head loud and clear and we all begin laughing. Maybe that is why some people learn faster than others. They have someone like Bogo who just talks regular and assumes I'll figure it out somehow. If not sooner, later for sure.

I can't say that Céline's slower and repetitive method is any worse than Bogo's, however, because by the end of the week's village visit, I definitely feel better at speaking and understanding French than when I came the week before.

When I'm not stewing about the whereabouts of my house, I pretty much follow Céline everywhere and she gets frustrated sometimes. Not just words I don't understand but so many things I see that I ask a million questions about. My village visit is mostly a success, however. Very peaceful, from the way people glide along when they walk by, to the way the dust floats up in the air when a baidjan passes by. Even the redness of the earth is peaceful, more red than other places I have seen here.

'Les gens dissent que c'est a cause des montagnes là bas. Il y'a de fer dans les montagnes et quand ça pleure . . .' Because of the mountains? The explanation a villager gives is plausible. Over a period of thousands of years, the rain that pours down the mountains reacts with the iron that the mountains have large deposits of, which has gradually, over thousands or millions of years, spread the color of rust throughout the land whenever it rains. Cool. Perhaps that may also explain why everyone seems to have a tinge of red to their skin in Zragbi. Is it reflecting up from the earth? Is it absorbed into their lungs and coming out through their skin? Maybe. Maybe not.

In Grand Noyaré, the Abé are more dark brown. Their people migrated to Cote d'Ivoire from Ghana. In Zragbi, the Bèté are a rainbow of colors. Their people migrated from Liberia and Liberia was founded by African-Americans in the early 1800s in an effort to return freed Black slaves to Africa. Presumably, this is after these former slaves had already forgotten their language and quite conceivably mixed with Whites to the extent that they would be alienated upon return to Liberia.

If true, I possibly have come home. These rainbow-colored folks and I may share the same not-too-distant relatives. Cote d'Ivoire is made up of ethnicities running from famine in the north, people running from being sold at the heavy slave trade port in Ghana from the east, and people running from Liberia to the west; all to get to Cote d'Ivoire.

In being here, I see that African can be any feature under the sun. Blacks in the States often attribute their West African features to what all-African features must be because American Blacks don't realize they are predominantly of West African origin. The Bèté among all the ethnicities here are the closest to what I feel African-Americans actually look like. Besides the food and the shelter, I have less to get used to in Zragbi than they do to me.

Northern Ivoiriens have sharper features. Bèté people have rounder features, fuller lips, and bigger eyes. You can be the darkest of Black here but with the thin lips and nose of a White person. No characteristic belongs to any one group once you've been to Africa.

Finally, it's time to say goodbye to Zragbi for the first time.

Steve meets me at the Daloa House.

"How was your village?" I ask with full optimism, but Steve gives me a grim look and we leave together in silence.

The first three months have passed and I am chosen to give the good-bye speech. Why me? Everyone thinks I am the best Abé speaker, but really all I do is memorize greetings, count one through ten, and say the few words I need to know—water, bathroom, and food. I write the good-bye speech in my limited French as heartfelt as I can make it. An Abé helps me translate this into Abé.

"Put this in there, too," the translator says, adding more sentences than he edits. "This too . . . Oh, this would be good, too." This speech is growing to be much longer than my French version. He is pulling from his ass.

"What does this mean?" I ask him about some of the sentences in Abé.

"Trust me," he smiles briefly, looking at me then leaning back in his chair on his right elbow with right hand on lips, and eyes up in the air as he creates.

Back on the same welcoming spots that we were in when we first arrived three months ago. The Abé dress up again, this time including us in our long, host-family-borrowed boo boo robes, pagne wrap skirts, and elaborate head wraps.

"You like?" Sam spins around smoothly and a little dust floats up into the air. His family adorns him with great fabrics and a cane to match. Big Daddy Kane has nothing on it.

"Woooh!"

"Go Sam!" yell different volunteers.

Laura has so many richly beautiful cloths wrapped around her that she could open a clothing store. Some volunteers look ridiculous, more so because that's the energy they give off, feeling awkward in their new haberdashery. I have something on that wraps my boobs up tight! No sleeves or straps to hold it up, just sheer wrap-around and tuck power under my armpits and another richly embroidered deep blue cloth snuggling into the fat of my waistline as wrap dress.

"How do you think it's gonna' be?" Steve asks me as I am called to the podium.

"I don't know hoooooow it's gonna' be, but it's gonna' be," I whisper strongly. Steve laughs out loud and slaps his knee. I proceed to shimmy on up to the podium after Denise delivers a good-bye speech in French, while flattening out the wrinkles in the paper held tensely in my hands for so many minutes.

I am surprised at the gorgeous wrap I am wearing, surprised at the enormous crowd, and surprised at the lovely Abé-transformed volunteers before me. As the words become real in my mouth, the crowd becomes ever quieter than before.

"Yaaaaaaah!" The crowd abruptly roars at some words. They nod in contemplative unison around at each other. Umhm, those must have been the parts I wrote. I finish with a soul-filled salute farewell and everyone in the crowd, save the volunteers who know as little about what I say as I do, jump in the air for absolute joy with their hands clasped or clapping rapidly together. That translator is good.

The next morning it's time to go. It's time to get on the bus and head back to Zragbi permanently.

"Baya-Gey! Baya-Gey! Baaaayaaaaa-Gey!" My host mom is shouting to the ground, the air, and the heavens. She falls down and Paulette runs to hold her up as I'm walking away with my luggage. Thank goodness Baya's back on her feet again, but when I turn around she collapses in Paulette's arms once more. I don't know what to do. I stand there and look at them. They look at me.

Grandpa stands up. He is a man that doesn't say much except when it is to shoo the kids the hell out of his way. This is a man who usually walks bent over, but when he has to carry a chair from one point to the next, can lift a heavy wooden one clear over his head and march to war.

Grandpa staggers up onto his cane that he takes with him

wherever he goes and starts to walk toward me. He begins to wipe his eyes and the shades that he always wears fall off his face to the ground. He starts to fall to the ground, too, but not before my old running partner is there to catch him. My departure is a death for them. This is too much to be real. What have I done to deserve such grieving? The kids stand around in the same fashion that I do; without a clue as to what is going on and wondering who died. It is gravely touching and I now know I will always have a home to come back to, but daaag.

Even after all of this, the ceremony and the soulful goodbyes, when the Country Director comes to express congratulations and bid us farewell off to our respective new adventures saying to me, "Wouldn't it be nice if this could be your village site?" I quickly say no. The grass is always greener on the other side.

7   In Your Face

The sun is already blasting brightness when we leave the Abidjan House at 6:00 a.m., and in another hour it will be dead heat. We catch an orange cab just outside, the preferred taxi color in Abidjan. Daloa cabs are green. As usual, the cab door is about one hundred tugs from falling off, but the cars run fast and well. All cabs and baidjans are unmistakably Toyotas, at least fifteen years old, and fiercely maintained to last another fifteen.

"Tu vas où?" asks the driver suspending his head over the passenger seat to see us, still keeping both hands on the wheel.

"Can we just say to 'la gare'?" I turn and ask Steve, not trusting my French past two words this morning.

"La gare de quoi?" The driver responds, quick on his feet, snatching the bit of French he can hear before we can get it together to direct our words to him.

"Le gare de NTT," Steve swirls around to answer.

"Tu va à Daloa là?" Yes, we are going to Daloa we nod. "Faut monter!" he besieges us in with just his voice. Steve and I look at each other and, although both visibly unsure about the French, start to comply.

"C'est combien?" I stop to ask.

"Five mille." Get the fuck outta' here. My New Jersey senses flood in. It only costs 3,500 CFA from Abidjan to Daloa and we aren't even leaving Abidjan! We just want to get to the gare first, okay? Our formateurs tell us it is an insult to accept the first price offered so we should always bargain, even if they don't end up changing the price. Discarding money without a volley of conversation is a bit anti-social to Ivoiriens.

"1 mille francs," Steve quietly demands and looks away waiting. It's really 'CFA francs,' but 'francs' is faster to say.

"Pour les deux, eh!" I quickly chime in 'for two' after Steve says the price. I add the 'eh' for exclamation in the same nasal tone I always hear Cèline add at the end of every possible sentence.

"C'est pas possible!" he cries, throwing his right hand up in the air and speeding off. What? Does he think we are rock stars, and not volunteers on meager stipends?

Soon, another cab pulls up and it is the same mess except this time we are the ones to tell the driver no thanks. Are we ever going to get a cab and at least make it in time before the tickets sell out? Shit. The third cab asks for at least three mille.

We are stolid by the fourth one, only moving our lips to speak. "500 CFA each," I stammer out. Driver number four looks off into the distance, nods in our direction without eye contact, and gets out the car to put our bags in the trunk. My soul says 'yeah!' but my body trips moving forward to hand him my luggage.

"Of course you know this means we have to give him something extra, him helping us with our bags and all," Steve finally speaks again.

"Whatever dude. How long we gonna' be out here trynda' get the right price?" I don't want to be here all day. It's getting hot.

Forget the Indianapolis 500. Weaving in, out, and around cars on the highway makes the scenery nonexistent. We can't catch a glimpse of it and my fear increases on seeing the gaping mouths of shocked faces in cars as we zoom by them.

"Man. I hope he's taking us to the right place. Maybe we're being kidnapped. This brother is on a mission," I look at the cab driver's face in the rearview mirror. He is miles away, could care less what we say in any language now.

From what I can squint in our mad dash down the highway, the common theme is garbage. There are only a few cities in Cote d'Ivoire that have access to modern amenities on a more regular basis; Daloa, Bouaké, Korhogo, Odienné, and of course Abidjan. The only thing that truly lacks in any of these places is waste management, which requires government awareness and investment, of course. Far from the problem of recycling, I first need to say the words 'garbage can.' No local government funds set aside for waste collection, so the people have to either create heaps on the side of the road or off in the middle of vegetation away from the street somewhere or they burn it themselves. It is capitalism gone wild. The influx of foreign goods does not match their capacity or familiarity with the need to dispose of things in a safer manner.

Many Ivoiriens still live the mindset of an organic lifestyle. They are not used to things that heavily accumulate but rather dissipate or can be used as something else. Having worked in New York City and knowing the massive amount of garbage each individual creates there hourly, I'm hard-pressed to find a good reason why Cote d'Ivoire should want to veer too far from their organic lifestyle.

"That sign looks familiar," Steve finally reassures me, but I have a better idea. How 'bout I jump out the cab like '007 and roll to safety? Naaaw. I would just be another splat on the highway. Relax Raven.

Before I know it, we arrive. The traffic suddenly congests as anybody who's anybody is trying to get their butt to the gare. Vendors charge toward our window and thrust their wares against the glass. The driver keeps yelling, "Il faut partir!" but they keep coming. They stand holding up their batik cloth, their peanuts, their little bags of bissap not saying much but hoisting products in the air and as soon as they see us, their faces spread outward in a smile and they scream, "les blancs, les blancs!" Shoot. I . . . ain't . . . White. You better say 'le blanc' and keep it singular.

But, it is unstoppable. The color of our skin is a magnet; mine only a few shades darker than Steve's. The cab driver is going crazy. "Quitte là! Faut faire attention! Oh!" Vendors are jumping in front of his car to get around to our windows. They don't see the car. We are two White bodies suspended in space. This combined with the fact that the line of cars unsuccessfully tries to split off into the various directions of all the gares, leaves us at a standstill.

"Even if you like something don't buy it," Steve warns. "We'll never get out of here then." The vendors are something else, but the apprentis are even more creative. They are the young men you can see, mostly in their teens to early twenties, hanging from the door of a baidjan. They collect the money of the passengers, figure out how to get and give back exact change so as not to lose their supply of coins, and climb on top of the roof to stack luggage as well as make sure it doesn't fall off. They are supposed to attract clientele and are not aggressive about it, but impostors give them a bad name.

Young men run up to our cab screaming, 'Bon arrivé!' and 'Il faut descendre ici!' or the infamous 'Tu vas oú?' They welcome us. They try to convince us that we have already arrived at our destination or try to find out where we are going so that they can lead us there and then ask for money. They are young men with shoes, full of holes, turned into sandals because the shoes are too big for their feet or their heels smash down the backs of them.

"Viens!" One yells, but where does this apprenti impostor want us to go? Steve and I look at each other confused. "Tu vas où?" he asks. I say nothing.

"Gare de NTT." Damn! Why did Steve answer? Our silence would have forced the kid to go away and Steve can see the gare just around the corner.

The young man looks around very anxiously. "C'est lá!" he exclaims. Okay. You know that we can see it for ourselves. But, you continue to stand there.

"I think he wants some money now Steve."

"Faut quitter ici. On a déjà arrivé!" The cab driver is very annoyed and yells. That's what I'm sayin'. Get outta' here. We've already arrived. As hot and boiling as we are in this cab, which probably hasn't had running air conditioning since the 1980s, Steve rolls up the window. You'd think after that the impostor would give up, but the youth runs to my side instead. If anything we've learned thus far, never give money. Because when you give away money, word spreads, and then we'll have ten apprentis, five women selling batik, two peanut girls, and one ngyamakuji lady here.

That is the problem in Abidjan. Young kids tired of working in the fields with their parents on land that is often owned by someone else, come to the cities with an illusion of riches they never gain because they don't understand the economic system. They come with the simple knowledge that there is more money in Abidjan. Once they get here, however, they are stuck with no money and nowhere to go, running the streets, hoping that some baidjan or bus operation gives them a job regardless of their level of formal education.

It is hard for kids coming from a true village, where people help just because they can, to come to a city where everyone is fighting for themselves only. What can we do? One hundred CFA francs here and there will never burn a whole in our pockets, but what is the greater solution for these kids? We are Peace Corps Volunteers and kids ourselves—mostly in our twenties—confused by the innumerable cultures, range of lifestyles, incurable and curable diseases, poverty, and richness all in the same place around us. We are not supposed to be intimidated by any of this. But, how can we help before having a firm grasp on the issues?

NTT is our bus—a big blue bus with yellow letters that have the NTT on both sides of it. It is usually on time and packed without having to wait very long for tickets to sell out. Someone is always going or coming to this gare that goes to Daloa. Maybe it is popular because the road it uses is an actual paved cement road. Unlike my gare that goes from Daloa to my site, NTT is protected by two high, side walls and a fence in the front. We get out, get our things, pay the driver, and lug our luggage to the back of the gare. Stacks of bananas, grain, and huge boxes line the walls.

"Is that going on the bus, too?"

"I hope not," Steve mutters.

When we finally reach the back of the gare, there is only a wobbling, black iron railing that I am not so eager to use to pull myself
up into the roofed waiting area. But, I succeed and turn back
around toward Steve to hand up my immense red suitcase. An older woman, wrapped in a beautiful orange and green skirt and top,
sits where I've stepped up. We look at each other with intrigue.
But, my intrigue is about how in the hell she got up here with all
of her wraps on when I barely managed to step up onto this three-
foot-high floor?

The benches are long and placed as in a church. Either we are
getting married, going to confess our sins, or are butt naked. People
stare at us and stare back at each other as we walk down the aisle.
Lines already form by the bus at 6:30 a.m., but when we reach the
ticket window no one is there. Steve peers down by the part of the
glass where the money goes.

"There is a person in there," he says.

Window shades cover all the windows and they've been pulled
down just enough to cut the cashiers off from view but enough for
you to see their hands when they take your money. These windows
are old, stained, and the brightest part of the entire gare is the
NTT busses alone.

"Deux pour Daloa," Steve requests as his face turns red from
bending down and straining to look up at the cashier's face.

Looking back and forth between Steve and now me, also staring
up at him from the small space below the window shade, the ticket
man slips out the words "sept mille."

3,500 CFA for me and 3,500 CFA for Steve. I slide my money
under the window and Steve follows. The ticket man peers down
and pauses at the 7,000 and then stares at the both of us still staring back up at him. I don't know about Steve, but I'm looking just
to see if this man runs off with our money and how I'm going to
find the door to get back there if he does.

"What's wrong?" Steve peers back at me. "Did we give the right
amount?" I nod a quick yes and look back up at the cashier, trying
to appear just as expressionless as he does. Man, this dude is crazy.

There aren't any windows in here. This small space is the only way he gets air. But, they are handling loads of money by the hour. They have to keep some sense of security I guess. People constantly putting down 3,500 CFA, is no small deal here. And, there is no perceivable door to the room. What do they do, come to work through the roof? After five long seconds of staring at us staring at him, he takes the money and produces two tickets.

"Maybe he was surprised that I paid for myself," I say. Steve shrugs and turns around. Or, maybe he didn't want to be identified as the keeper of money.

We spin around to find seats and the people stare and look away, stare and look away again. They want to stare but don't want to be caught staring. I hope that my staring back helps them make up their minds, not done in an evil way, but you know. We find a space toward the back and crash down on the benches that sway to the sides a bit as the benches do at the Daloa gare.

"I'm hungry," Steve proclaims and out comes the last bit of a PowerBar.

"Where the hell did that come from?" I cry out. People suddenly glance back at us unafraid this time. "Where did that come from?" I repeat softly.

"I didn't eat any breakfast," he responds. I hadn't either. We are starving and there is not going to be any rations sharing I see.

"I'm going to get something to eat." Steve announces popping up, not looking back down at me.

"From where? We're not supposed to eat any street food."

"Look at that store behind us. That doesn't look like street food. There ain't nothin' in there but ice cream and stuff."

"There's gotta' be more than ice cream. Go ask," I quickly change my mind about being picky.

Discussion goes back and forth. Steve strains a little to ask what the stand clerk has and the clerk makes expressions of confusion while raising water and ice cream bars to show what all he has. What a disappointment. Nothing!

Steve sits back down and whips out what is left of his Power-Bar. I stare. I don't want it. It is brown and funny lookin'. Definitely not in the States anymore. I'm sure we won't find a PowerBar in the entire country. I'm sad, but Steve has energy . . . now after eating, of course.

"Maybe we need to put our stuff over there," Steve is anxious. People are busy lining up to give their luggage to some man sitting in a shaded space up against the wall below. We jump down off the waiting area floor, dragging our luggage down with us. Oohw. Ugh. Awh. Heavy. The bus is parked alongside the shaded area. Bags everywhere. We receive a ticket for ours. But, then I regret it when I see what is being stacked under the bus along with our things.

"My knapsack sure isn't getting checked, too," I whisper to Steve. His eyes scan the lower compartment. The plantains that were piled in bags along the walls are now packed back against the sides of the bottom of the bus. Some plantains poke through holes in the bags with gooey tips from being ripe. Some bags are full of bright, red palm oil seeds making red oil stains through their sacks. Overall, the bottom luggage area of the bus has a funny smell from a range of things placed under here at one point or another. Who knows what my suitcase will look and smell like once it is pulled from underneath here?

I hold onto my knapsack tight and get on what appears to be the line for the bus. Where is the line anyway? People are just walking about and shoving their tickets in a man's face. He picks tickets from the crowd, order known only to him.

Tall, short, medium heights. Deep brown, black, reddish-brown, light brown, bluish-black, coffee brown. Truly curly, curly straight, straight stiff, tight curls. Thick, thin, heavy-set, overweight, paper-straight. Babies, old ladies, men with canes, young girls, preppy young men. Merchants, teachers, doctors, farmers. In one single line, there is every kind of person and they all travel together.

A community in the true sense of the word. No separations here. No wonder we fight and disagree in the States. No one can expect to see this gamut of people with their different colors, shapes, languages, and probably beliefs all together in one tiny area. Here in Cote d'Ivoire, community is common. Common + unity = it's common for everyone to be together. Everyone is moving, travelling, living, and breathing together. No unknowns to imagine the worst about. Everyone is right here, right in your face.

We get on the bus toward the back, and I sit next to the window putting my legs and knees up on the back of the chair in front of me. Either that or sit up completely straight for five hours. There is no other way for me to lean back. Steve's and my seat are fused into one.

"Shoot, I dropped my ticket." I lean straight forward and reach down. I have to turn my head and body to the side, mashing my hair into the back of the seat in front of me, trying not to mush my nose into the window to the left of me.

"You got room?" Steve gives me some space, but my butt is unavoidably up against his lap. Worse than him stuck in the middle is the woman to his right who has to step her right foot out into the aisle for balance.

The seats are dark green and worn with holes in places where they have been worn down from body parts without enough space. The bottom window cannot be opened, but the top one slides open after a few pushes, tugs, yanks, and grunts. Steve jumps up to assist me in the final push.

"Il est poli," comes from somewhere.

"Look they're calling you polite now. Better than 'White man,' ain't it?" We laugh a little, but self-consciousness keeps us from laughing too hard.

The wind is calm outside, but you wouldn't know this by the way it roars through our window as we start to drive. It whips me in the face, but Steve beads in sweat.

"Il faut fermer la fenêtre," I hear a lady's voice directly behind my seat.

"I think she said something about the window, Steve."

"It's hot as hell in here. There's no air-conditioning and she wants us to close the window?"

"Just a little? It'll still be cool if we leave it open a little."

Steve makes a half gone mad, half worn-out face, so I take that as okay and start to push it. It closes completely 'cause I have to push it hard. I open it again and it comes all the way back. Wind bombards us. Hair stands straight up and back. Faces turn scrunched up and sour.

"C'est quoi ça?!" a middle-aged, suited man behind us shouts.

"Sayqwahsah? Saayqwaahsah, Saayqwaaahsaaah," I sound his words out under my breath. "quoi, c'est q . . ." Oh, it means 'what is that?' or with his tone, 'what's up with that?!'

"Faut fermer la fenêtre! Tu es fou ou bien?!" another older man cuts off my audible reflection in a roar. Daaang! They are co-bustin' on me. Don't call me crazy! I'm just tryna' work with this crazy-ass window! I should have left the damn thing the way it was. The same woman who complains first complains again.

"Oh! Close the window!" she wines in French placing her hand over her forehead. After a few nudges forward and a few nudges backward, I achieve just the right amount of openness to keep big mouth lady behind me quiet and White man from drowning in his sweat.

Being right underneath the window, I get the first hard whips in of the outside air. As long as no one yells at me, it's fine. Ugh. 'C'est quoi ça' is right! What iiiis up with that? I put my head against the window to relax with eyes closed when a baby starts wailing out of nowhere. I open my eyes and it gets even louder. It's the seat directly in front of me. Leaning up against the glass again, a little baby peers back at me then looks away. Each time she calms down, she looks back at me to get some more, and the look on her face makes me feel ashamed. Her eyes widen in surprise, her mouth slowly opens, and she starts shaking her head back and forth with her eyes closed in a 'no, no, NO!' head flurry.

"I had that effect on babies back at Grand Noyaré," Steve plain-ly notes.

"How do you know that's why she's crying?" I protest. Before Steve can respond, the woman holding the baby answers.

"Il a peur de toi." Afraid of me? Man. That's bold to say. Never have I had my color thrown up in my face like this by White and Black, young and old, all at once. The woman in front of me finally decides to switch the baby from her left shoulder to her right which makes me feel worse, but what is more important, my pride or my damn eardrums?

I settle back against the window again. The fear that the baby will look back once more to scream soon goes away and my attention veers off out the window. The city starts to disappear. No more buildings. No more street lamps. No more sidewalks. No more overhead bridges. No more big stores. This time to Daloa, I take everything in. Steve is in his world and I in mine.

The sides of the highway immediately shoot up into steep hills that have shacks at the top with palm trees all around them. A few people walk up and down these hills. Masses of clotheslines with clothes hanging out to dry cover the hill. The clothes are discolored, worn, and torn, but their owners place them gently because those are the only clothes they have. But, soon even the clotheslines disappear and the people walking through and around them disappear as well. The hills become higher and greener as we speed down the highway.

"Haaaaaa," I involuntarily exhale. Suddenly, there is nothing. Land explodes around us. I have never seen so much land, real land, stretching out as immensely as this. Land has its own identity. Land has its own rights.

An hour passes. Two hours pass. By the third hour, we reach Yamoussoukro our third time. The stranded Basilica is around somewhere. My stomach growls. I still haven't eaten yet. Steve hears my rumble and boasts, "I'm gonna' get something here."

"We're not supposed to eat off the street, man. Do you wanna' get sick?" I whisper just in case someone by some chance speaks English too.

"Man. I don't care. I'm thirsty. I'll just have to take my chances."

I frown, more upset that I am too afraid to make the same choice. Steve disappears off the bus and down some street. Shoot. Where is he going? I look at the garages in this expansive Yamoussoukro bus terminal and off in the distance I see bathrooms. Looord, here's my chance. If I don't go now, I have a two-hour wait left.

The bathroom is old but like any other bathroom. I open a

door, take a step up, and close the door behind me. I turn around toward the toilet. Oh. Excuse me. Hole. Another hole? I can't take it anymore. Not like I'm gonna' sit on public toilet seats, but at least a toilet bowl allows you to avoid looking straight down into the hole where everything goes. It is cramped in here and the hole is right back up against the wall. Facing the wall to do my business is not an option. Not even squat-facing the wall is possible without squirting everything in sight. The hole is flat and there is no semi-igloo-shaped hood to curb the pee like traditional Japanese toilets would. The only option is to turn around with butt toward wall, but how in the hell am I going to make it in the hole without rubbing my butt up against the wall?

"Yuck." Disgusting. I straddle the hole facing the door, keep my back straight to keep from falling forward, and lift my butt up. Quite a physical feat.

"Shit!" I missed it. Hold. Reposition. Let's try again. I make my back as straight as possible, lift my butt up as much as I'm able while holding both sides of the wall to keep from falling over, and go to town. It's working! Done. I start washing my hands . . . Oh no. The bus!

I bolt out the doorless entrance, down the stairs, past the garages to where the busses are lined up by the front of the terminal at the gate. So many busses have pulled up since I've been gone and all of them look alike! I run all the way up to the first of ten. I frantically run back to the last one. This isn't it either. I run to the third one. I'll just get on this one and check to see if it's mine. But, how am I gonna' know it's mine unless I run all the way to the back and chance not seeing my bus leave? And, I am so worried about people noticing me that I never take the time to notice who else is on my bus.

"Over here!" Steve yells just as I am about to get on a third bus. I run over to the second bus and Steve has his head sticking out the side window.

"I had to tell them to wait," he exclaims when I reach my seat. We both know this is a big deal because that means he had to explain the whole scenario of me off in the bathroom to a hurried bus driver—in fucked up French.

"Thank you so much. Going to the bathroom was a heck of an ordeal. Y'ont even know. Whew." I squeeze past Steve to the window and plop down in the seat but have to straighten back up immediately to conform to its flatness. Then, out of the corner of my eye I notice it—the wetness and coolness of it. Steve has bought a small, plastic sachet tied at the top in a little knot. This he turns over, pinches a bottom corner between his fingers and bites it off to suck out the juice. A chunk of ice floats in the middle because it is 'bien glacé.'

"Is it cold?" I ask just to drive myself crazy with jealousy.

"Yeah," is all he will admit, too concentrated on keeping the juice from squirting out.

"I don't care," he squeaks out—about getting sick that is.

The sweat drops on his forehead slowly disappear. 'Bissap' is what they call it and the flower it is made from has the same name and color—a deep purplish-red. Ivoiriens boil the bissap petals in water so Steve knows it is somewhat purified. I was sick for two of the three months at Grand Noyaré just trying to figure out what to eat and how to eat it, always feeling on empty. Hear no evil, see no evil. That's how I'm gonna' get through this temptation. But, then Steve pulls out another one.

"You gonna' be shittin' all over the place, man."

"You can't ruin this for me. We're gonna' get sick anyways so why not enjoy it?" Umh. Good point. There is no way to protect ourselves from everything out here waiting for us. The Ivoiriens get sick from unpurified water as well. How discouraging it must be for them to live this way all of the time.

The universe conspires in my favor, however, with the young teenage boy below now walking up and down the side of the bus with a Styrofoam box strapped over his shoulder.

"La glaaaace!" he screams at the top of his lungs. I throw the window back and flag him down.

"C'est combien?" I reach out the window before even knowing the answer to my question.

"Ceeeeent francs!" Every time he speaks, he advertises. Where is my 100 CFA franc coin? Down in my jeans that I shouldn't even have on as hot as it is, I get lucky.

"Tiens," I thrust it forward and he takes it. Vanilla ice cream wrapped up with a stick on the end and logo around it; this is made at a company and not at somebody's house. Aaaaaah. Cool, vanilla-tasting, yes, and squidaly-oops-ah delicious. Before the young boy gets away, I produce another coin and he fumbles through his box to quickly get the most frozen one. When I turn to boast, Steve's already got me beat on bissap number three.

We pull off from Yamoussoukro. Every few miles is a road that leads off to some village out of sight, except for a few people around or a small store shack at the highway's edge. Vegetation springs everywhere. Light green, dark green, regular green, algae, and chartreuse; lively trees and plants laugh at us along the wide road.

Getting used to the bumpiness of the ride brings on a doze until a strong gust of motherly wind flaps in through the narrow space in the window and my lungs expand. The land vegetation thickens. Two people standing next to each other with both arms straight out and connected by a finger touch, would not be as wide as these trees. They are an odd grayish-white color. The bases are several feet thick but shoot up thinning all the way to the tops that poof out into an absurdly tiny broccoli shape. The trees are so high that the sounds of the birds, singing at the top of one, float to my ears in only a whisper until one of them swoops down by the window and I can hear the sweet, high tweet their voices actually make.

With each breath my lungs relax more. Do some places have more oxygen than others? Beyond fresh, it is mystical. Drunkenness creeps in from it. My mind expands, heart pounds less forcefully, and ears pick up every stillness unseen. Flowers bloom in the heart. Vines grow from arms. Plants sprout from feet. Air takes the body over. This new world breathes for me. What surreptitious misery for those in places with less green things than people.

The bus pulls to the first of two Gendarmerie stops just before Daloa. The brown earth in Abidjan contrasts the deep, orangey-red here. Deep green, orangey red, and velvety brown colors, in the skin of several women and girls, flood the eyes as they flock to our bus.

Too much air. Too much color. Too much life not even considering the sounds of so many languages being spoken all at once— these, too, swoosh in as another passenger thrusts a window open, throwing his arms quickly out to reach the offerings.

"Biiiiiiiiiisaaaaaaap!" sings the first voice.

"Arachide! Banane!" demands the second.

"Les oeufs!" rings a third.

Divide 50 CFA by 600 CFA. Less than one-tenth of a cent. That is how much in American money I pay for the first boiled egg I sink my teeth into. I could buy a carton of eggs for one cent. The little girl that sells me my first egg wears a loosely tucked wrap skirt that drags a bit on the ground and a sleeveless top. She sets the silver platter full of eggs on top of a cloth that is wound up on top of her head.

The egg is still warm as I crack open the shell. She passes up a miniature piece of paper wrapped like a big tear drop. I finish half of the egg before sprinkling what's in this paper onto my egg and am disappointed to late discover how good this salty, spicy, red pepper seasoning is. I duck my head out the window again. Another egg and I am in business but still not satisfied.

"Arachide! Banane!" the voice of a little girl demands as she carries her tray up over her shoulder. "Arachide!" What the heck is arachide? She glides closer and roasted peanuts come into view. The plantain lying next to them doesn't look like much with the skin burnt black on the outside, but I purchase one and pop a piece in my mouth only to soon discover that the smoking process deepens the sweet flavor just as much as boiling does. Back and forth the mouth goes between taking a bite of roasted plantain and shoving peanuts into it. I'm not in control. All this simple goodness I've been missing!

Do I dare find something to drink? Plenty of bissap girls and women pass by, but bissap is too sweet for me. A young girl at another stopped bus waits for the Gendarmes to finish so she can sell. Ugh, she's got bissap, too, but what are those sandy-colored sachets? She catches me staring and risks a dash across traffic to our bus that waits to be checked.

"Ça c'est quoi?" I point down at the sandy-colored sachets of juice.

"Ça?" she points at the bissap to confirm.

"Non. Ça là, à côté," I point to the ones sitting next to the bissap.

"Ça c'est la ngyamakuji." The what?

"Ngyamakuji," I repeat her 'nya' sound. She repeats herself once more on seeing my blank expression.

"Here. Fifty francs," she then offers the price as she raises one up to me—quickly giving up on the pronunciation lesson.

"Mais, ngyamakuji c'est quoi?" I hesitate but proceed to insist on further detail.

"C'est le gingembre." Gingembre? Sigh. Another word I don't know. The heat is attacking me because the bus is not moving and there is no longer air rushing inside the windows. Let me just try it before I pass out.

Ginger! Sweet but fiery, it instantaneously brings me life. The sachet is wrapped very tightly so the juice squirts out strongly and I'm forced to finish quickly. As usual, I buy another one.

"You wanna' try this?" I turn to Steve. But, he is now on bissap number four. Where is he pulling these things from? I buy another ginger juice. The eggs, peanuts, plantain, and ngyamakuji are better than any potato chips or candy bars.

After passing through one more Gendarmerie stop, we are a few minutes from pulling into Daloa. On entering the city of Daloa, there is an old billboard promoting powdered milk for babies as the road slopes upward. The last five miles to Daloa slope sharply upward then sharply downward, but the ups are much longer than the downs. We are at high elevation and the air percolates.

We pass some school buildings on the left and fairly sized houses on the right. Some land sits abandoned with nothing more than baby plantain trees sprouting up in the midst of high grass and debris. There is no grass in front of the houses, only light or reddish-brown earth with smooth lines spread across them from the women who sweep it with small, straw brooms. Japanese Zen gardens come to mind.

The city enlivens upon reaching the center. Young kids and teenagers sprint from one side of the street to the other to join their friends in school uniform, to join their friends in rags, or to sell water, homemade juice or donuts, and other goodies to a potential customer.

All ethnicities descend on Daloa and one speaks to anyone who speaks their language, raggedy-looking or not. Ivoiriens drive on the left side of the car and left side of the road. Taxis speed back and forth. Baidjans pull off packed for far away destinations with apprentis hanging from outside the front passenger door. Luggage piles up high on every other vehicle. A barely visible swirl of dust is in the air and never settles as there is always some sudden rush of action.

We pull into our blue and yellow NTT gare, half the size of the one in Abidjan and not far from my gare. As expected, my red suitcase comes out a few smudges more than before. Steve and I grab our luggage, throw our large knapsacks over our shoulders, and hail a green cab. It isn't as much of a hassle to catch a cab in Daloa as in Abidjan. We are back at the Daloa House in a flash.

"I'm staying here tonight before going to my site," Steve tells the air.

"Me too," I spurt without thinking. Our Daloa House Leader has bought wood to put together a mini-bar in the front room and it's turning out pretty nice. No alcohol stock but a cool place to eat.

Glad to be with so many English speakers. I need a break from French. Being the only Black volunteer is the last thing I'm thinking about, although when the house guard's eyes meet mine, I know something's up. The guard's duty is to keep watch on the house at all times. But, the volunteers have him cleaning up the yard, hand washing their clothes, and going on errands to the store.

"Hey petit . . ." I hear a volunteer call after the guard. Doesn't that mean 'little one?' This would all be a little more legit if some CFA change ever passed between them and the guard, but no. Nothing. Yes, some White volunteers have a few lapses of master-itis, but most are not so disconnected, thank goodness.

Music? Do I hear American music? It sounds so good not because I'm a rock music fan but because its familiarity comforts. It echoes through the open doors, out to the patio, up the coconut trees, and floats out onto the street. No cacophony of sounds puts me on alert. No cars, no hum of machines, no factory or building noises or TV alert me. No doors are sealed enough to separate us from the night and the infectious air in our lungs. We eat and laugh, play cards, and listen to music and one other. This kind of natural fun is rare. Nothing fancy in our surroundings, just our fancy personalities. Naturally, the day finally hits us and we fall out.

French bread is the morning adventure. The store on the corner has lots of posters glued on its inside walls and around its concrete front wall. A tin roof covers the tiny space. A thick bar gate lays open.

"Gum, please." A young boy and his little sister walk up to buy.

"How many?" the owner barks from behind the counter. Several other kids walk up to the storefront asking for various items. But, why is it that they never enter? The kids stick their slender, dark brown arms through the gate bars with money in their hands. He brings their purchase to them and they drop the money in his hand.

The owner isn't Ivoirien. Maybe Moroccan. He has an Arabic accent and sure does keep a suspicious eye. I walk around the store and feel that eye on me without much of a look in Sandra or Steve's direction.

"I'm gonna' get yaourt," Sandra declares instead of 'yogurt,' just falling short of speaking French to one another. We mix French words in where we are used to saying the French version so much that we can't think quick enough to say it in English. Sandra obviously eats a lot of yaourt then.

"I can't eat yogurt in the morning man." To this, Sandra gives an Ivoirien shrug and 'unh.' She has certainly been here a while. I glance around more anxious to find something to buy, more so that I can show the owner I have money than that I really want anything at all. Soon, my anxiousness trumps my lactose-intolerance and I give up on actually finding something I like for some pizza-shaped cheese in small packets, eggs, and a long, skinny loaf of bread instead.

"225" is all his lips budge and he stares at me. Dag. Can I get a 'francs' on the end of that at least? How I'm gonna' be in Cote d'Ivoire surrounded by millions of Ivoiriens and a billion Africans beyond that, dealing with an African himself who'd rather be more friendly with Sandra and Steve than me? And, he and I are the exact same color—that's some Houdini magic, psychological disembowelment if you ask me.

Poof! I open the gas pipe up too much and flame shoots out in all directions of the kitchen.

"Shit man! I'm fuckin' gonna' burn up trynda' cook some damn eggs!" I yell out to anyone who can hear in the house.

"Dude! What aaaaare you doing?" Sandra exclaims in her characteristic West Coast voice. She rescues me, showing me how to open up the gas aperture just enough to catch the flame from the lighter, which has to be held really close to the burner but without burning my hand off or having flames shoot up my arms. I'd rather go out, cut up wood, and make a fire than deal with this shit. Peace Corps makes a sailor out of everyone—curses ring from our mouths without a wince.

"I'm fuckin' hungry as hell," grumbles another volunteer into the kitchen so I drop some cheese chunks on my eggs, stick them in between the bread, and pass it to him.

"Here you go."

"Oh, thanks," he takes it with eyes opened wide and leaves the kitchen quickly with sandwich in mouth. Volunteers are very generous with each other. We have little money in U.S. standards, but in Cote d'Ivoire we are equivalent in salary to what are called fonctionnaires or civil servants and a farmer might consider us Grand

Types. Taking turns paying for meals or cab rides is standard procedure since we know it always comes back around. No doubt we copy this from Ivoiriens who always share their last, knowing that next time someone will do the same for them. One night in Daloa easily becomes two.

We get up early the next morning despite another late crash and set out for our respective gares at 8:00 a.m. Sandra tags along with Steve and me.

"Hey you guys, my gare is over there so I'll see you later," Steve smiles then up and hops off. Sandra and I watch him disappear and then Sandra disappears.

"I'll be right back," she says, and with that I am truly alone for the first time in months.

"Where are you going?" someone asks. I turn around and see half the cook's face, a pair of sparkling, coal black, smiling eyes, miniature jet black afro, and warm brown skin blending into the color of the shack as he looks at me from inside through the small, square hole cut into the wood.

"Zragbi," I report.

It has been a while since Sandra left. My baidjan might pull up and whisk me off before Sandra returns. I sit inside the Zragbi gare shack with the same characters I met the first time I came with Bogo. Money Hands is there, counting the money folded long ways and sticking out from between his fingers. There is the beautifully black, dark-chocolate Senoufo man who is always smiling as well but with his entire being. And, of course, the cook, who doesn't ever come from behind his long, rickety wooden table where he creates behind a flat gas stove on a long table bench. Sandra busts through the back entrance of the gare.

"Dégé, girl. This is the best 'yaourt' you will ever have." Ugh, again with the yogurt? Sandra has already broken hers open from the bottom, sucking it out while handing me one of the other two in her other hand. It is the biggest, knotted, plastic sachet in all of Cote d'Ivoire.

"Dang. Are they that good?" I doubt. How many good things that I never knew existed can I discover here in a matter of months? I've had so many good things to eat—what happened to all the starving Africans on TV? We eatin' good.

"Raven. Oh my Goodness. You have to try it."

I flip it over and stare at it a bit. The texture is thicker and whiter than other yogurts and there are little brown dots of something throughout it. Sayqwahsah? It isn't just yogurt in there. What is that?—C'est quoi ça?

"Those are grains." Grains my ass. But, as with anything new in this place, I am learning to trust and dive in. I bite a bottom tip off and to my surprise it doesn't come squirting out into my mouth. It percolates just like the air here. Stark white, thick, rich, creamy, and not too sweet, the texture is amazing. The grains give it an even greater taste. A complete meal. All of the nutrients and fiber I need. Hate to sound corny, but it is simply nutritious.

"I want another one," and this causes Sandra to frown down at her third.

"My own I mean."

I turn around and walk out the back. Sandra follows me up in the rear. It's not long before we stumble upon a beautiful young girl standing with a silver saucer full of dégé, selling her yogurt in Jula language. She is excited to see me just as soon as she sees my excitement to see her. I fumble through my bag for change and give her fifty CFA francs with a smile. Ooh, it's good. And, ooh, is that my baidjan leaving? Through the back of the gare I can see it and it's already full.

The apprentis quickly pile everyone's luggage on top of the baidjan and I detect a little strain when one apprenti picks up my crazy, red piece of luggage. Another apprenti runs to help him hoist it up while a third is already waiting at the top to pull it up, over everything else.

I step into the baidjan hesitantly as always. The roof is low and the seats are all different as if they come from various discarded cars. They are strategically smooshed in together to get the most out of the space. I go to take the far back, but the driver ushers me up front next to him. There are only two seats up here and unlike the back, I have a fully open window that works and stretch my legs out without having to worry I'm putting my feet on someone's things or that I have my knees in someone's back from behind a seat. Sandra runs up to the passenger's side.

"Bye," Sandra says with the Peace Corps smile that means 'I don't know when I'll see you again, but I'll see you.' I am sad to see her go.

How does a young White woman walk around here the way Sandra does? Not because she naturally swivels her hips or even because she has no problem speaking French with a good Ivoirien accent but because it is obvious that she is comfortable with who she is. The way she carries herself makes Ivoiriens forget she is White before they even know much about her. She doesn't give a damn . . . in a good way. She disappears off into the crowd again except this time for good. You'd think she's been here all of her life and has no intention of leaving.

Sandra is certain of why she's here or, if not, she knows how to make the unknowns of this journey a part of it. I, on the other hand, can't stop wondering what in the world I'm here to do!

8 SAYQWAHSAH?!

"Zragbi! Zragbi!" Money Hands yells out trying to get one last person into the baidjan to fill it up completely and as luck prefers it, one last person arrives. Thank goodness. So many hours have passed since Sandra walked off into the earlier heat-haze of the day.

Once the baidjan van is Ivoirien-packed, off we go back down the main Abidjan road. Those same two Gendarme checkpoints along the way stand between us and Zragbi. Of course we have to enter them and everyone hopes to be waved through. Some passengers are from another country but manage to live here for a while without papers or some stay in their village so long that they haven't renewed papers in town.

One Gendarme is ready for us standing sharply, right at the edge of the road. He waives us down with a smile on his face already. Black boots make his feet and legs twice their normal size. Hoisting his arms up on his hips once the car rolls to a stop in front of him, he is covered in green camouflage clothing and hat.

Usually, these 'Men of Arms,' as the term means, wave us

through without checking IDs because the Zragbi drivers go through this checkpoint all day long. This is their area. However, these men sometimes conduct the perfunctory look-around required.

"Ça va?" The Gendarme peeks his head in on the driver's side.

"Yes," the driver peeps out, now nervous.

The Gendarme smiles over at the driver. This sitting back and staying low that I'm doing, is not really going to hide my face. Walking from my side of the vehicle slowly around to the driver's side, he finally catches something out of the corner of his eye, clicking his head up over to where I sit.

'Who is that?' must be what he guns in French next. The driver feigns cluelessness, struggling through his French to prevent full-on engagement. He is very nervous. Maybe this Gendarme has a reputation? The Gendarme's smile turns to an unsatisfied scowl.

"Don't speak when he talks to you," now rolls smoothly in French out of the driver's tight mouth as the Gendarme is now walking back over to my side. Am I about to get pop-glocked? My stiffening body resembles the driver's as the Gendarme speaks to me.

"Ça va?" he asks. I pretend that I don't understand him. "Carte d'identité?" I give my best confused-face. "Your carte of identity," he then brings forth in Franglish. I reach in my bag and produce my ID card. Volunteers carry their passports everywhere. He looks at my card and then back up at me. Looks at the card again then back up at me. Over and over again, he does this cross-checking every damn feature on my face. Finally, after directly staring a while without shame, a smile comes across his face that I only see partially because I look past him to avoid straight eye contact.

"Liberian girrrrrl!" he sings sticking his face in the window closer to mine. What? Michael Jackson? The built-up tension keeps me from laughing when I should. It is funny however—getting serenaded with Michael Jackson at a checkpoint. I guess I do look Liberian or Bèté. Whatever it is, I look like somethin'. He gathers I am in no mood to laugh and a quick exchange goes on over me between him and the driver.

"No . . . no . . . no . . ." the driver responds to his questions very emphatically. The Gendarme gives me a final once-over and backs away from the car, waiving us off with his long, shooing right arm and hand. The other passengers exhale, glad that I steal the show and that they don't have to deal with him.

The road to Zragbi is as long and bumpy as the first time, but this time I'm more nervous. I don't know anyone in this baidjan or the cultures and languages to which they each belong. Plus, I'm alone this time.

I'm happy to be near a window and I lovingly absorb the immense landscape. Dunes stand up along the road every 1,000 feet. Ants build their dunes wherever water abounds. There has to be water underground permeating the soil, allowing the ants to mold the red earth into tall, red mounds that produce odd, imposing shapes within the pyramidal structures in the air.

The trees are still so high and some gray with bright green rings of color on the bark. The land on both sides of the Zragbi road has been planted on at some point and is cleared compared to the dense trees tucked in the background. Pockets of water start to appear every few minutes alongside the road. We pass Grézuou on the way to Zragbi, and there is no visible human action. The next pocket of water is a little larger, stretching underneath the road to the other side, with a couple of boys sitting on the edge and a third in the water swimming. They have swimming lessons out here? How'd he learn how to swim? But, we are all swimmers, aren't we? Any human being alive was the first sperm to get to the egg out of the hundreds of millions of others all in that one shot. Why wouldn't kids figure it out?

"Ça descends," I yell as Zragbi approaches, but I have no need to because everyone gets off here. The market is in full swing on Monday. Where did all these people come from? Many more villages must exist beyond here. People also fill the baidjan back up and continue on down the road that splits and goes off into two opposite directions. The road to the right goes up toward Seraguhé, another nearby village. Grézuou is mainly of the Bèté ethnicity while Seraguhé is mostly Jula and Senoufo; two Muslim ethnicities who usually live in the north of Cote d'Ivoire.

Zragbi is a hodge-podge of Grézuou and Seraguhé. There are Bèté, Jula, Senoufo, and small numbers of numerous other ethnicities. Zragbi brings this trinity, and more, together on market day. It . . . is . . . packed and far more populous than on average when everyone is off farming in the woods.

I weave my way quickly through the crowd and hope that the others off the baidjan are more interesting to the villagers than me. That is going to be pretty difficult seeing as I have this huge, red suitcase. This damn red bag and damn yellow skin color. I keep my eyes up and my chin down. The hospital is straight ahead. Just keep going. You can make it.

I weave through the market folks as quickly and seamlessly as possible, but when I arrive at the hospital it's just as packed as the market. Sticking out is unavoidable as everyone waiting in line is ailed or carrying something in the oven and have nothing else to watch. Bogo sees me and motions an index finger for me to wait. No problem. A few minutes later he jumps up and rushes me off to his house. Dare I ask it?

"Is my house ready?" Maybe my French is no good or he doesn't hear me.

"Put your bags inside the house," he says without a glance toward me.

"Is my house ready?" I ask again.

"No." Bogo goes off to work. Guess more than language is the problem.

I'm taking a walk. Céline is at the hospital working, too. Not quite sure of my direction, but the same route back through the market and across the main road should be promising. Dodging doo doo is par for the course. I'm starting to know my doo doo pretty well. Chicken poop versus sheep poop versus cow poop—each has its own special quality.

"Aw, shit!" I take a turn into a patch of grass and almost step in human poop.

Different textures, smells, and sizes; I can tell which animals are around by the trails they leave. As soon as I see tiny, hard, black poop, I hear a sheep baaa-ing nearby. Women are at their houses bending over large metal or bright-colored, round, plastic basins. Barefoot babies not big enough to walk ten feet without falling but that can manage a good waddle-walk, waddle their way around courtyards, disappearing behind houses only to pop back up a few moments later with goofy faces or crying because they hurt themselves while their mothers cook or clean the courtyard.

This must be the Jula quartier. There are no Bèté here from the languages I hear. The Bèté are on the other side of the market. This segregation is strange since most Bèté speak Jula although I've never heard a Jula speak or understand Bèté at all.

One's relationship with land is evidently different here. Getting from one path to the next necessitates that I walk through someone's backyard. No one has a fence or any other type of barrier. Back home, you step on someone's land and the response you get sometimes . . . well, you might as well have just stepped on their face. Land is a part of an American's sense of self worth. As I pass, men, women, and children stop to watch me. Is it the intrusion or my skin?

"Bonjour!" I greet them as I see them greet each other . . . nothing comes back.

Around 17:00 p.m., the sun still blazes at its best and Bogo is off. The Filles de Salle, Céline and Oyo, assist the Sage Femme, which means Midwife. The Garcons de Salle assist the Infirmier, which is Bogo, the Head Nurse. Although consultations are done for the day, if an emergency arrives they must go back.

"I'm going to take you on a tour now," Bogo says.

I am meeting all of the Chiefs in the villages of the area and some random Grand Types living in between villages, neither here nor there. One of the Grand Types has his own car. Not even Bogo and the Sage Femme have that.

"Raven!" He softly yells with a French accent, leaning back into the baidjan. "Ça descend ici. Faut descendre." What? Huh? Again? Isn't our village back there somewhere, where I dropped off my bags? I'm sick a' this. If he takes me to one more village, I don't know what!

"D'accord," I gather up my things and climb out the back.

We enter this next village, Grézuou, through a courtyard and a circle of twenty men form around us as soon as Bogo and I sit down. Fine too. Bogo goes through the same whack introduction as in the Zragbi and Seraguhé villages, except this time they have lots of questions. The men speak in Bèté, which Bogo struggles with and pretends to understand. He takes a stab at Bèté by translating everything to me in French, but another man keeps correcting him mid-sentence.

"Do you understand?" I want to find out if I'm listening hard for nothing.

"No, but I speak Dida and it is similar to Bèté. I understand some words here and there." But, it really isn't a pleasant sight watching Bogo fumble through pronunciations and trying to use Dida words in hopes that they are similar enough to Bèté.

"Ananaaaa . . . eh, aa . . . zu . . ." Damn. Just speak in French, man. The mosquitoes are coming out. I don't want to hear you mess up in another language that I'm trying to learn! Evidently, Dida is to Bèté as English is to German. But, this is not going well for him.

Everyone here speaks some modicum of French, more than Bogo's Bèté for sure, but they all refuse to speak it and I never meet the Chief of their village either. Or, he is never formally introduced that way.

"They want to know why you are here," Bogo turns to me to translate their question as if he doesn't know either and wants me to tell him so that he can tell them. Oh, I know you don't want me to speak now. You all in the hot seat and tryin' to pass it off to me. Na'ah, no way, not happenin'. I stare back at him blankly.

"What kind of projects?" they push on. They pressure Bogo to break down exactly why I am here. No one has mentioned it since I arrived, even on the initial village visit. I forget, too. I must be getting used to my station as 'La Claire.'

"Working with the schools, the hospitals, and maybe business-es," Bogo finally breaks to tell them in French. I'm shocked. Is that what I'm here to do? Business? I don't have an M.B.A.!

"Businesses?" one man repeats questioningly. Now the men start speaking in French. They give me a once, twice, and thrice over, then one main gentleman to my left smiles, says a few words, and the meeting adjourns. They are satisfied and happy with the explanation of my presence. Money has entered the conversation. C'est quoi ça? No more explanation needed. I even get a song. You can't imagine what it's like to be sung to by twenty healthy, young Ivoirien farmers.

The striking feature of Grézuou is the mansion, or mansions I should say, surrounded by a black iron, ten-foot-tall gate. Where did this come from and why hadn't I noticed it before? Darkness tiptoes up on us, but still I can see that the house is large and re-gal. Does some Ivoirien queen live here? Does some king live here? The mansions are worn down and have been around for a while. No constant upkeep, but there are plenty of kids and older adults walk-ing inside the grounds.

Maurice is not there—said to be the owner of the two mansions. So Bogo settles for the neighbor next door on the other side of the gate in a smaller yet relatively bigger house compared with the usual two-room houses that most people have. Two-room means front room and back room if you are lucky enough to have that much.

"Please have a seat," says the voice of a very tall, dark-skinned man. He doesn't belong here. People in Zragbi tend to be my 5'9" height or shorter. He must be of another ethnicity but speaks Bètè. Are those his children or his wives? He relates to them in the latter way. They are too old to be his children but also too young to be his wives. They all wait on him hand and foot. Bogo gives me no formal introduction, but I assume that if this man is being intro-duced to me then he must be a Grand Type of some sort. That is what this travel from village to village is all about anyway. To get to know who's who before I get down to business—whatever that is going to be. I don't ask any questions. Words whiz past me as usual. I miss some and catch others.

'La Claire . . ." is one of them. How many times are they going to call me 'clear?' Sounds like a weather forecast. But, I guess that is my only characteristic as my speaking is still poor and my function will be hazy until I find out what my site wants to do.

"Have some soda," the tall husband says. A young woman of about eighteen runs forward to her husband with a long, thin glass of Fanta orange soda in one of those 1950s glass bottles. He places it before me.

"Non, merci." My stomach is bursting ready to explode. 'No, thank you.'

"Drink." So, maybe he is offering this to Bogo and not me now?

"Non, merci," I repeat. A perturbed look erupts on his face. Bogo begins to squirm in his chair in the same way he does when trying to use his Dida in place of Bètè.

"Mais, il faut boir, eh!" He is using the emphatic 'eh' at the end of the sentence, leaning forward grabbing the bottle from the top. He shoves it up toward my face. I don't blink. I ain't drinkin' that shit. I have been traveling all day in crouched baidjans with plenty of red earth swirling up onto my face and in my hair from the rides, a belly full of soda that I don't even drink back home, a headache from trying to figure out and remember all of the conversations in the many different languages that balloon around me all day, and now at 21:00 p.m. you want me to drink another crazy ass soda!?

"Non."

They look at each other. The only thing keeping this tall gentleman from cracking the bottle over my head is that Bogo hasn't said anything yet.

"Il faut laisser." The man then leans back at Bogo's words, still with bottle in hand. Bogo to the rescue. Jerk. Spends the whole day trying to make me look bad, not even breaking down what it is I am in Cote d'Ivoire for to the Daloans we meet, and sometimes not translating while laughing in my face. And, here, now, he finally has some heart to stand up for me when it least matters.

The independence I grew up with as an American gal rises from my chest and I can't keep it down. Maybe I can't protect my image for lack of real French-speaking ability, but I am forever going to stand up for my stomach. The subject changes to I don't know what, and then we get on the road back to Zragbi.

The night catches up to me at Bogo's house. It's live. People on the porch, people inside the house watching TV, people leaning in the doorway trying to see the TV, and Céline getting her business done in the round space called a kitchen of four outside pillars, and each a little thicker than my rusty runner's legs, topped off by a thick straw roof that points to the top. Four large bricks create a square with a space that has thin logs placed inside. The enormous, black pot sits angrily, flames shooting up the sides on top of the Bricks.

I don't think any other house has a TV and there are only one or two channels in Cote d'Ivoire on regular access TV. One of them brings to Ivoiriens a famous Brazilian soap opera. Tonight's episode features a woman passing for a White Brazilian living in the house where her mother, who is obviously Black, is the maid. They keep each other's secret. The Ivoiriens are so intrigued with this story yet form confused looks whenever I say I'm Black. Maybe they need to see my light-skinned father and dark-skinned mother to believe me?

Céline makes me love Fufu. Southeastern ethnicities usually make Fufu while the Bèté make Futu so I am surprised to see Fufu instead of Futu on my plate tonight. Tonight's accompanying sauce is peanut sauce with chicken. My normal gag reflex, from not knowing when to swallow or chew the sticky substance, subsides and my mouth takes control. Delicious.

Bogo's two daughters are there but their mother is not. Jijina and Eliane are an interesting pair. Jijina has the pastel brown color of my own sister and stands permanently erect. She is average height for twelve and the top of her shaven, clean head comes just under my chin. Her entire face is chalked white. This can't have the same meaning as the white clothes the Abé wore at our welcoming. A child so young, putting herself in mourning? Eliane has not done the same.

"Allons pomper?" Jijina asks me, standing still staring straight ahead. Still, this is the best invitation since being here. I perk up. Jijina is shy but tough and her erect posture, I soon figure out, is due to the work that we are about to get into.

Eliane, the younger sister who meets my chest, appears from nowhere and after a knowing look from Céline, off us three go to the pump. Eliane feigns little girl but, as soon as we get to the pump she springs forth a wealth of life, information, and laughter.

Unexpectedly, the neck of the pump squeaks, sucking in air as it comes to life and a gushing sound overwhelms Eliane's chattery voice. The pang of metal working against metal, creaks into my ears. It comes from the middle of the school courtyard—inside a roofless, four-sided wall, slightly higher than my head, with an open entrance on the side as wide as two young people.

"Tu sais pomper?" What kind of question is that? Is the fact that my eyes are wide open at the wonder of you little kids throwing buckets and basins full of water up over your heads not sign enough that this is an endeavor never before experienced?

We step up into the space. Several small basins surround the pump. Some are full of water. Some are empty. Some are partially full. Some are plagued by cracks weighted down with too much water and too much upward and downward force lifting or placing them. A girl walks in, in a beautiful church dress, and the zipper traveling down the back that's open, doesn't work. The belt is hanging from the side. Some parts of the dress are torn, other parts stained, and still other parts have complete gaping holes sometimes exposing her ten-year-old underwear full of holes. Maybe I just love the dress because she stands in it with dignity. She could wear a trash bag and make it haute couture. Her brown skin gleams under the light and her lower back has the characteristic arch that sticks her belly forward. How does she stand so erect with her back so deeply and naturally arched at the same time?

I have the curve in my back, but my posture cannot compare. Her head lifts as well, a little bird about to sing and she flits around as one. A cloth sits on her head to keep the bottom of the basin from digging into her scalp—she's tired but ready to go again. At the pump she stands triumphant, tosses down her green basin standing at ease with hands on hips, making her elbows stick straight out to the sides, and legs spread apart with flashy red plastic sandals that barely stay on her feet. Waiting in the pump line is less appealing than chasing the dog with the other kids just outside of the pump wall, so she abandons her green basin, not forgetting to remark her place in the hierarchy of water waiting, and runs off to catch a glimpse of fun underneath the tall, village lamp light that glosses everything in a mysterious, pale orange night vision. While waiting in line, I receive a few stares and questions are thrown to my new guardians Jijina and Eliane.

Water sparkles and girls laugh and cut their eyes at boys who love to misbehave in front of them and who also never pump. Braids, bald heads, strung-out perms, and little afros all waiting triumphantly at the pump. The pump stems out of a round concrete-mixed base that reaches up to my stomach. On the side directly opposing the entranceway on the other side of the pump is a thick, ten-inch slab of step. Lining the outer edges of the inside pump area is a thin drainage space. Another slab of thick step on the side of the pump is to the left upon entering. Eliane places our large green basin over the entrance-opposing slab, our gray one below that, and Jijina steps up to bat on the left slab.

Jutting up from the round concrete in the middle, the pump is a large metal apparatus with a long metal arm extending out over the left slab to the waist of anyone who steps up on the slab. At the end of this arm are two small bars. Jijina, taking hold of these bars and swinging her upper body up and back, with arms straight, manages to suddenly swing the large metal arm way up into the air as high as she can reach with her 5'6" frame, stopping once in a weightlifter's final pose before crouching her body inward to pull down the arm again with all of her might.

Her face hardly changes its solemn expression. One, two, three times she performs this motion with strength, speed, and a slightly perceptible bit of strain on her young frame. About the third pull down, the screeching sound eeks out again and pockets of suppressed air come forth from the part of the pump over the back slab. The pump is resuscitated again breathing forth blasts of air and small then large streams of water waves spill out into our round, green basin thereafter.

"Eliane!" Jijina screams at her sister. "Faut prendre ça là!" Eliane is dancing around the basin and nodding her head from side to side, singing some Ivoirien song that she has heard on the radio, in too much complete bliss with herself to notice that the water is just missing the basin and splashing onto the floor.

"Excusez-moi," she says in a charming, French male actor imitation, feigning to frantically push the basin back in an exaggerated way to everyone's delight. Jijina is the only one not amused, of course, for Eliane's blunder means several more weight lifts for Jijina than she wants to spend.

Finally, after listening to several conversations in a combination of native languages with a few French inserts for words they can't think of right away in their own language, Jijina wobbles off of her slab. Eliane quickly jumps to one side of our green basin full of water, waiting wide-eyed for instructions from Jijina, but none there come. The drill is already known. Jijina grabs the bland, color-stripped, torn, extra cloth from around her waist and carefully wraps and shapes it around four of her fingers. Not too tight but not too loose. She then places it on her head. Eliane crouches down sumo-wrestler style, grabbing her cloth skirt wrap up slightly revealing strong, gymnastic, nine-year-old thighs. Jijina, on the other side of our green basin, braces herself and looks off over the wall into the distance as if making sure no one is coming. Eliane moves forward and grabs her side of the basin.

"Faut pas prendre comme ça!" Jijina reprimands.

"De prendre comment?" And, Jijina's eyes pierce Eliane as if to say, 'girl, you know good and well that ain't the right way to grab the rim!' Eliane frowns for the first time then moves her hands around the rim until she figures to grab it as she would the rim of a man's hat placed upside down on Jijina's head, thumbs facing skyward. I gotta' see this. How these little kids gonna' put that forty-pound basin of water on Jijina's little, round, shaved head?

When it begins, everyone waits inside the pump frozen to catch any spilled water with their thoughts. Jijina pulls her body up and back in the same manner of motion that she has swinging the pump bar except twice as fast. This pulls Eliane forward which is the only way it can work because Eliane has to then immediately step up on the slab where the basin sits previously in order to compensate for the two-foot difference between the two and thereby be able to help Jijina plant and steady the basin on her head. No strain or hesitation, just a moment of intense concentration and up it goes. Sssssswoooop. Jijina wobbles a little more and after pushing the cloth to help steady the basin, the two-legged gazelle glides away.

Eliane stays, throws our second, gray basin on the back slab then stands on the left one. Now, Eliane is half Jijina's size. How's that gonna' work? Sure 'nuf, Eliane takes to the challenge immediately. She, too, looks off into the distance to brace herself. Her up until now quizzical and comedic expressions disappear into the face of a serious little woman. Do work, girl! Little Eliane is twice as strong as Jijina, throwing the bar up into the air rapid fire and what she lacks in arm length, she makes up for by jumping with her gymnastic thighs to push the bar up as far as it will go— airborne every time. Water gushes out and I adjust the basin to catch the thick spray of water.

"De porter ou bien?" Eliane asks, pointing at herself. Hell yeah you gonna' carry that shit. Maybe I should be more compassionate as she is duly tired from having to pull twice as much energy out of her little frame as Jijina does, but that's not my reason for not carrying it. Eliane isn't going to be able to put that basin on my head. I'm much taller than she is, so I should be the one to put it on her head. Even the back slab isn't going to be enough for her to step up onto and help me place the basin on mine.

Buzz sparks up around me. Usually, most of the young girls waiting in line are so determined to get their water pumping done and get out of there that they spend no time talking and all the time focusing their energies on the person at the pump, subtly urging them to hurry it up and get it over with. They aren't disrespectful as I am an adult, but they are visibly curious and questioning who I am and why I don't just hurry up and put the damn thing on Eliane's head. Eliane untucks the small cloth around her waist and winds it slowly around her hand to shape it for her head.

I test it first. Whew. I can't even lift that thing up a small bit from the side without causing water to splash out everywhere and straining my poor little fingers. Dang.

"On va faire maintenant," Eliane forewarns. Aw shit. Aw shit. Okay. I can do this. Remember how Jijina did it before with Eliane and move quickly. Legs spread wide, we both bend over at the waist and lower our knees to get ready and take the right grip. She gives me one quick look in the eye and up she goes. Oh! I gotta lift, too! The true weight of it becomes stressfully clear and the heaviness causes me to come in fast. I have to because I am ruining Eliane's momentum by slowing down to think about what to do next. She can't lift it any higher and my hesitation has the basin now suspended in air between us with all the momentum we came up with destroyed. I'm gonna' have to heave it by myself because just me picking it up using my height is already enough to bring it to Eliane's head. Water is spilling out the sides.

'Does she mean to tell me that she made me lift this thing up and can't even get it over my head?' reads from Eliane's eyes, but she isn't arrogant about it, just frightened. Thankfully, in this exact moment, Jijina comes back and rushes to Eliane's rescue, who by this time is worn out by having to steady the bucket and figure out how to communicate to me to move more forward and lift the basin up higher so that she can squeeze underneath it. Jijina grabs Eliane's side, pulling me forward.

Jijina adjusts the rag underneath the basin for Eliane. Pausing just a moment to catch her balance, Eliane briskly walks off with her basin, grasping the rim and keeping it steady. The incident with me leaves her with water streaming down her face, but somehow Eliane manages to keep only a drip every ten steps from spilling out of the basin as she switches her hips in a speed walk back to Bogo's house. Jijina throws our now-empty green bucket down and directs me up to plate.

"Faut pomper," Jijina orders, which from her mouth bends in a friendly tone. She quickly tilts her head sideways and back to suggest 'come on.' Everyone is waiting. Saying no is not an option. This is my child initiation and with children is one of the best ways to pick up a language at an easy pace and in context-rich situations because they are always doing something. No worries about having to figure out discussions on politics. No pressure to take it more than a word at a time.

The pump is five times heavier than it appears. The slab that I step on doesn't help, with bits from the corners chipping off. Getting a good grip on it to balance myself as I lift the metal arm is awkward. I lift the bar up halfway and I'm still not done. I bring it up to the top, but the top is only half of the pump. A full pump is all the way up and all the way back down. On coming down, there is a sensation of air being somehow pulled up by my downward force. Coming down is harder than pulling the bar up! One. Three sets of my nonsense efforts go by and nothing comes out. It has just been used so the pressure is built up enough. The water should have come out by now.

"Il faut faire comme ça," Jijina says as she comes to show me how quickly and forcefully it must be done, putting her weight and back into it. Air makes a squeaking noise as it blows out of the spout and water gushes forth again but soon thereafter stops. "Il faut faire maintenant," she steps aside to let me continue.

I step back up, take my flip-flops off so my feet better grab the crumbling concrete slab, and close my eyes trying to forget that everyone is staring at me, wondering where I'm from and why, at wherever I am from, I don't need to know how to pump. All of my weight goes into bringing the bar down. This is worse than college weightlifting. Let's just pretend I'm in the Olympics and this is the last lift for the gold.

Water flies out after one full pump. I can't believe it! I did it! I almost stop amazed, but then the eyes of the girls still resting on me tell me that their intrigue is over. I need to hurry up so they can go home, eat dinner, and do their homework.

Soon the basin is full. With her eyes, Jijina asks me if I will car-

ry it or will she. My arms are flaky and drained. How did I get myself into this? Ugh, it's wrong to complain. Jijina is involving me in
her life and I'm learning. She performs the ritual of wrapping her
rag around her hand to prepare it for her head. There is no such
talking or chatter between us as with Eliane. She heads right for
the basin and just knows I will follow. I do. Clean and jerk it. The
crowd roars or at least the one in my mind does. Jijina makes a few
adjustments and we head back to Bogo's.

Happy to eat, Eliane jumps from her tiny stool and dances. Her
rhythm, so swift and smooth, creates imaginary beats and Jijina
claps and hoops, "oh, oh, OH, oh!" The Logobie, it is called. The
Logobie dance is the image of someone climbing up a rope and it's
funky. You can go up and back down. You move your shoulders
drastically as you climb or slip back down the rope. The Abé don't
do this dance. I can't be so surprised. Blacks in New Jersey definitely don't dance the same as those in Detroit or Washington,
D.C.

Bedtime. I step into the house and head for the back rooms. I
take a sharp turn to the right and to my surprise, there are already
several people back there sleeping on the floor. Young men, women,
and children and damn . . . he didn't put my mosquito net up. Is
he trying to kill me? I keep asking the brother when my house will
be ready and he keeps telling me soon. If you're not going to get
my house ready, at least put my net up. Who are these people?
Patients? C'est quoi ça?

"Do you think it's okay to sleep without a net?" I ask Bogo.

"Ça va." It's okay, he says. "Tomorrow." Taking no serious eval-
uation of the situation, I go to sleep. I mean, we all go to sleep, all
seven of us with me on the only bed in the room. The mosquitoes
bite me all night long and although I rarely get headaches, I don't
make the connection between my splitting headache the next morning and the tens of mosquito bites I have.

I'm not sleeping here no more. Can't even put up my damn net.
Céline prepares a bucket of water for me and I clean off in the
shower room separate from the house in an attached wing that is
cemented everywhere, is the size of a closet, and has one small win-

dow vent up toward the ceiling with cob webs in every corner. I wrap a pagne around myself and run from shower to house. Everyone there the night before has already cleared out.

Céline and Bogo step over to the hospital and I take a walk around Zragbi again. My head starts pounding once more. Maybe it's dehydration. Let's go to the store. I know that there is one around the market somewhere. I spotted it before on arrival while walking through the market with all of my bags.

Upon reaching the market, there are actually several small stores, some more shack than store. One store near the edge of the market sells aloko and poisson right outside of it. Maybe I need food. First, I grab a plastic sachet of water out of an ice cream freezer inside the store, pay five francs, and head toward the aroma.

Aloko is fried plantains in I don't know which language. Poisson is fish in French. Put those two together and you have Ivoirien fast food. Young school kids mob the tiny appatam that covers the two women cooking the aloko and poisson. McD's ain't got nothin' on it. Big, fat, juicy slabs of sweet, fried plantain cut long and fish perfectly floured and seasoned. Achèké comes with the meal as well. Achèké is dried-up, soft, yellow strips of manioc, from the same manioc that goes into Futu, and I smoosh it together in my hand to pick up plantain and fish with it. A slab of spicy something is packed in the plantain leaf that holds all of this food together. Mmmmm. The Bèté love spicy food.

"Bogo? Ma maison est prête?" You better answer 'yes' my house is ready.

"Non, mais ils ont la clé." A key? What key? And, who is they? They have my key?

"Ils ont mon clé? C'est où?"

"C'est par là, là. Chez le pharmaciste." Why does the pharmacist have my key? Is he pulling my leg or what, and why can't he just go and get the key for me? Man, shit. I'm going to get that key today. I can't keep living like this. Bogo is crazy. What am I supposed to do . . . sleepin' in his back room with all ages of mankind, no net for two years, and getting eaten up by the mosquitoes every night? Heck naw.

With no street signs and no distinct roads that allow me to use a landmark on the corner, all I have to go by is that the pharmacy is beyond the market. So, I head through the market that morning fully fed and on a mission while Bogo and Céline are at work at the hospital and the whole village is empty except for the young ones too young to walk or work in the fields and the few 'commercants' who stay out at the market during the week to at least sell the basic groceries—tomatoes, baby eggplants, onions, and dried fish.

Shelves of medicine fill the space behind the counter. No one has bought anything from here in a while. To the left is the pharmacist's waiting or living room, and he walks inside from the back of the counter where a woman is sitting outside, working her mortar and stick to death, repeatedly bending forward and down in a fluid motion to get whatever it is in that mortar to the consistency she seeks.

The pharmacist has on no white jacket or special clothes, just a nice colorful shirt and some shorts, wearing them proudly with his stomach heading south and his chest soon after. He is sweating but greets me with a huge smile and suddenly frowns at the last minute when he realizes he doesn't know who I am or what here for.

I hesitate never knowing what French word is going to come out of my mouth until it comes and I stress over conjugation. He stares at me and looks around at the young man who is also behind the counter.

"Bonjour," I say because he won't say it, still staring and wondering what in the world I might want. "Bogo a dit que vouz avez mon clé?" I continue politely.

"Quelle clé?" he returns my question with a question. My key, that's what key.

"La clé de ma maison." Introducing myself is probably a better way to start, but I just tell him the key to my house is the key I'm asking about.

"Bogo?" he repeats rewinding to the first thing I said. Not asked as if he doesn't know Bogo but in disbelief that Bogo said that or anything else to me at all.

"Bogo, l'infirmier." You know, Bogo. The nurse. The head of the hospital.

"Vous êtes l'americaine?" What game is this? He knows I am 'the' American?

"Oui." Upon my affirmation, he steps into the living room and produces the key so quickly that I wonder if I had just stepped in and simply said the word 'oui,' would he have known who I am and just produced the key no questions asked. He hands it to me with hesitation. I want to grab it and run.

Relieved and happy that a key actually exists, I take another stroll heading down the Zragbi main road that leads back to the Abidjan road. It's only a little ways before I spot a path. Is it alright to walk through here? Fuck it. As soon as I do, I see a man sitting on his porch, carving something with a knife. He must be used to strangers, sizing me up instantly and heading toward me. I am something he knows or at least knows not to be afraid of. Either that or I'm about to get stabbed.

"Ça va?"

"Oui, ça va," instinctively my guard stays down as we greet each other.

"Are you lost?" Yeah, I am lost. Lost in Zragbi with nothing to do and no one to talk to.

"No, I just wanted to walk a little." And, then what comes over me I'll never know, but I tell him everything just to be free of my thoughts.

"I am American. I came here with Bogo, the nurse, as a volunteer to help the village, but he didn't give me my house key so I went to the pharmacist for my key, and now I want to open my house, but I don't know where my house is because no one told me where it is." Aaaah. One big run-on sentence of release in French.

"De t'aider?" I don't know how you're going to help me find this house but . . .

"Okay."

We walk in silence back to the other side of the market and past Bogo's house. Maybe he knows although there is one moment where confusion slows his pace. He never stops once, however. Zragbi is his village, a few thousand people. Why wouldn't he know where the house is likely to be? The only uninhabited place in the joint is quite likely it.

"C'est ici." We arrive. "Donne-moi la clé." I give it to him. He steps to the door in a wide gate one would use to one's own house. The frame of the first door is all frame and no screen so that when pulled, it falls forward on its hinges crookedly and with a loud creak. First with a tussle and then a jostle, the main wooden door opens and the house breathes the relatively cool air from the outside on the inside. He disappears into the darkness. All of the windows are closed. When I see him again he has apparently surveyed everything and his feet and sandals are covered in a thick powder of gray dust.

From the perspective of my back to the house, there is a big open yard canvassing it, a house immediately to the left that leaves only a small sideways passage between us, and a house off on the other side almost facing mine but more so facing the bottom of the small hill that goes down then up toward Seraguhé. To the right, lining the street is a less than bosky patch of green that camouflages little.

My new friend walks out into the courtyard and stands right in the middle of the dry, red earth, twisting his head and waist to the left and right. His eyes take him to the other side of the house on the left and after a few moments, he resurfaces with a small wicker broom of arm length.

Sssssshew, ssssshew, sssshew . . . sails a loud whisper from inside the house. I just met him and he is already inside goin' to town on all the dust and dirt. Soon, each 'ssssshew' is accompanied by small cloud storms of dust and dirt swirling out of the door and up into the air. He comes out and finds a makeshift dustpan of cardboard, goes back in, sweeps everything up, and throws it in the corner underneath the window that is in between my front door and the outdoor bathroom.

After lots of loud whispers, clouds of light brown dirt, and a few dead and nearly dead baby bats living inside my house; my new friend emerges with dust all over him from head to foot. Then, he opens all the windows, which open from the outside ironically, each with one big wide slab that opens upward instead of two that open outward from the middle. He takes advantage of a few sticks to prop them up.

"Merci beaucoup," I thank him sincerely and off he goes. A service rendered for free. Should I be giving him something? There is no sign that the gesture is done for reward and I am so pleased to find a Good Samaritan that I'd like to keep it as that. Treating him any other way defeats the purpose of me being here. I have to start acting as part of the community. What an entirely awkward beginning here in a new place with no proper living space given. Taking up the Peace Corps Director's suggestion to stay in Grand Noyaré might have been a better idea after all.

Back and forth I go from Bogo's house, moving all of my things in a flustered hurry. I ain't sleepin' with ten thousand mosquitoes again. I grab my big, red suitcase, my medium-sized bag, and my little red bag along with my large blue travel pack on my back and manage to lug everything to my house at once. As the big, wooden door hangs slightly off its hinges, I pull it up by grabbing onto a nail that sticks up out the top of the door and this makes the lock properly align for me to insert the key and open it.

My house breathes in again, a furnace inside. The aluminum roofing seals the heat in even though the roof is not sealed tight. Can I live in here? There are no window screens so I dump all of my things and go back to the market. Lucky enough, I spot a store that sells nails, a hammer, and a wiry material good enough to work as a screen with its tiny holes.

Eagerness starts a racket. I cut the screen material to fit into the windowless windows and the screenless screen door, hammering them onto the frames with lots of nails. The mosquito net goes up too but up over what? Oh God, I need a bed. Well, sleeping under the mosquito net on the floor here is better than sleeping on a bed with no net at Bogo's. Furniture is needed, too, for the kitchen and bedroom.

All of my things lay locked up in the house. Out again to the market to see what can be got. I walk by Bogo's house toward the market and Céline catches me just in time with the phrase that I hear from everyone in a number of languages daily.

"Where are you going?" Céline asks, raising her chin up to point in my direction.

"I'm going to the market."

"For what?"

"A table and a bed."

"Je crois que l'atelier et là." I know atelier means workshop. Okay. So, the workshop is somewhere over there? Céline points. No directions. Great, Céline. Now, tell me how to get to New Jersey.

Several eyes at the market wonder if I'm going to buy something and several eyes just wonder. The earth under my feet swells up and covers both in little, light, reddish-brown clouds as I walk. My ears perceive noises of clanging and wood being thrown up against things off in the distance.

There is no front wall to the shop. I don't want to scare anyone and prefer to appear to them so I walk up slowly, stand there, and wait. They throw down wood and pick wood up. Sawing, hammering, fitting, and aligning pieces. One older man in search of something squints up and around noticing me here. He waits for me to speak probably because he doesn't know what language I speak in. Who am I? Where am I from? What quartier in the village am I living in?—are his thoughts.

"Do you have beds?" I muster to share the goal of my quest in French.

"Oui, on a ça," with a smile he answers 'yes, we have that.' By this time, the two, tall boys still at work squint up as well, wood dust in their eyes. They give a telling look to each other and keep working. One has a bit of a smile on his face and makes a remark in my direction. They speak in yet another language that I have not heard before. However, I feel no ill energy in it.

"Can I buy it today?"

"It takes time."

"What?" I ask him to repeat. He has a very thick accent behind his French. It is leagues more thick than Céline's or Bogo's. I'd like to hear his native language to figure out the phonetic pattern so that I know which sounds he is replacing or naturally omits from

French due to the differences with his own language. The kids speak Senoufo, but his language has got to be different from that.

"Two days," he plainly states. Oh, okay. The next two days will be me and the plastic prayer mat then.

"How much?"

"Ça depend." The price depends on what? Depends on how much you feel like janking me for?

"Ça depend de quoi?" I probe further.

"There are many types of wood," he puts one foot out to faintly point at random samples around him. Aw, come on with the wood types man. I just wanna' bed. Just make me a bed!

He shows me the samples up close. One type of wood is mahogany colored. Another is lighter but just as strong looking. I guess that's all they have in stock, wherever that is kept.

"C'est de bon bois," he assures. I can see they are good. No need to say that. But, how bad is the cheap stuff? People shouldn't think I got all the money in the world. My silence from indecision prompts him to bring out a third type of wood.

"This is cheaper," he pulls a sad piece from behind the others.

"Is it good?"

"Yes," he says but shrugs a non-verbal 'I guess so' and an 'it will do' at the same time. It looks alright. I just need something to sleep on. Now the price. He knows what's next and his eyes sparkle.

"It's not expensive," he delays with giving me the actual price. The weight of the silence following this makes his last word stick in my mind more. Should I jump in with a price or will I go too high and ruin the bargain? After several more seconds of silence and me staring blankly at him and then blankly at the wood, I decide to wait him out.

"Faut faire 15,000." Fifteen thousand CFA? Ivoirien, please! I lower my chin so that my eyes bulge to express strong incredulity. I look back at the wood again, walk up to it, and touch it. My silence works because he then feels the need to assure me of its quality twice. "C'est du bon bois. C'est du bon bois."

After twelve more long seconds of silence I repeat his price to him, "15 mille?" I almost add 'Ivoirien, please' out loud in English, but I don't want to be disrespectful in any language so I resolutely swallow the air I just let in from being about to say something.

"Fine—10,000." Well, alright! Goin' down in fives. I like it! I really don't know how much a handmade bed should cost or how much with that type of wood, whatever wood it is, but he sounds like he has at least gone down from a lottery price to a high price so I surrender. Aiy, wait a minute. I need a table to create my kitchen area, too.

"It's 15,000 for both." Oooooh, boy. A table is so simple to make. How is he going to add on 5,000 for this tiny table when that's half of what the bed now costs? I want to be over with it. I surrender again.

"Okay . . . merci," I thank him.

He nods a 'thank you' back at me. Umh, maybe he is staring at me because he expects a down payment but oops off I go back down the road!

Every time I get a piece of furniture, I think of another piece that needs to go with it. A bed frame requires a mattress. What am I gonna' do? Sleep inside the frame? This is a mess! But, the day is long enough, and as much as I really want to tough it out on the hard cement floor with sporadic cracks in it that bite my back, I am going to do my best to get on up to Daloa and get a mattress. The spirit is with me because as soon as I get off the baidjan the first person I see points me in the right direction.

The store people carry the mattress back to the baidjan for me. Oup, I need a stove. I get a small, two-burner flat stove with a big gas tank. Now, I have never had to carry a gas tank around before and probably shouldn't be slamming it down and putting it about the way I'm doing. Pots, pans, and utensils. A third trip around Daloa, I make, and all the while the three Muslims—Money Hands, Big Smile, and the Cook—are nice enough to watch my things. No contract. Words are good here. A fourth trip has me with cans of white and red paint to achieve the pink I want throughout my tiny, two-room abode. And, it's not like we get an additional stipend for all this stuff I need. A volunteer's house is supposed to be set up before she gets there! But, whatever. Once I do it, it will be done.

"Dégééééééé!" The Dégé girl's shout saves my life. Big, sachet handfuls of dégé.

My gare has a room in the back where you can see Muslims in transit taking the time to pray and the only word I understand from their prayer is 'Allah.' God. God, thank you for this cold dégé on this scorching day. I said it once and I'll say it again. Doesn't sound like much and the grainy description may turn a mere observer off but oh my. It turns this lactose-intolerant into a lactose-intolerant, lactose lover. The taste of a dégé yogurt sachet on a hot-ass, Ivoirien afternoon is downright scandalous.

Just when my mind drifts off past my weariness, the heat, and the flies that want to know what's up with me not sharing my dégé with them—here comes big butt. He is really a little butt with a big head, no-key-to-my-house-carrying, Denzel-wanna-be-a-doctor but isn't saving anything except the money that he hoards from the medicines he sells from the pharmacist at five times the value— Bogo. He immediately smiles. Big head. Don't smile at me. Smile at my dangon mattress!

"Tout ça c'est quoi?" What do you mean—'what's all this?' That's how you greet a person? Of course my archenemy would appear when everything is better.

"My bed, my fire, my things," simplicity redefined.

"Tu prépares?" Bogo looks around for someone to accompany him in laughing at me in disbelief that I know what to do with pots and pans. "La Blanche prépare!" he yells in laughter. The Muslims that own the gare crack a smile then pretend they are too busy to listen to the rest of the conversation.

I wince. The word 'La Blanche,' which I hear every day for the next two years and in loud decibels, is rapidly gaining equivalence to someone suddenly dragging their nails across a brand-new blackboard. I wince again playing back the word in my mind. I don't hate White women, but I hate being called what I am not. It's equally insulting that he knows my name and chooses another instead.

"Je ne suis pas Blanche," I reject his claim. My defiance goes unacknowledged to which I wince again. Instead, he asks if it's me who's going to pay to transport my things.

"No, you are," I smile and he slowly smiles back not wanting to pay, then sees it as a chance for him to show off not only paying for my ride and the cost of transporting all the luggage but sending me back immediately in a passenger-less baidjan . . . so that I can blow up when my gas falls from the baidjan by myself.

Money Hands and his business partners whip glances back and forth at each other. A miracle has occurred. They don't have to wait in the heat for every possible space in the baidjan to be bought up and filled. They quickly summon two apprentis to keep my things on top of the baidjan steady during the ride.

An older gentleman, who I'd never seen drive before, jumps in the baidjan, and Bogo nods his head again adding, "Faut la prendre" while waving off at the baidjan with his hand and looking away as if it is something he does often. Dude, whatever! I'm not impressed. 'Take her,' you say? Psh! Take this! Take my key and give it to me when you should have! Like I'm supposed to shack up at your place with every last person you wanna' let spend the night because they're visiting the hospital and you ain't even there. What kind of homologue is he? Oh, I forgot. He's not anymore. He has passed me off to Céline already. Good thing he paid though, 'cause my allowance is running out!

The baidjan drives me straight up to my door and helps me unload everything. Should I give them a tip? Naah. If people are going to accept me, I've got to start doing as everyone else does. Plus, who knows what else I'm supposed to have that's missing that I don't know is missing yet. Gotta' save the cash.

Céline cooks me a hot meal any time of day and that is just what I get as soon as I go up to see her. I try again to 'piler' the plantains, but I have no life left in me. I eat, say my good night to Céline, and push my body on over home.

I slide the mattress in the corner underneath the only window in the bedroom, the window underneath which on the outside the good Samaritan threw all of the dust, baby bats, and random wood pieces earlier. I gotta' get rid of that stuff. There is still a bit of light left so I rush to nail in the mosquitaire completely. No more risks. It's so hot that I sleep naked on the mat. A bit of air seeps in through the shutters but not enough.

Sleep doesn't come. My head is hot and pounding with a headache. Another night like the first back again. When I lay down, the pounding is worse. Standing up is only slightly better. Let's go see Céline. Maybe she will have something. Every step I endeavor toward Bogo's house is measured. Too much exertion makes blood surge to my head in huge, pulsating bursts.

"Céline? My head hurts."

Her eyes tell me that I don't look well. I can't stand much longer. She comes to where I sit to put her hand to my head and the other to the back of my neck. Her hands are normal temperature but cool compared to my body. Every breath I take, every beat that sends blood throughout my body up into my brain, I feel. I am a clock slowly winding down.

And, there is a bump on my right arm that started out as a pimple yesterday but has since swelled into this large, hard bump on my skin. I show it to Céline.

"C'est le firon."

"Firon?" I question, not even certain that I pronounce it correctly.

"Le fi-ron," she replies even stronger this time, seeming convinced the longer she looks at my arm and into my eyes. "Yes. It's from the firon. It's that." She lifts my head up and looks deeper into my eyes, seeing something that scares me by her response to it. A frown stays on her face and she scurries to the open doorway leaning in to yell to Bogo who is lying on the side couch facing the door watching television.

"Bogo. Elle est malade." She quickly tells him that I am sick and a few other things as well and maybe I might understand them if I did not have this headache pounding so loudly in my ears. No. I probably might not have. Bogo responds in true Bogo fashion. Unconcerned, he speaks twice as fast. No words are distinguishable.

Céline is trying to be patient. This firon thing must be a trip. She asks Bogo something again to which he very slowly replies, "They say that the volunteers are supposed to take care of themselves. That we can't help them so let her help herself."

Dang! It's like that?! But, I don't even have the blood to make me angry. All of it pumps into my temples one heartbeat at a time. Céline turns to me, places one hand on my forehead and the other on my neck again explaining, "C'est le firon. La petite mouche en brousse qui donne ça. Mais quand ça pousse . . ."

I interrupt her through my headache, "Quand ça pousse??????" When what pushes? From where? And how? From my arm?! It's a little fly that lands on my arm and puts something in my skin, you said? Awww, no. Not the kid. I can't get sick out here. I just got here. I was sick during training already. This is highly inconvenient. Reliable medical aid is a good seven hours away and it's nighttime. Well, maybe one or two hours, but Daloa City hospital is no Abidjan hospital.

She continues in metered words, "Quand ça pousse, ça va finir."

Okay. So, I have to wait for something to come out of my arm for this crazy headache, no, migraine to stop? "Fine, I'm going to sleep." I don't know what else to do and somehow manage to fall asleep in spite of the headache. I do, however, wake up every hour with the same headache. Every hour, I say. If I stay completely still, it subsides a little, but as soon as I move that creates a relentless surge of blood pumping to my head.

Am I just a head? I forget about my legs, my arms, and the rest of my body. Will my head fill up with blood and explode? The blood pumping is so intense it has a sound. I can see it. I can hear my heart beating faster, working harder and harder to rid myself of this thing. Keep your eyes closed. Let's get some sleep. Every hour I wake up until finally I sleep long enough to wake up and it be daytime.

'They say they are supposed to take care of themselves?' Who says that? I don't know what these things are that are happening to my body. Why is it that I can't get out of bed because my head feels heavier than my entire body? Why is it difficult to move? Why, when I move, does the blood in my body surge to my brain? I shoot up out of bed out of habit and if all thunder and lightning doesn't come crashing down inside of my head—Pulse! Don't rush yourself. I can't think. I look up at the shutters and the light coming in doesn't register with my eyes. The light shoots straight back to my brain. Ugh, too bright. Are my eyes working? Why don't I blink at the light? Nothing is filtered. Everything I see, my mind cannot perceive. It goes in, stinging my very brain. If I had a mirror, I'm sure my eyes would be fully dilated. My pupils are not working. Do I have brain damage?

I have to go outside and take a bath. It's getting hot in here. I can't stay in here all day. I try to get up again, except this time I crawl, not walk, to the entrance of the kitchen. I use the frame of the middle doorway to pull myself up. Aaah, it hurts. Movement hurts. Even the little bits of sunlight coming in through the two adjacent windows out in the front room hurt my eyes.

Jijina and Eliane help me partially fill a big, blue, plastic water barrel I buy in town. I fill a new bucket with some of the water but can't carry that much so I have to empty some back out. Not yet fully unpacked, I shuffle back to the bedroom and sit on the floor to forage through my suitcase and find my pink soap box. Time lapses. I find myself simply staring into my suitcase. Then, I remember what I am doing. Washcloth. I find the washcloth and time lapses again. Even thought needs a moment to be realized. My movements become completely that—movements. Hand up to wall. Leg up. Push up. Foot forward to walk. Stop. Turn around. Pause. A look up at the shutters just to blink away in pain from not being able to take in the little bits of light.

Aren't you forgetting something? Right leg forward to turn around. Okay. Turn. Look down. What are you looking for? My right hand travels to my head to hold it from the pain. Of course, the soap box drops out of that same hand because I forget it is there and can only focus on one thing at a time. The lone bar of soap slides across the room. Forgotten. Still holding my head. Am I dying?

No. Dying is not like this. I can still walk. I can still breathe. But, everything is not everything. Everything does not exist because I can only perceive one thing at a time. I have become used to the door creaking open every time I exit or enter, but the noise this time leaves an indelible scratch on my brain. All I can do is stay alive. I get outside and a child passes by without saying anything. They normally salute me with 'La Blanche!' but he knows something is wrong.

This outdoor bath space is much better and larger than the closet at Bogo's house. But, then I am paranoid, looking up and wincing again in pain from the sunlight. It is my first bath outside ever in life. Can someone see me from the trees? Fuck it. Wash. Finished. I get the essential parts. I can't believe I went to bed dirty like that after all the walking around the village, getting a mattress, and buying everything else in Daloa and then coming back down to Zragbi. I want to lie down again as soon as possible, but lying down hurts. I tuck myself into my favorite blue, white, and yellow pagne with strapped, matching blue top, but now laying here on my mattress on the floor, it comes undone. I didn't do it right. Oooh, somebody help me. But, I don't yet figure out how to help myself . . .

I struggle upright and give myself the heave of life to stand up, getting caught in the big, white, flowy mosquitaire. Pressure shoots to my head again, pounding more—this time too intense for me to keep my eyes open. Everything in my reality is too bright, too loud, and too much to comprehend. I open the door and the orangey red earth, too, glows hard into my brain. Is it reaching my cortex? What is a cortex? Is it searing my brain cells? I throw my head up as people automatically do when going outside, but the sun attacks hard into my eyes, shuddering me right down to my very bones. All regular bodily function desires shut down. The desire to eat, the desire to sleep, the desire to go to the bathroom. I resign myself to some more sleep and turn back around. Maybe, more rest is all I need. Maybe, if it is so hard for me to even move, that's an indication that I shouldn't be moving at all. The impending heat forces me nonetheless to go outside around to all of the windows to open them so as not to fry to death. I forget about the screen door coming back into the house and the ensuing slam is a man inside my skull hitting me in the back of the brain with a hammer. How can Ivoiriens have a productive life with firon constant?

Maybe I am feeling slightly better because when I wake up next it is 15:30 . . . the next day! Shit. I slept more than twenty-four hours straight. Did I temporarily slip into a coma? Jesus Christ! After taking all effort possible to lift myself up and out the door, I turtle to the market, sliding right by Bogo's side entrance in hopes that no one detects me. A walk that normally takes three minutes has me still walking fifteen minutes later. I am so worried that people are going to think I am crazy, walking through town, barely able to open my eyes or move with any kind of normal stride. Only short scuffs make the cut. One foot moves halfway past the other foot continually until I manage to get where I sometimes remember I'm going.

The market isn't closed, but all of the places there are to eat a meal, are—aloko, poisson, and achèké or the lady who makes sauce and rice dishes nearest the hospital. Céline's cooking would be nice, but I don't want her to see me. Paranoia returns again. This is the first time in my life where I sense a great loss of control. What if something goes down and I can't defend myself or get out of harm's way because I am disabled like this? Passing by Bogo's side entrance again, I speed my step up to three-fourths past the other foot. Improving, but my eyes refuse to open more than the filter my eyelashes provide. I pass a woman on my left and worry that I appear strange to her in my stiff, slow position, but masking my pain and discomfort is only extra strain. I keep the shuffle pace going and surprisingly she looks at me, and then looks straight ahead showing some recognition on her face of my discomfort. I expect a 'Ça va?' but no 'are you okay' leaves any part of her mouth.

The knowingness in her face hits me. I have malaria! Céline lied.

Oup, now I remember. Those three white, large, button-sized pills in all of the blue medical cases we each receive before leaving to our individual sites. Was that what I was supposed to take when I felt it coming on? What else is in there? I open up the case. Bandaids, bandages, syringes. Syringes? They certainly didn't show us how to give ourselves an injection. When Americans get sick, we call 911. That's it. How do I help these people with healthcare when I struggle to survive myself? And, how is Steve making out?

9 LOVING YOU AND LOVING ME

D idier is married to Désiré. Their house faces the street and is in between mine and the one facing me in our courtyard. Their children, from youngest to oldest, are Dowa, Bri Bri (Bree Bree), Louie, and Margot. Dowa and Louie are the boys. Louie has a chronic ear infection and it affects his rhythm, movement, and perception; often a lot slower than the other children but happy all the same. Dowa is the youngest but very smart. He talks fast, walks fast, laughs fast, runs fast, and eats even faster. His personality is very strong and he reacts to everyone and everything in an absolute fashion. The first time Dowa and I meet, he wakes me up out of my sleep.

"Uuuuunh," I start to pick up from my slumber. "Uuuunh, unh," I hear the voice again and wake up. Is someone hurt? I listen some more. "Uuuuuunh." Shoot, sounds like someone's going to the bathroom. Is someone in my latrine shower? I peer out a crack in my thick, green, louvered shutters from the bedroom. Nope. My door is as locked as it was earlier this morning. I get out of bed to go to the front room and peek out the front window over my gas stove.

It's Dowa, squatting down right in front of his porch taking a dump. Do I have the right to look? Should I be giving him privacy or should he be giving me mine away from his doo doo brown machinations? My goodness. Am I in a parallel universe? Maybe I'm not really seeing what I'm seeing. Maybe he's playing a prank. But, the strain on his face and in his naked, brown, little boy body, grabbing his knees to give him an extra push, say it is so.

"Uuuuuuuuunh!" And, with that, is the last definite push and the end of a long pile of mush that folds out onto the rest of the light brown pile—your regular, brown, ice cream dream. I spend so much time disbelieving that what I am seeing is real, thinking it has to be a holograph, that I don't see Dowa staring right back at me. He is in as much amazement that I am staring at him while taking a shit. He even has the nerve to give me a look of disgust. Half asleep and wiping sleep from his eyes, he grimaces and cocks his head as if I am ruining his morning ritual and how dare I watch him. 'The audacity of this woman to come here and watch me doo doo. Why . . . I . . . never!'

I draw back my stare. This isn't my world. I just got here. Girl, my mind cannot compute. I'm missing something for sure, either information or a part of my brain fell out somewhere between getting off the plane and getting malaria. His mother, Désiré, cleans it up later when she wakes up.

Bri Bri is the second youngest and just as bright, although I never see her leave any droppings. She is much more inquisitive. She knows only a bit of French, but she works it out.

"Yes?" I respond to her one morning as she stares at me inquisitively.

"Je t'aime," she slowly eeks out but does so with force in her deep, cracking, six-year-old voice. Her voice is becoming deep and womanly like her mother's already. Her dimples are even deeper and this is accented by her purplish-brown, chocolate skin that forms chocolate swirls on both sides of her lips. Dimples and a sharp jaw line just like her mother's. Her smile is so spirited that it makes me enjoy her porch visits. She is a mini-adult and she understands even the subtle things going on around her, in Bèté or not. She is all eyes. Is she joking by saying 'I love you?' She laughs after everything she says.

"I love you, too!" I respond in kind and she abruptly grabs my arm and kisses it. I grab my arm back alarmed. She laughs again and grabs my arm again and this time, lays several more kisses all over my arm. My arm is no longer a part of me at this point and then I realize she is admiring my skin color. Moments like these can create a child's idea of beauty so I quickly grab her arm and kiss it back with as many pecks and smacks as her lips have done on my arm.

"Non! Pour toi est bon!" she yells proving my suspicion right.

"Non! Pour toi est plus doux que pour moi. C'est joli. C'est chocolat!" Against her claim, I insist her skin is sweeter than mine, that it's pretty. 'It's chocolate!' I tell her. This makes her laugh and cry out in more delight than before. She grabs at my arm a third time and feigns going wild in admiration of my color. Black Americans struggle with color, too, so I'm glad I am here to reaffirm her.

".Je veux pour toi!" she pleads that she wants my skin color.

"Non! Pour toi est le plus joli." I insist hers is the prettiest and with that we feign wrestling to grab at each other's arms to plant kisses.

My real grandfather and I are visually quite a contrast, which is never a consideration until the day somebody forces me to pick. The day I am forced to choose I don't know what to do. I didn't know what race was or that it even mattered. I was confounded that after all the hard games the other kids and I played together, they could suddenly ostracize and compare me to the only two White girls in primary school.

"You're not black like us! You're white like them! Go over there with them! Look! Is her skin like ours? No! You're not black! Are you? What are you?"

"Um, what?"

"Look at yourself! You're white!"

"I'm white? What?"

When I came home after school that day, I went straight to my parents' bedroom to stare into the mirror. I touch my skin. I examine it. I think about it like the little girl tells me to but still don't understand. What is this thing about color? When my mother enters the room, I try it out . . . putting my hands to my cheeks and stroking them, I questioningly proclaim, "I'm white. I'm white. I'm white . . ."

"What? What are you saying?" My mother stops short while searching for something in the room. Well, the sound of her voice is enough to tell me I'm mistaken about something.

"Mom, I'm white."

"You're White? I didn't know that. Who told you that you're White?" I shrug my shoulders.

"Well, if you're White than you don't live in this house 'cause a Black family lives here." And, that solves it. I am what I choose to be. We all are.

Some people think I'm Latino, but Latinos and Black Americans have different histories that change their emphases. For example, a dark Puerto Rican might not say to me 'I'm Black' although they are aware they have African ancestry. They may just prefer 'I'm Puerto Rican' because they feel this more completely defines who they are—just as an Ivoirien won't say to another Ivoirien 'I'm African.' They will share their ethnicity because that expresses their culture.

Genes are a tricky thing. You can't always see what's there. Your skin color is your own skin color only, not the skin color of every person that was ever in your family tree. I know I am multiracial. Do you? We all are. If the color of offspring from first to third generation and even first to second can change drastically after mixing, think about what the last one thousand years have done to you.

Whatever my parents are is what I am then. If my Dad says he is Black then I am Black and if my mom says she is Black then I am Black. Based on those two things, 'Black' has always meant more to me than just color because my parents are light and dark. Light like me or darker like my sister, I am 'Black' through and through. That is my culture. That is our self-prescribed identity as are all identities self-prescribed. Reality is what we make it.

I am my language—I am Spanish. I am my color—I am Black. I am my region—I am Middle Eastern. I am my religion—I am Jewish. People's experiences dictate their emphases and those emphases are not mutually exclusive even though most people do not bother to explain 'the everything else' that they are—who could?

Skin color makes up less than .001% of our DNA. Color reflects very little about where we come from or our differences.

10 À L'HÔPITAL

At least one funeral, even in tiny Zragbi, is something to expect before the month is up. I can't tell if it's normal or not, but there are way more children than adults in this village.

'I almost had my bac,' Céline often reminds me in frustration. She nearly achieved what is called a high school 'baccalaureate.'

Cote d'Ivoire has seven years of secondary education following the French system—four years of 'collège' and then three years of 'lycée' where you specialize. Once you finish lycée, you have your bac, and can then go on to either get a good job or attend a university.

Céline got pregnant with Laudine just before finishing lycée. Luckily, however, because she is so smart, the village chose her to be one of the Filles de Salle at the hospital. Assistants are honorable positions here. They do just as much work as the Midwife and Nurse. This makes Céline a volunteer, too, and she is paid by her village any way they can, rather than by the government as are the Nurse and Midwife.

From time to time, I go up to the hospital where I am supposed to help but never really do. There really is no pressure on Peace Corps Volunteers to do anything other than what they expect from themselves. I'm still trying to learn to communicate well in at least one language.

Céline has to get up whenever someone needs assistance. A woman's water may break. She might be having a miscarriage. Someone might be dangerously ill. Nine times out of ten, however, if there is a woman at the hospital it is pregnancy-related. I see a few pregnancies and I say a few because that is all I can stand. The hospital can't afford the proper instruments they need in case of a real emergency. It is very risky to put your life in the hands of the Zragbi hospital, but they do as good as they can with what they have and it's better than having to have a baby off in the darkness somewhere in the middle of the night.

On the women's side of the hospital there are two main rooms in constant use. The room on the right is for consultations, baby weighing, and gynecological examinations. The room to the left is where everything goes down.

Céline gets requests at all hours. One comes today at 17:00 in the afternoon. The sun still glares. I sit around waiting for Céline to cook up something for me to devour in five minutes when a little kid runs through Bogo's yard.

"Tantie?" The little boy calls Céline 'Auntie' out of respect.

"Someone is there," he explains sweating with mouth wide open trying to suck in air after doing a full-out sprint.

"Unnnh," she affirms that she knows he speaks of the hospital.

"Come," Céline calls me and we walk over.

"Put her on the table!" The Sage Femme/Midwife is already there. This one thing she says is the only thing I understand besides a few other directions accompanied by obvious gestures. Anything else, I only understand with my eyes. The girl on the table is seventeen.

"C'est un Mossi," says the Sage Femme to Céline. Céline begins to eye the girl suspiciously. Is being from the Mossi ethnicity bad? The accompanying aunt is a much older woman wrapped in cloths around her head and covered all the way down to her toes, speaking Senoufo. La Sage and Céline know her language at least.

"She doesn't speak Senoufo?" Céline asks the relative in Senoufo and the relative silently nods her head 'no' as she peers up at Céline embarrassed. The relative comforts the young girl, but the girl is really all alone. Is this another girl taken from far away to be someone's umpteenth wife as was the frightened girl I saw captive in the corner of that house of so many women?

"The two don't speak the same language," Céline shares with me.

"Which languages?" I ask confused.

"She speaks Senoufo and the girl is a Mossi," Céline finishes the last part with a bit of disgust in her upper lip. "She is from Burkina Faso," she adds. This is a mess. The girl has no family here. I'm scared and I'm not even the one pregnant. But, the Sage Femme and Céline act coolly.

The girl's eyes shoot around. La Sage Femme slaps her legs open and the girl is surprised as her privacy is invaded, not knowing what is to happen next without anyone who can give her an explanation. Maybe this is her first time in a hospital.

Her eyes shoot from face to face and finally rest on mine. For a second, she has fear in her face. Am I the doctor? Is she being prepped for me? I am the only one not yet doing anything. I see her going through these thoughts in her head, more and more nervous.

"She is going to help us," Céline replies to the young girl's thoughts by speaking to the aunt in Senoufo, momentarily pointing her head toward me. This reassures the aunt who suddenly smiles my way, then looks back at the Mossi girl with reassuring eyes. The aunt gives her an additional pat on her left hand, which she has already been holding, combined with a few obvious words of encouragement in Senoufo, but the Mossi girl doesn't really understand nor does she respond. She just keeps her gaze on my eyes one long while, and I'm afraid to alarm her by not allowing her to read them.

"You're going to help us, isn't that right?" Céline then translates what she just said in Senoufo to me in French with a snicker. In the midst of Céline scurrying to the left, La Sage Femme scurrying to the right, and the aunt trying to block sun from the girl's eyes by the curtainless window, holding the girl's hand and switching her weight back and forth from one foot to another, I become solid stone. I'm a little American with no formal training. No training period. Our three-month training is primarily for us to get used to the climate, the food, familiarize ourselves with a few of the languages, learn how to take care of ourselves, teach people a few simple things to prevent A.I.D.S. and malaria, and maybe throw together a latrine project or two. Not for this.

The young girl is nervous again. My eyes now tell her I have as little clue about what is about to happen as she does. Shit. I'm not helping. Everyone moves around me and finally I have enough sense and consciousness to get out of the way.

Whatever happened to 'scappel?' 'Knife?' All those instruments you see on TV in those hospital scenes. Where is the tray of prepped instruments? There is no hand scrubbing or gloves. They've gotta' have gloves. Are they simply going to reach in there and pull it out? No one has a doctor's mask over their mouths and the window is up through which a few flies enter.

La Sage Femme has to slap her legs open again and what I finally see, I do not understand. She has no vaginal lips, no clitoris, and no hole readily identifiable down there. She has been circumcised in the worst possible way. There are different degrees, I have learned, but this is the worst. Any part that is sensitive to enjoyment is cut off. How is a baby going to come out of that?

I'm moving. I can't watch this and have no right. This is not a show. Why do I have a right to be here and watch this? Finally, La Sage Femme sits down after having found an incisor instrument. It looks okay, but has it been sterilized? La Sage Femme cannot, of course, communicate with the girl and all that the aunt can continue to do is pat the back of her hand. Brace yourself. I mean me, not the girl.

I now stand by her head to block out the sun assaulting her through the window and when she looks up at me, I give her the best smile I can, regretting that neither one of us know what is happening and how much worse it will get. She smiles back right before crying out from being cut in a place so personal.

"Aaaaaaaah!" she screams. La Sage Femme starts to cut from somewhere in the middle all the way to her anus. Her vaginal lips were sewn shut in the final part of her circumcision years before, and all of it is now fused-together skin that the Sage Femme must open back up.

"Push," Céline says strangely calm in Senoufo. The aunt then says a few words, to which the girl obviously does not understand, to which the aunt gestures with an outward swing of her arm down in the direction of the action. La Sage Femme and Céline take turns slapping her legs open. The girl struggles with the pain, the cutting with no anesthesia, and worst of all that no one can explain it in the Mossi language to her as it happens. After more slapping of the legs and not much more than plain and perfunctory urges from Céline and La Sage Femme to push, the girl slowly understands that if she does not push, she might be here all afternoon and into the night.

Her teeth grit and right when her legs falter from the effort it takes to push down her diaphragm, smack! Another slap stings her legs to keep them open. Why are they being so hard? Are they like this at every birth or are they just upset that this is the trillionth baby they have to deliver and after-hours to boot? Are they mean because she is a Mossi or are they trying to get this little girl to not ever want to have a baby again or come to this hospital? It isn't her fault. The husband is probably twice her age and she is very far from home if she could not at least have someone with her who speaks her language. Umh.

A smell rises in the air precipitously. "Ça sort," the Sage Femme whispers vaguely to Céline. What's coming out? The baby? As the girl pushes, out comes a lot: mucus, blood, and a chunk of doo doo protruding from her anus that La Sage Femme swipes with prongs into a silver pee receptor tray. She does it quickly with a grimace on her face, noticeable only for a split second. Then, she gets back to work.

I don't have to be on that end to smell what comes out. It subtly sneaks up on you; breathing things that have been in any woman's womb for months can't possibly smell great. I'm light-headed. The smell takes over my consciousness and I find myself shaking my head to stay clear and standing. I grab for the wall by the window to the left of the supine girl. The strong sunrays fortify me again.

"There is no air in here," Céline complains. Her too? I thought I was the only one. I am avoiding all future 'assists' from now on. I mean, give me a break. I'm only twenty-three. I'm a Health Volunteer, not a doctor. Has Bogo not explained what I am here for yet? Maybe he doesn't understand either. I'm sure he finds a way to slip out of homologue information sessions given by Peace Corps if he ever goes to them.

Oyo is the other Fille de Salle who assists the Sage Femme with Céline. She has the kind of deep, glistening, dark, mulberry brown skin that emanates a mystical energy. Hers is the kind that reflects onto you and makes you darker just by standing next to her. I'm sure if I had a special instrument that could measure ultraviolet rays, she'd be giving them off. It's as though her skin absorbs the sun's rays instantly and pours them back out. I can feel it. Oyo is the same medium height as Céline and La Sage Femme, but she dresses differently. She is Muslim and Senoufo and more traditional in the sense that she rarely deviates from pagne wraps. I never see her without the fula she wraps into a coiled snake shape on her head, the edges of the cloth draping down her back. Her hair today is individually wrapped in the same thickness as braids with black, shiny, flat, plastic strings. Around in a circular pattern it goes to seal in every bit of hair all the way down to the tips. Each thick section of her long, wrapped hair is then pulled back and pinned up, sticking straight out in the shape of a sugar cone.

Oyo comes to the hospital the next day, which makes it La Sage Femme, Céline, Oyo, and me in a room the size of a kitchen in a small apartment. The women of Zragbi and beyond haven't come for consultation yet so I don't know how all of them and us are going to fit in here. I get to the hospital before Céline. She enters in a modern outfit that covers all but is slinky and shows the shape of her powerful, slim, trim body. The dark purple dress is long, velvety, and the top has rhinestone buttons along the V-neck. Its shorter-than-short, tight sleeves pronounce the cut of her arms. Céline has to be at least thirty but is in much better shape than I am. Many people in Zragbi don't know their age or when they are born. The year of birth on their carte d'identité may or may not be correct if they aren't born in the hospital. Some birthdays are chosen randomly when registering for an ID.

Some have their birthdate changed so many times that they can't remember the original one. Children have to be a certain age for their school grade and if for some reason they aren't, because of sickness or having to take time off to help their parents around the house and in the fields, then they adjust their age in Daloa for a small fee.

"Ah, Céline, before I forget," the Sage Femme slides Céline a crisp 10,000 CFA bill without a look.

"Merci," Céline smiles shortly holding her happiness in, never knowing from where, when, and in what form her compensation will come.

It is weigh-in and vaccination day and women and men come from Zragbi and way beyond it. Weigh-in day coincides with one of the biggest market days of the week. People come to make their presence known as well as buy or sell what has been cultivated in the fields. The line starts from the consultation door with some people on the floor, legs stretched out, and some people sitting on benches. Women have their babies pagne-wrapped on their backs, heads peeking out from underneath their armpits to feed from their breasts. One woman is outstretched on a bench with her hand on top of her forehead exhausted from the heat, exhausted from the line, exhausted from waiting, exhausted from whatever ailment she might have, or all of the above. There are several more people standing by her, waiting with her, or waiting for her to get up and share the bench.

These lines take hours. Some men stand up straight. Some men in brown or tan slacks are tired and shift their weight to their left hip or their right just as the women do. There are as many men waiting outside the Infirmier's door as there are women waiting outside La Sage Femme's door, but most of the men have nowhere to sit with women sprawled out on the benches. So, if they are trying to hide their visit to the hospital, it isn't going to work because the men's line snakes from the inside hall to the outside along the hospital wall in plain view of the tens of people passing by every five minutes to enter or leave the market.

Vaccination day is something to see. Little kids gather around the hospital in shorts and torn T-shirts or just shorts or just a T-shirt. They get in a line and Céline treats them one by one in rapid procession on the hospital lawn.

"What is that?" I ask upon seeing the children with their heads tilted back and a drop of liquid placed on their tongues.

"Vitamin A," Céline informs with her Ivoirien French accent. 'Vee-tah-meen Ah.'

"Just one drop?"

"Just one drop is good." Vitamin A prevents diseases such as goiters.

Consultation consists of a lot of things, one of which is not privacy. I am back in the room again along with Céline, La Sage Femme, and Oyo. The door is left open. At least two people wait anxiously at the door to be called in, another person is just stepping inside past them, one stands at the door entrance with her baby pulled to the side sucking from her right breast, another stretches out on the doctor's bed, another places her baby on the scale to be weighed and marked in the book by Céline, and still another sits next to Oyo, who is giving vaccinations to pregnant mothers. It is an orderly chaos that keeps the line moving.

"You wanna' try?" Oyo eyes me with a vaccination needle in right hand and a woman's arm in her left. The woman doesn't even blink at Oyo's suggestion, releasing herself to whatever the hospital decides. But, I have nothing to prove and no one's precious arm is going to be my playground. Some women's arms have old scars and some new ones forming from needles either put in too shallow or too deep.

"Non, merci," I nicely decline. Oyo and Céline smile at each other.

La Sage Femme has litmus paper, which she dips into pee samples that the women give. Sometimes the paper comes out yellow and sometimes it is purple. Some women are well hydrated and fine while others have hypertension. La Sage Femme herself is a big woman, over 300 pounds at 5'6" inches. She waddles from side to side when she walks in the long, flowery dresses she wears to the hospital. Half of her entire face droops from one eye to the right edge of her lip as if she had one time experienced a pummeling and very severe stroke.

"You have to stop eating the salt," La Sage Femme leans forward with one fist on the desk to tell the woman with a dark blue fula wrapped around her head, sitting opposite her on the other side of the desk. Hippocratic Oath? Forget about it. Everyone in Cote d'Ivoire and America is gonna' know this woman has hypertension now. Her green blouse dips down off her left shoulder as she squirms in her seat the way a caffeine addict told not to drink coffee or a child with cavities told to stop eating candy would. Salt?! If these people out in the middle of nowhere with no processed foods in sight can have hypertension, then I guess I'll be dead in ten years. Salt does not seem to be part of the body's evolutionary plan anywhere.

"Like the Whites," I hear someone say in French in the midst of business.

To which La Sage Femme replies, "Mais, elle est Blanche."

I'm trying to keep out of everything. I prefer to be a quiet observer with nothing yet to get nor give but gain an experience. Céline is talking about something which compares White people and La Sage Femme has just come back with, 'well, she is White,' pointing with a piece of litmus paper in my direction.

"Je ne suis pas Blanche," I straighten up and defend myself with the usual. Well, everyone swings their head up and over, including the two women each with one foot in the door trying to catch a glimpse of the action. Only the babies suckling their mother's breasts don't care. But, there is nothing to see because as soon as I protest, La Sage Femme backs down smirking satisfactorily at both her jab and my immediate block. She certainly knows how to wake me up. There is no time to speak, only absorb. On top of all the activity going on in this tiny little room of two adjacent shaded windows, everyone speaks in their own language. French words leave La Sage Femme's mouth and Céline translates them to yet another woman, now standing at the corner of the desk, into Bèté. Then, Oyo yells in Senoufo, which causes another woman to walk in and sit down for vaccination.

"Thank you," the woman who just received an injection from Oyo says in Jula as she jumps up.

"You're welcome," Oyo replies heartily switching from Senoufo into Jula. La Sage Femme then turns around to the window at her back because a young child asks her a question in Abé to which she replies in Abé. Is La Sage Femme Abé? Hmm. Didn't know that. The young child runs off with new orders and then just as fast, La Sage Femme swirls back around responding to a question that Céline poses in French about the weight of the infant currently being weighed. An unfamiliar language then presents itself, but still, La Sage Femme manages although stumbling through it.

"Céline? How do you say . . ." La Sage Femme asks Céline for help with the words she searches to address the new woman on the bed table behind the chair in front of La Sage Femme's desk. La Sage must have wanted to express something like 'Wait there. I'll examine you in a second. I have ten other people in the room and I don't know who needs help next and who is already being helped.'

I must be correct because suddenly out of my fog I hear "Pahdré!" My slouch straightens. "Quitte là!" La Sage Femme yells as she comes around her table to where I stand, sandwiched between the bed, the back of Oyo's chair, and the medicine closet.

"Haaaaaaa!" Everyone bursts into laughter and bright smiles breathe happiness into the shaded room. The women seem nervous that I am there without knowing why. La Sage yelling 'move from there!' reassures everyone that even being an unknown entity, I am at least okay enough to be yelled at.

I squeeze over to the right from behind Oyo to La Sage's chair. I put my butt up on the open windowsill. I look down and ogh! Two little eyes glare up at me. The sylph in the beautiful church dress with the completely shaven head at the pump is back, but this time there are two of her. Her twin has her back up against the wall, out of sight of everyone else, but she instead smiles at me. The glarer hands me a plate of food up through the window that makes La Sage grunt and instruct me to 'met ça sur' the table. I do. Lunchtime is here and the trinity of La Sage, Oyo, and Céline rush to get everyone in and out.

An exchange in the unidentifiable language continues between the woman on the doctor's table and La Sage. La Sage turns to Céline and asks for 'la clé?'

Céline quickly throws her a bunch of keys formerly sitting by the good-smelling food. The young woman and La Sage leave for an examination. This departure causes a woman waiting to slump her shoulders in despair that she may never be seen today. At least she has her foot in the door! The line behind her is treacherous.

"Elle a 3 mois," La Sage announces when she and the woman return. Céline frowns. The young girl is three months pregnant.

Why such long faces when so many other young girls walk around the village pregnant? What's the difference? Right in this moment, an older man enters the room past the increasingly sulking woman with one foot in the door. They allow men back here? He wears a small, flat, cylindrical hat that stands up from the middle of his thinning, miniscule, white curls. His robe is pure white and long with short sleeves and brown and green embroidery stitched along the V-neck. He sits down right next to the young girl that is three months pregnant on the bench before the baby-weighing machine. What a shame that she is pregnant and all she has is her grandfather to take care of her.

"C'est son mari?" through successful straining I understand La Sage interrogating Céline.

"Unnnnnh," Céline says 'yes' giving her signature, deep version of 'unh huh' without taking her eyes off the record book she checks in her hands. I do a double take. This eighty-year-old man is her husband?! First I see a vagina-less vagina, now this? What is going on in Zragbi? Women have the short end of the stick for sure. A teenager has to carry the child of some old man. Will she have more?

A few women in the room show interest. Other women don't care or are used to such sights just wanting to get their consultation and go. It doesn't happen often enough to desensitize La Sage but often enough that the older man shows no shame in his face. His 6'3" frame does, however, shrink a bit being surrounded by so many women and no way to hide the truth which all of Zragbi soon knows. The silence says abortion is not an option and that isn't done in Zragbi anyway.

The trinity willingly crashes after a long day of baby weigh-ins, pregnant mother vaccinations, consultations, urine testing, and all other problems that women have out here with no easy access to a well-supplied and staffed hospital and prescriptions for medicine at the pharmacy they can't afford. The quiet of the early morning returns to the room and I am gladly not the cause of it this time. I'm tired and I don't even do anything. I sit back up on the doctor's table and stare out into space. Oyo, Céline, and La Sage do the same. I have seen blood, pee, poop, and heard the private matters of so many women I don't know and may never get to know the names of.

How do they do it? All day long in this tiny little room, allowing five or more patients with babies on the hip in the room at once, never knowing which language they'll have to help or consult in, and sometimes having no language in common at all—having to step out the door or over to the market to find a willing translator. That is the strength of the hospital; taking whoever comes, whenever, however, and using whatever resources they have or can create to solve the crisis. This is what a hospital should be. So much paperwork and money is involved in getting treatment in the States and even then you might still get a horror story. Imagine the trinity with more supplies, Oyo and Céline with more training, actual salaries, and free medicine. Whew.

Oyo sucks on an ice cold and tellingly spicy gingembre sachet,

Céline has profoundly purplish-red bissap showing on her tongue every time she laughs wide, and La Sage finally gets to finish the lunch I place on her desk a couple of hours ago. Céline pulls up a chair to the left of La Sage who faces me now in the patient's seat, and Oyo is seated in her chair to the right close to the other window. They talk for a while, but I am far out in my thoughts, my skin seething from the heat bubbles trying to break into sweat down my face. What am I supposed to do with all this newfound information? How do I start a project from all of this? Luckily, I am not too absorbed in my mind's confusion to miss the entire conversation. A few words pique my interest and turn on my French strain meter.

"C'était comme ça!" Céline cries out in astonishment while simultaneously gliding her hands across each other in opposite directions creating a loud slap. "Il n'y avait rien en bas! C'était quoi ça?"

Oyo merely shakes her head and sticks out her lips in an 'I don't know why' gesture with her eyes to the ground and then focuses her eyes off in the distance. "Je ne sais pas pourquoi c'est comme ça. Ils faisaient ça depuuuuiiiiiis . . ."

"Il font ça encore?" My mind rewinds to play back the conversation from the beginning. Céline's hand gesture and the words 'en bas'—they are talking about the pregnancy yesterday. Céline is astonished that the girl had nothing below. 'Flat like a board' she signifies. All Oyo can say is that they have done that since time immemorial.

"Who is 'they'?" Céline inquires to Oyo whose Senoufo ethnicity is obviously one of the ethnicities that perform female genital mutilation.

"It's the women that do it." The women do it to each other? "The women gather a bunch of little young girls each time and do it one after the other."

"What?" Céline goes on in disbelief, but La Sage just listens having finished her meal. "I couldn't do that. They did that to you, too?" Her probing shocks me.

Oyo simply answers with a nod. Then, even though it appears as if she will go no further, she quickly contributes, "I don't feel anything."

"With your husband?" Céline seeks confirmation but more quietly now.

"Nothin'. I don't feel nothin'." Oyo's lips stick out again. She zones out at the floor for a few seconds, a moment of silence which the two grant, and then up at each of them and for a moment over at me. Time stops to allow this personal share. She keeps shaking her head back and forth resigned to the fact but resultantly also showing a tinge of satisfaction at the thought that her husband can't satisfy her no matter what he does. It happened long before him, but he is clearly not valuable enough to her to elevate him to more than what he will never be able to do for her.

"I couldn't give up my . . ." and then Céline gives a sweet grunt and squeezes her legs tight giving out a loud shout of a laugh. La Sage gives her a look of agreement then glances back at Oyo with concern.

"But, I didn't do that to my little girl. I don't see why. It's not necessary," Oyo adds. La Sage nods and smiles lightly. "I'm never going to do that to her . . . unh um."

Can this just be written off as a cultural thing? I'm trying to think of immediately painful things that Americans do to themselves? There is male circumcision, but that does not take away any sexual feeling in the penis, does it? Female genital circumcision has that specific goal, however, whether only the clitoris is cut off or every single sensitive part of the outer vagina is. If this is a cultural thing, what is then the definition of culture? Webster's dictionary says culture is 'the skills, arts, etc. of a given people in a given period.' With that definition, can female circumcision be defined as a skill if it's done well? What would make it 'done well' and what is the benefit to the woman? If Oyo's daughter grows up to be condemned for being of the few in her quartier not circumcised, is that culture? How can something, which you can be condemned for not also doing, be a skill or art if you are obligated to do it? Getting an infection from not being able to urinate or menstruate normally because your exits have been tampered with? Maybe it is cultural, as large groups of people do it, but it's one of those cultural aspects—like America's preference for colossal, pollution-creating, gas-guzzling cars—that only do harm.

Céline takes me to the fields with her on Saturdays when she doesn't have to go to the hospital. We cut through people's connected backyards in the quartiers on the other side of the main Zragbi road.

"Let's stop here," Céline says as we approach a large well. I always get my water from the schoolyard pump. It brings the water from deep under the earth's top layer, away from any potential contaminates that may penetrate from the surface soil. The pump structure itself seals the water up so that nothing can go in or come out of the water source—only the air that is pressured by us pumpers to bring it way up and out of the spout.

The well, on the other hand, is only sometimes covered with an often random sheet of wood that doesn't insure no one has accidentally or otherwise dropped anything or themselves into it. Too, well water is the water that has naturally risen to the earth's top layer from below, so, it is exposed to the top soil and also gets depleted of the nutrients found in water pulled from below the earth's top layer.

"Ça va," Céline assures me after seeing my pursed lips. We stock up on this water in the Jula/Senoufo/Mossi quartier in plastic water jugs and a bucket before going any farther. As we jump back onto a main path that leads us out into the open fields and toward the cultivated forest areas, young Jula girls head back. They go out early in the darkness to gather wood for breakfast or to scare the birds away from their crops. We pass them between two bushes on either side of us. The bushes are plush and green with long, green leaves. As each fula-head-wrapped girl passes Céline and me to our left, they pull off a long leaf, tear off the flesh from the stem, and eat it.

"They eat that to not get pregnant," Céline shares disgustedly
after they pass. But, after seeing my first and last baby delivery in
Zragbi and that eighty-year-old man, I can't say I wouldn't do the
same in their shoes. What voice of resistance do they have otherwise?

Some ethnicities among Zragbi women, however, do have more
autonomy in their relationships with men and all the women in
general are just as physically strong if not stronger than their male
counterparts, regardless of ethnicity. Women take many functions in
Cote d'Ivoire. Cooking, cleaning, field work, taking care of the children, and more—those things are exceedingly challenging because
they are so organically done from scratch.

Bogo has one function: to go to the hospital and work until the
early afternoon. Then, he is off to Daloa. It is seldom that he
spends the night in Zragbi for more than two days at a time. He
does whatever he wants and maybe that's because he isn't from
Zragbi. He rarely divulges information about himself.

Why didn't he ask to be an Infirmier in his own ethnicity's village? Maybe fonctionnaires aren't allowed to work in their village
for reasons of conflict of interest? For example, if a relative needs
medicine but can't afford it, then you as the nurse might be more
likely to give it to them for free. La Sage is Abé and she is also the
only Grand Type of her ethnicity in Zragbi. Many of the teachers
here are also not of any ethnicity native to Zragbi.

Bogo says that Jijina and Eliane are his children, but they don't
resemble him or each other at all. No affection or sweet words flow
from him to his girls the few times a week he is home. He only orders them around and without eye contact. He's more so taking
them in, the same way he allows random folks to sleep in the gues-
troom at night or watch TV because they don't have one. La Sage
unofficially adopts orphaned children as well—the twins included.

He is just like me. No family. Just in the village on assignment.
His front doors stay wide open from morning 'til night. There is
regularly someone new. Many benefit from Céline's cooking if
they're around at the right time, and then never to be seen again.

I don't go to the hospital anymore. They keep trying to get me to do stuff and I am not here for that, nor am I qualified for it. I'm not going to take advantage of the opportunity to stick needles in people or deliver a baby just for fun! I am really supposed to be giving sensibilizations to the villagers about malaria and A.I.D.S., but I feel pretty strange walking up to someone and telling them how they should be doin' it—even stranger whipping out the wooden penis and condoms Peace Corps provides us with to show people how to use them. I think that would require a five-year assignment, not a two-year one. I've got to first learn some of the languages in Zragbi before I can start telling everyone what to do. But, even harder than telling people how to have sex, is explaining the process of A.I.D.S. itself.

He died from pneumonia. He died from diarrhea. She had skin cancer. How do I explain to them that there are illnesses and then there are illnesses that look like other illnesses, really resulting from the H.I.V. virus, which has weakened their immune system to any illnesses prevalent in their environments they would otherwise not die from?

"He just shit himself to death," Céline tells me about someone who died recently. Who shits themselves to death? He probably died from having A.I.D.S.—not being able to fight the subsequent diarrhea because his immune system is now so weakened by the H.I.V. virus. The H.I.V. virus then turns into A.I.D.S. once it has taken over the cells in the entire immune system.

However it is that I'm going to do this, I for sure can't begin anywhere working with Bogo. He even tries to touch my boobie once. Stepping out of his house while getting something for Céline, Bogo steps in. He passes me and says something. I can't understand him so I turn around and when I do he is right there. His eyes beam with excitement. In a flash, his hand snatches up toward my right breast trying but failing to squeeze a piece of me between his thumb and forefinger. I instinctively step back without yet having processed from what I am protecting myself.

Did he get it? Did he touch it? So slow to process the meaning of the act, I don't step out of the house right away. So, he tries again, a smile breaking across his lips thinking that I want it. I step back again, but this time he just gets my nipple through my shirt. I cock my head to the side. What? I am part angry and part confused. Does he think I'm from here?

I don't speak. Who do I tell that Bogo touched my boob? Do I yell it? It's not rape, is it? What is it? Will people laugh if I say something? I don't feel the presence of any laws hovering in the background to discourage the wrong-doers or encourage the victims to speak up. So, I'm either going to stay and deal with stupidity as it comes or leave outright. All of these thoughts thunder through my mind until I realize he is still standing there.

My anger bristles so intensely that his wicked smile finally reduces to at least a plain one and he turns back around to continue on to his room. You supposta' be my homologue and we create projects together and you snatchin' boobies? What are other volunteers dealing with? Would he do that to a White volunteer?

How many women does he really have if he would do something like that to me? He is hardly in the village. What does he even do anyway besides sit at his desk and prescribe medicine to men who can't afford it?

I wake early the next morning. Maybe Céline will go to the fields again. If I want to do anything, I've got to let people know by sunrise and Céline always insists I come over for breakfast at 7 a.m. When I get to Bogo's house, she isn't up so I turn around back down to my house thinking she is still in bed.

"Pahdré!" she loudly whispers with a smile, heading toward me. Huh? I beat her here? We must have woken up the same time.

"You don't live here?" I ask.

"No, I live down below." But, she is always up so early making Bogo's breakfast and doing other housework for him that you would think she lives with him. She lives down by me a couple courtyards below, near the Chief that lives at the bottom of the hill. There are so many houses in the Chief's courtyard area that you would think several other families live there, but actually it's one huge, extended family—all cousins, uncles, aunts, grandmothers, and grandfathers, and multiple wives of the Chief—Le Chef.

She briskly sweeps the yard, made messy with bits of debris from visitors the night before. It now has smooth, rainbow strokes across it from the long, straw broom that is a broom without the handle. She grabs it where the white string at the top ties the tens of skinny straw legs together. Smoke wisps soon sneak out from under the appatam where she cooks Bogo's rice dish. After she finishes, she disappears back toward her house and when she comes back up again she is fresh.

"Look Pahdré. Look at my hair," she says producing a photo after putting the final touches to her hair. She must have gotten this when she went back down to her house. This picture is from the early 1990s. She has an egg-white cotton dress on that reaches down to her calves, puffy shoulders, and her hair blooms out thick, full, and black all over her head. Beautiful. Maybe it was hot-combed, but I never see anyone using a hot comb around here. It must have been a mild perm because it is somewhat straight although puffy. "Maintenant, ce n'est plus comme ça." When she says this, I at last take my eyes off of the beautiful photo to glimpse at her hair for which she is correct in saying 'no longer looks like that.' It is breaking off at the edges, thin, and hairline receding.

"You need to trim your ends," I say. But, this falls on deaf ears. She combs it so much as if doing so will reshape it back into the hair in the picture, but it does not. She has access to perms that leave her with major breakage but no upkeep information to prevent damage. Really, it's the chemicals. A lot of the little kids have bald patches on their heads from perms gone bad, leaving it in too long or not putting Vaseline around their forehead, ears, and all other hairline edges before slapping on the skin-eating, burning, white perm cream.

"If you cut your ends then your hair will grow back full again." Her roots are a thick forest, but I can see through the straggly ends. Poor Céline. Poor Ivoirien women. Poor Black women around the world. I stopped that madness long ago. Even though Blacks in America can afford better perm maintenance, no matter how shiny and fabulous we think we've made it, we've still lost our hair.

"There is a woman at the hospital," a child comes running into the courtyard saying again. The child leaves and Céline paces back and forth.

"Raaaaugh," she snaps and stomps creating a red cloud around her legs. Céline has had it. It's like damn—I just got up, sleep still forming in my eyes, I cooked breakfast for my family, now for Bogo's, I didn't get much sleep last night because a late pregnancy came in, and now at seven in the morning I have to start again?! She wants to scream but holds the stifled yell I hear gurgling in her throat. She pouts and stomps her feet up and down, pounding her fists on her thighs and no one but me is there to see it.

Céline deals with everything although not always gracefully. I, on the other hand, regularly quit. Céline knows I don't want to see another pregnancy so I go back home and leave her.

Back at my house, a dramatic shift comes over me while sitting on the floor of my kitchen staring out the window. One moment I am thinking—What am I going to do today? Who will I hang out with?—And the next, I want to rip off my clothes and run down the street butt naked. What? I feel my synapses ready to fire to make my body go. This is not normal. These are not my thoughts and it is only through a logical deduction of about two minutes that I finally conclude butt naked is not a good idea. It is this medicine.

The impulses come in waves. No real hallucinations or cataclysmic dreams as others complain. One volunteer dreams he is a kangaroo with a baby in his pouch hopping around in Technicolor. I do occasionally have thoughts I've never entertained before, crying frantically in tears I can never anticipate or explain.

I stand up in the kitchen, take my Mefloquine medicine with me, walk out to my latrine, and watch it spiral down the hole. Yeh, I did it. I'm sick of this shit. The thought of getting malaria again pales in the background of the urges to do crazy things on these drugs. I'm not going to lose it out here in Zragbi with no family for a million miles. I've already had malaria twice so maybe this preventive malarial medicine is not working.

Mefloquine requires a high dosage because you only take it once a week. Those heart pains I used to have in Grand Noyaré for the first hour after taking it, this sporadic depression, and the insane impulses are overwhelming. Nivaquine is an older medicine that malaria strains have built up a resistance to in many malaria-endemic, West African countries, so it's not popular. Doxycycline is once a day. The Peace Corps doctor says we can switch to that if we want, but I need a break from all drugs right now. Logic is not logical right now.

Feeling free after disposing of my Mefloquine forever, I return to the hospital hoping the morning delivery I escape from earlier is miraculously over. I do visit the hospital periodically, but I do not stay long. Céline and Oyo's male counterparts, the Garcons de Salle, do not make the hospital any more appealing.

The Garcon de Salle is operating when I return. It is a woman receiving treatment on the men's side and why do I know this? It is because the Garcon de Salle leaves the door wide open. She is barely lying on the bed table with her elbows propping her up and one leg hanging off of the side. Both of her breasts are exposed and the right one has a gaping hole in it which the Garcon de Salle makes with somewhat of a knife, walking back and forth to Bogo's office with blood on his gloves asking for more gauze, not knowing what to do with the hole he creates but stuff her breast with it.

I have a Peace Corps workshop coming up in Abidjan and wait outside Bogo's door to tell him as he is supposed to come, still officially being my homologue and all. A line forms by Bogo's door so the only place for me to stand is by the Garcon de Salle's room. I wait by the door long enough to get the large whiffs of alcohol that pound me in the face every time he scurries by me to ask Bogo another question and I don't mean medical alcohol. The hole is more than an inch deep and in sloppy square shape. Is he trying to cut her heart out?! Drunk as a skunk, eyes blood-shot red. Why does Bogo allow him to operate on her like that? She is losing her mind, gritting her teeth, only sucking in air between pursed lips every five seconds, wondering when it will be over, what the hell he is doing, and if he even knows.

How is levelheaded Céline with a man who runs such a ship?

Maybe she could not avoid him as she works at the hospital with him. Maybe she loves him. What will happen if she decides not to be with him anymore? One thing for sure, she can't get rid of me. Céline feeds me. She teaches me how to speak Bèté and French. She makes me laugh. I fiercely try to learn from Céline because she is always fiercely teaching me. I frustrate her with my ignorance about everything Ivoirien, but she never gives up and so I soak it in. I ask her so many questions, it's a phenomenon she doesn't sock me in the head with her big, marmite pot. 'Na wupuri kada kada, dey!' She tells me in Bèté that I'm hardheaded when I do not agree with her on an issue.

Another lunchtime arrives and Céline breaks from the hospital to make Bogo's meal . . . and mine. We are cooking underneath the thick, straw-roofed appatam or I should say Céline is. I watch her extract the red palm oil from the bright, crimson, acorn-shaped nuts in her mortar. Red oil smears all over her fingertips.

"Je peux t'aider?" I insincerely offer to help and for a moment she is about to hand me the stick until the last time I try flashes before her eyes and she changes her mind.

"No, that's okay. I don't want you to get tired," she laughs at her poke, the ostensible gap between her two front teeth leaping in the air as she merrily throws her head back.

"I'm not going to get tired," my face scrunches up even though I know it's true. "That's you," I poke back. She is ready to battle now but pleasantly surprised that I know the who-can-tell-who-off-the-best game without a real insult.

A big, long, loud noise then cracks the silence—a simultaneous combination of middle of the lip smack and tip of the tongue suck, not the lip smacks in the States that peep out the sides of mouths. Hers follows with a loud, nasal, and from the gut "huh!" as if to say 'please!'

"You over there!" she shouts. 'I could neeeever get tired! You— that sleeps until 10 a.m.!"

"Ha-haaaaaa!" We both start laughing.

"Tu viens plus a l'hôpital," she jerks serious. So, I get serious back.

"I don't like coming to the hospital," I say surprised by my so long sustained candor. The Bètè always say their real feelings so I'm going to, too. It's refreshing. "I didn't go to school to learn how to make babies come out. I don't know how to do that," I struggle in French to find the words 'deliver a child' and 'no formal training' but opt for simple words although probably childish-sounding to Céline's ears. "I don't want to hurt someone because I don't know what I'm doing."

"On va t'apprendre," she promises.

"But, I don't want to learn. That's too much responsibility for me."

"We are going to call you Pahdré," she suddenly decides as she smack-sucks with lips, teeth, and tongue again.

"Padre?"

"Yes, Pahdré. That's your name."

"Padre? Isn't that Spanish for 'father?'"

"No. Pahdré is Bètè," she demystifies the origin proudly. "Pah Dré!" She enjoys saying it some more. 'Pahdré' is a Bètè name with a popping-hard, aspirated stress over the 'P' in the 'Pah' syllable, followed by 'Dahrey'—a phonetic version of the final syllable. There is also 'Mahdré' and that isn't Spanish either. They are both actually two words, many phrases in Bètè ending in 'ré.'

"Faut reflechir . . ."

"Il faut reflechir?" I repeat after her. I put my head back to reflect. 'Reflechir,' 'reflechir,' 'reflechir,' what is that word? In doing so, I figure out that I'm doing exactly what the name means. I play back her words and translate for myself.

"You must reflect," she translates. "Think about what you want to say before you say it because everyone is listening to you. Everyone wants to know what you have to say.

"Finish what you start," she pushes on to explain the deeper meaning. "If you say you are going to do something, then do it. The projects and all that you say you will accomplish here. You have to do the projects that you say you are going to do and finish them," she goes on in French never ceasing to pound the plantains in her mortar. The confusion on my face disappears. I have gotten so used to people here not expecting anything of me that I have started to fulfill that perception.

"Céline, what if you found out Bogo is seeing another woman?" My turn to jerk serious on her.

"Je prends ça television!"

"You—are—crazy! You gonna' take his television?" I bend over in laughter.

"Huh!" she forcefully exclaims in disbelief that anyone could doubt her ability to react, heaving her chest out before stepping into the house. Take his television? That would hurt anyone anywhere.

She then steps out of Bogo's courtyard and into the path toward her house so I follow.

"Abidjan!!!!" yell three younger men coming from the other direction.

"Abidjan!!!!" Céline greets back and grins with her fantastic, big, white teeth. She is strongly beautiful and walks with confidence.

"Why are you saying Abidjan?"

"That is what they say every time they see me. They think I am too stylish to be in the village. They think I am not a villager but someone who comes from Abidjan."

Interesting. A class distinction in the village. A desire to be from somewhere else—that the city is better than Zragbi. I'm not yet entirely familiar with village life, but I'm not amorous of city life either.

I finally get the chance later in the day to ask Bogo if he is coming with me to the Peace Corps workshop in Abidjan and, of course, he isn't. Céline does all his duty.

11 Two Things

What was her name? That Mossi girl . . . She died. The baby never did come out. They just kept slapping her legs open and trying to get her to push. She never could catch her breathing right. Internal bleeding. They got up over her from behind her head to push down on her stomach and push the baby out the way they said they often did in a difficult delivery. The young girl couldn't take it.

"The baby has gone back in," La Sage told Céline, still standing over the girl's increasingly lifeless body. I was there for that part. The head had crowned momentarily but gone back inside. They rushed her to the hospital in Daloa City, as rushed as one can with Ivoirien transportation. Once there, she died.

The Muslim men singing as they carry her body up the road to Seraguhé comes through to me in my sleep this morning. I wake up to see ten Muslim men hoisting up the casket that holds her body. They carry it much higher than I have ever seen and it is not because of their uniformly tall heights.

"La li, la li, la . . ." they sing; a combination of Senoufo and Jula men all in long, dark robes. I hear something besides sound coming out of their voices—if it's possible to hear what's not sound. It is sadness and joy at once. It is beauty and pain in one. The singing lightly hypnotizes the Bèté children standing next to me as we stare together from my porch.

"La, la, laaaaa, li, li, liiiiii," the children imitate before catching themselves. How can any child fear death when it's treated like that?

"Pahdré. This is our mother," I am introduced. Mother? It seems like everyone is everyone's mother around here. Everyone calls every woman 'mama,' but this woman is too old to be any person my age or younger's mother.

"Oh, mama? On à amèné quelqu'un pour toi. Regarde. Regarde," they call out to their mother, persistent that she sees who they bring for her. "She is light like you," they lovingly tease.

La Vielle is crouched in a fetal position, so visibly worn out. She is not dark at all. She is lighter than me with wisps of hair that lightly curl into the air. Two sisters explain that this is their grandmother, everyone's grandmother, the live ancestor that makes all the people living in this courtyard and beyond related; over 120 years old. La Vielle is likely the reason the people in Zragbi are a little more red than brown.

She slowly peers over her shoulder back at me and quickly pulls her body back toward the wall into its crouch as if to say, 'go on now.' Seeing her deteriorated frame and weather-beaten skin when she peers back proves every single one of those 120-plus years they claim she is. She waits to die.

During the day of the funeral, according to the sex of the deceased, women or men gather together and sing. I have no idea what they sing, but it's a melodic jazz sound that harmonizes and it's a part of their mourning.

"Pahdré!" A woman calls me from the street in front of my

house. "Come sing with us," she flutters with delight. The group has five women in it and by the time we get to the market area, not too far away, it has twenty easily. Everyone knows the Bèté song we sing and I do mean 'we.' I mouth the sounds that I can catch as best I can.

"Ah! Pahdré!" They scream and laugh, falling into each other, loving my support. Dance-marching through Zragbi, we sing.

The night of quadruple-times-a-grandmother's funeral, Céline tells me, "We stay up for three nights. We don't sleep." I don't stay up for three days straight, but I'm up late every one of those nights. Women get together with their backs hunched over and undulating as if they are planting seeds to a song, bent over the entire time dancing around in a continuous circle. After wearing themselves out from dancing and a quick break, the instruments materialize. I receive a drum with a stick whose end shapes into the hook of a hanger. The tip of that hook is covered with rawhide and I use it to hit my drum nonstop. A multitude of regular drums and other instruments are brought out. The playing is freestyle. One young man sings while playing his instrument.

I lose track of time easily having also thrown my watch down the latrine hole with my mefloquine. How many people are up? That is how I know how late it is. Different mourners get up to dance again in a circle for the onlookers, normally relatives who have come from far away to attend the funeral. As with the Abé, great dancing is acknowledged with a full body tilt to say 'well done' or 'yeah, you tore it up dawg.' After each personal, freestyle, impromptu dance, people with money throw it at each dancer's feet and that money pays for funeral expenses and supports the bereaved.

"Aaaaaaaaah! Wuh! Hooooo!" A woman suddenly tears out of her house crying. She tumbles onto the ground, screaming in agony, falling right on top of an infant whose head pounds into the ground. The woman, delirious with sadness, is still unaware of what she has just done and another woman rushes over to pick up the weeping infant, whose hand holds her own head. The Bèté give themselves time to completely reflect on the life and death of the deceased and once these three days end, they move forward. The mourning energy is an energy that pervades everything and these three days are filled with more life than what might happen any other day. On the second night of La Vielle's funeral, the Chief shocks us all by picking up the microphone to speak. He never speaks. "La Vielle," which respectfully means 'Old Lady' in French "lived for a long time and married twice. Her first husband was a French man. They had children . . . I couldn't believe that this woman could be light-skinned and Bèté, done all she has done, been married twice, and live in Zragbi," his Bèté translated into French for me by a family member. Relatives circle roun' him standing at the mic, some smiling at him, some staring right into his mouth soaking up every bit as if he may never speak again.

"Now, when I see Pahdré, I guess it's possible." Well, I guess that's a compliment. Goodness. How did I get thrown into this?

The Chief is old himself, in his seventies at least. If he has trouble believing her stories at his age, then she has got to be 120-plus! It is odd to me too, however, with such little knowledge of how people interacted during her time and who was actually around. She was a light-skinned woman maybe even treated as White sometimes, her marrying a French man and all. Or, maybe she was just accepted by her husband for what she was. She spoke Bèté and lived with the Bèté. But, she was very light as well so who knows how far back the mixing goes—it was either the French who had to have pulled down their pants as soon as they stepped onto land or the White Americans before African-Americans were sent back here and migrated from Liberia. Liberian girrrrl!

I don't stay in Zragbi for the third funeral night but take a break at the Daloa Volunteer House. I get to the Daloa House and go into town. Should I walk or cab it? Feels like ninety degrees, but I know it's got to be hovering over one hundred degrees. This is some bullshit. Every time I step outside I start to sweat. Can I get a warm-up at least? And, this red earth just keeps sticking to my sandaled feet.

On my walk, I pass by a building with a ten-foot tall, black, iron fence enclosing its few acres, but the gate is wide open. I look but don't see anyone. A couple more paces go by. A gallop sound spikes up off in the distance. Those sound like . . . those sound like hooves. Naw, can't be. The gallop gets closer and closer. Dare I turn around? Oh! A horse?! It comes charging out the gate and rounds off down the street just two feet from me but not in my direction! Are they training horses back there? Are there other ones coming? I spin around again. Boy is that going to be a surprise to someone else walking down the street. I hope it doesn't get hit by a car. Shoot. I better pick up the pace and get this walk over with.

A shortcut path with high grass presents itself, giving me the moment of shade I need and a break from public view. No smell of piss, what I normally expect when walking through tall, grassy paths in the city. Wow, I get to the sidewalk and there isn't even as much as one car on the road. I don't have to make a dash for it. I cross. Perfect. Let me just step up onto the sidewalk here . . .

What—in—the—world . . . Just my eyeballs look down to make sure that I don't trip stepping up onto the sidewalk when down by my feet what do I see? Did you guess yet? Un serpente! I yell in my mind, but my heart maintains itself and more so as I pick up that it does not want to bite me. If it's coming from behind me . . . that means . . . it followed me all the way across the street! It must have been happy, too, saying, 'oh, how nice, no traffic' as we both happily mosey across the street, no cars barreling down on us.

Right where I step up on the sidewalk, I stay. It is a baby at two feet long. Less than an inch thick, it bristles and coruscates a bright, fluorescent green and moves very slowly. A green mamba— one bite and I will be dead in less than four hours. Bitten is what I should be now ten seconds later. Instead, Baby Green presses on, slithering by at two inches from my sandals, up into the foot-high grass that reaches back to a woodshop now in front of me.

Snake is my world. I do not see or hear anything else. It might as well slither on top of my feet as close as it is. Up into the grass it goes, no bite, not even a bump into. Oops, I'm sorry, Baby Green. I didn't see you there. Go right on ahead.

I am transfixed and stunned that a snake could leave me alone so close. This is the second time—the first time on the way to a funeral in Seraguhé with Céline and another friend—except we almost damn near had a conversation this time! I can't move. I wanna' watch it. It's so beautiful, so surreal, such a sublime moment in nature! Bristling green in the sunlight, it stands up and waves forward and back, poised in my direction. Baby Green blends right into the tall grass. I lose sight of it for a second, but it hasn't gone anywhere. It harmonizes with the grass blowing in the soft, warm wind. Maybe it thinks the grass is a bunch of other Baby Greens.

"Hsssssssssssss," I hear. At me? I thought we were tight? What's up? But, I still don't move.

"MAIS! IL Y A QUOI?!" jumps into my ears accompanied by the customary one hand clap that then opens up toward the person's face and ends with both hands facing skyward waiting for a reply.

'But, what iiiis your problem?!' The deep, dark brown older man with jet-black hair repeats this hand gesture again sitting in front of the woodshop he likely owns. The smack of his lips and an impatient sigh-huff officially pull me out of my trance. My head scans up the grassy, little hill toward the six-foot-tall man with legs stretched out in his wooden chair only a little farther from the snake than I am.

"IL-Y-A-QUOI!?" he slows down to repeat all four syllables. He must think I'm just staring at him like a 'fou,' another crazy. If I could only get out the words. I first point where I have been looking for all these mystifying seconds. Next, I squeeze my brain to recollect the word for 'snake' in French.

"Un serpente!"

This same older man that sits back relaxed as if he will not get up for food or water springs up. He looks hard. Looks back at the young men and boys working, pauses frightened, and then yells 'Go and get it!' in a mixture of languages.

Go and get it?! Who thinkin' 'bout 'go and get it?' One tall, thin kid with wood-sawing arms rushes out next to the man but turns back and calls a smaller kid standing closest to the door. The youngest picks up the closest weapon to him, a long piece of wood, and charges toward it with a taller young man in tow. I don't know if this is good or bad, but I sum up that all of this is bringing the snake right back to me. Back to me? Oh. Run!

I dash down the street, throwing my head back to see them smacking away at Baby Green. She leaps into the open sewer along the sidewalk and they keep smacking away, nasty black water shooting up all over the place, getting on the youngest's white shirt as he moves his head every time the water pops up. Did they get it? My chest heaves. I glance down where I finally stop running to find a peanut woman glaring up at me asking 'what in the hell is wrong with you?' in her eyes.

"Un serpente," I answer. She slowly rises to peek over at the spectacle, holding on to her loosening pagne. They slap away. She sits back down just as slowly as she stands and laughs.

"It's your brother." What? That's just what Céline says about my other snake encounter. Do I have a connection to snakes? My Chinese zodiac sign is a snake. Maybe I was a snake in another life or however all that human-as-animal analysis stuff goes. I don't need to understand the connection however as long as it keeps me alive.

I wake up to go to the bathroom in the middle of the night as usual. I walk out my door into the darkness, leaving my front kitchen room light on to guide my way. I do my business down the large, rectangular hole that is my outside toilet, return to the house, and head toward bed. When I re-enter, however, I notice an ant scurrying around on the floor, lost. In my slumber I put my sandals back on that I had just taken back off, and smoosh it. Back to sleep I go.

Again, I have no idea how much later, I wake up to go. But, this time, when I happen to survey the corner, the squashed ant is gone. Was I dreaming when I killed it? I check the bottom of my black sandals. Nothing there either. Where did it go? I noisily scratch the little bush of hair on my head, still sleepy but growing more and more awake as the enigma grows.

I stand there a good two minutes fearing I might be on some residual mefloquine trip despite having thrown it all away. Just before I lose motivation to stand there any longer, up the wall in the corner, I spot another ant crawling down.

Is this the same one? After it finishes defying gravity and reaches the same surface I stand on, I flatten it out and wait. Soon, a third ant defies gravity, charging down the wall at a steady pace. I wait. The third ant has the career of wanderer as well, wandering right upon the second ant I kill. It sniffs the second ant all around its body, slowly walks away a little, and then even more slowly walks back to the corpse to sniff again. Yes, it's dead. Once this third one finally confirms this, it goes crazy.

It circles the ant in one direction three times. It circles the ant in a counterclockwise direction two times. It paces nervously back and forth, visibly showing itself to be shaking! Its head wobbles, too, in an emotional frenzy. After a several-minute display of grief, it trudges over to the body, picks it up with its mouth, as close I can determine, and transports the body vertically along the wall out of sight.

Sensitivity to death pervades everyone and everything here. What is wrong with me that for experiment's sake I could kill two ants?

Cows are the same. Herders often travel by foot from the north with their cows and cross right through Zragbi. A few wear conical, straw hats—the kind that have the shape of a wide ice cream cone, just shielding their eyes and face from view and the sun. On one such occasion, upon descending the baidjan into Zragbi, I see these herders running around everywhere. All of the cows have broken the herd and the herders try to round them up.

"Ahhhhhh," one cow runs toward me wailing blindly. It isn't the mooooo I expect but a strangled sound that interrupts the air. The cows are screaming all over. I jump out of the way and if I had been the target, I certainly wouldn't have made it. The eyes of that cow are spooked and glassy.

"What is going on?" I ask the first person I see along the road.

"A cow has died," and with that the man points to the corpse a few yards from me. The cow is sickly and pale, struck by death itself to the ground with flies swarming it, red-veined eyes bulging, and foamed tongue hanging down and out to the side. This cow is pushin' up daisies. I'm getting away from this thing before I catch whatever it had.

"Aaaaagh! Oooioooogh!" more gurgled throat sounds wrestle their way out.

"They are crying," the man clears it up for me. "They grieve the dead cow. I don't know when the cows will settle down. It may be all night."

Same as the ants. Same as the people. Death impresses me as more immediate here, stirring up a release of deep passion for loss of life. I've never had anyone die in front of me or seen a dead body right after it has died, and I don't know anyone else who would show the great and sincere emotion of ants, cows, or Bèté people. All of that plus the roach discussion in Grand Noyaré and the Green Mamba incident in Daloa make me see that we all feel loss.

Death happens so often in Zragbi, however, that the response is not always consistent with how the Bèté tend to react. One evening in Grézuou with Céline, she and I came upon a house with all its lights on and tens of people standing and sitting around in the yard, in the path out in front of the house, on large rocks, or leaning up against the house's low wall that lines the path and not really saying much.

"There is a woman dying inside this house," Céline reports what someone reports to her. I've never been allowed to be around someone dying growing up. Should we call 911? Oh, no 911 here.

"What is happening?" I ask, suddenly on alert. So, Céline goes inside as she has the right, people living in nearby villages often being at least distant or marriage-related relatives. When Céline re-emerges, exasperation kidnaps her face.

"It's a woman. They say she was living in Abidjan when she got really ill. So, she went to the best hospital there and they told her that what she has, there is no cure. That there is nothing more she can do but go back to her village and die here."

"What? I don't understand that?" At this point, Céline has her own questions and turns away from me to start talking to others in Bèté. I sit down by some kids my age or younger. One young teenager comes up to our group and illustrates the scene.

"I went in there. She has all these dark marks all over her skin and she's all thin and skinny like this," at which point he drags his left and right hands up their opposing arms and legs to emphasize her skinniness. "She is like this," he tries to whisper with his body bent over toward those of us sitting down on the ground, but his voice carries a bit loudly. He pulls his cheeks together in a fish mouth imitation to show how the poor woman has withered down to nothing—literally skin and bones. "Her eyes are sunken deep in her face like this. They say it's A.I.D.S."

A.I.D.S.? Well then, Céline's report about the Abidjan hospital, which I also know to be top-of-the-line with advanced equipment and more, telling this woman that her illness has no cure, makes sense. This makes the only time that I will ever hear an Ivoirien attribute a death in the village to A.I.D.S. The description that the teenage boy before us gives of dark marks all over her body as a symptom also makes sense. She probably has the skin cancer form of full-blown A.I.D.S. The young teenager toggles between Bèté and French animated.

"She is in there sucking away, trying hard to take in every breath. They are just standing around her bed waiting for her to die," and then he makes a fish mouth again, himself sucking in air every two or three seconds through his protruded lips. We are all frozen watching his breathing imitation when he bawls out laughing. The other kids and I, sitting by or leaning up against the wall, look to each other for how to react to him. Céline turns around about to upbraid him when weariness forces her to simply stare. She relaxes her body and begins to laugh incredulously. She deals with death as her daily job. It must feel like some huge joke to see people dying all around you all of the time. When death gets a person to the point of comedy, you know Ivoiriens have seen it too much.

All of us are waiting for something to happen either way. The Bèté do not believe a person will die until she is actually dead. Still, impending death initiates a complex range of emotions tonight. If I had been told the same, that nothing can be done and that I just have to wait here with my loved one and watch them die, what would that do to me? A handful of people outside the house are depressed with fear, others stand with furrowed brows, and others laugh at the mystery of the scene that presents itself so extremely and incomprehensibly as to border on the ridiculousness. Obviously, no one has seen death go down quite like this before. What is this? This thing called A.I.D.S.—is it real? Where does it come from? Sorcery?

There are only two things: the living and the dead. Maybe to the Bèté, dying is just a function of living, and that there is no such thing as dying when you are alive. Dying is certainly not absolute. People can and do recover from critical illness. My greater question is, however, why didn't the hospital give her medicine to prevent her from developing into full-blown A.I.D.S., or maybe she went too late?

Up early the following morning, out for a run, and about to bucket-bathe myself when I see several all-day-and-night funeral visitors already up and searching for breakfast. People are arriving to Zragbi steadily this morning. Who died this time? I gotta' get my green, soja bean sandwich quickly. I don't want the word to spread that I'm up early running. Of course I cannot get too far before a sound, early-morning harassment.

His eyes are bloodshot and the alcohol floats to my nose from him ten feet away. Stankin' ass. He is only one of the few well-known drunkards in the village. He stares at me in line, having just finished my run and rushing to get my beloved soja sandwich for eight one-hundreths of an American cent. He stares at me so long that I have to stare back and when I do, he barks.

"Pahdré! Why are you here? White woman! Go back to France!"

"I'm not from France. I'm from America." Oh whyyyy did I reply?

"Why are you here?"

I start to say I'm a volunteer here to do community projects, but I stop myself. I haven't done anything yet except an impromptu malaria session with one woman out in the fields. When I ask her where she thinks malaria comes from she says, 'It's when you stay out under the sun too long and it wears you down.' In that moment, with sweat beads pouring out my every known orifice and no shade that could make a difference, I didn't see how my mosquito explanation could compete with the sun. I mean, it is pretty expletively hot out here and the symptoms are similar to heat stroke. So, I opt not to say anything that time. A planned approach is needed.

"Go home," he threatens. Ugh, is it the skin again? The French musta' really done Ivoiriens wrong over here. We don't even yell at White folks like this in the States. He pushes me.

"Pahdré, go back in your house. We don't walk around in our underwear outside here!"

"I'm not in my underwear. These are . . . are . . . are . . ." a stutter forms and I cannot finish the sentence. What is the word for 'shorts' in French?!

But, then I remember. What am I doing coming out here like this? A lot of women wear shorts underneath their pagnes, but I didn't think they had nothing under that. I never do see women walking in shorts only, however. Ooooh.

He paces back and forth around me, lightly pushing me from time to time and I take it. I don't know why. Maybe I have a Superwoman complex. Maybe I feel I'm invincible because I've never been attacked. Maybe I know that if anything goes down I've got the fastest legs in Zragbi. Each time I receive an aggressive nudge, I fall right back into the spot I hold in line.

"Pahdré, go put some clothes on!"

I've never even spoken to him before. I don't know his name, have never shaken his hand, and was never introduced to him. But somehow, beyond 'La Blanche,' he knows my name is Pahdré.

"Pahdré!" he yells. I try to check him out periodically when he isn't glaring at me. He does more pacing than anything else. I eye the Soja Lady and she eyes me back, hoping our looks to each other all stand for 'yeh girl, I gotchyu.' There is a circle of paralysis around him that no one dares enter. Bodies are stiff and eerily the only talking is soja transaction related. No men are around, only women and children. People are buying it up and there is no actual line, just a bunch of people closed in around her on her miniature stool and foot-high table with her pagne pulled up between her legs.

Everyone knows who got here and when, but every time I go to buy, drunkard jams me up with his nonsense. She slides her soja bean blend of vegetables and spices into soft pillows of bread and I am so hungry. I just ran six miles for goodness sake. Every time he distracts me someone goes ahead.

How angry is he getting? I look back to check again and the meanest eyes are right there to greet me. Does he really expect me to leave just because he says so? His teeth are mangled to the point where he can never completely close his mouth. He is drunk and this isn't worth it, but by the time I come to that conclusion and look back for the umpteenth time to check the soja bowl, all of it is gone. Soja Lady just stares at me as she wraps up her things.

I walk away and when I get inside the house, I lock the screen door, push the heavier door slightly closed, turn around, open my mouth, and pause the way a child does right before a cry, falling face first to the ground.

"Puh, hoo, hoo, haaaaa," I softly wail then sob, stifling myself in the most pitiful, choked-up manner. My forearms spring forward instinctively at the last second just breaking my fall. My lips then moosh into the floor. My nose, too. Tears pour out from my face. I feel completely ashamed for—I have no idea what. The sadness wells up throughout my body. I am stuck here in this time and culture warp, unable to identify myself how I'm used to, in the way I want to, and no one with which I share this same, now mental, problem. Yes, mental.

Not many days pass before drunkard wants another confrontation.

"Pahdré! Leave here!" he barks. I must not be seeing the color history or acknowledging him in a logical, sensitive way, but how am I to get around an immediate frontal attack? So, I attack back. The only reality I see in front of me are his sharp and mangled yellow teeth he surely ruins from drinking, his bloodshot eyes, and the way he speaks to me.

"Tu es villain," I say calmly.

"I am ugly?" he questions in surprise, not believing I would call him what people have likely called him at one point or another and what likely causes him to drink in the first place. His whole attitude is unattractive and that is all I can see.

"Yes," I confirm.

"I am ugly?" he is hurt but suddenly calm with anger looking straight at me.

"Yes."

"Je vais te boter," he says. Hmm, 'boter?' I don't know that word, but I'm sure he means 'I'm going to knock you into next week' as I see he's now charging toward me. I calmly ignore him, turning to close the windows since it is getting dark. I reach behind the wooden enclosure for the big slab of wood that keeps it open and out. I'm ready to leave its permanent print on drunkard's forehead if I see his hands come near me.

Didier flies into the few feet of space between drunkard and me to hold him back just as I stand firmly with my hands gripped around the long slab, hiding underneath the window, waiting. I know that Didier and Désiré are nearby listening as I am going around from window to window throughout our useless exchange. I didn't expect an intervention as no one intervenes during the soja debacle, but then again, no men were around at that time. Either way, after Bogo's boobie touch, the Baby Green slaughter, and the shoves just the other day, I am now resourceful.

"No. No. It's not good. Leave her alone," Didier pleads as he struggles to pin drunkard back. Hmph, he really is going to hit me.

I leave that night back to Daloa yet again, the most recent funeral still going on, as I think will be the thing to do during any funeral from here on out. However, I'm not leaving until I tell Céline everything. I try to leave right after speaking with her but not before Céline then speaks with Le Chef, her own house being in the courtyard right next to his.

Céline sits down. An older man who must be the Chef's brother sits down too. I sit down and then Le Chef exits his house.

"A na na . . ." Céline fires up slowly in Bèté. 'A na na' means 'he said' or 'she said' and is used at the beginning of just about any story. But, that's all I can catch. The Chief parts with small grunts at the end of every pause in Céline's tale.

Five minutes pass and I'm sure Céline must be adding in colorful details that I don't even know. Gee, the story is not that long. What is she saying? But, I know not to interrupt. I understand nothing until the Chief's brother speaks up at the end of moments of silence, which punctuate the end of Céline's description.

"If it was an animal acting like that," the brother says in French staring off in the distance in front of him, "we would kill it." My eyes burst in spite of my attempt to show no reaction. The Chief says the equivalent of 'okay' and then everyone gets up and leaves in different directions. So? Now what?

"I told him the story," Céline says, still with stern wrinkles pressing into her face. I was going to leave into Daloa, but I decide against it. I don't know all what was said, and I hope they don't really kill Drunkard.

12 MORE THAN A.I.D.S.?

On a visit in downtown Abidjan today. Riding in taxis can be peaceful. You have the comfort of another soul in the vehicle with you and no words required. It's a service, but to me it has divinity in it, as long as there is no accident of course. Sandra and I are on our way to—the—market. The Abidjan main market in Cocody has everything including clothes, food, jewelry, and I can also get my hair 'did.' I won't get my hair done today however. I have more spending power than I've ever had in my life, even on my volunteer stipend.

I love this market—not particularly for all of the interesting Ivoirien and other African countries' cultural items possible to obtain for near nothing, which I ought to be ashamed of but a love of the people who run it. All currencies should be equal. There is so much here. It's an open-air market with few merchant spots defined or separated by walls and the major part of the market has a roof that lets in most of its light by the entrances through which people pour.

The people in the market are real to me. They don't sit posted at their spots. They mingle with the other merchants, amicably examine the quality of their competitors' goods, laugh, smile, sell their wares, and sometimes step in to sell the wares of their merchant neighbors if a neighbor has run off to grab lunch, make prayer, or fulfill a sudden errand. I walk around and soak up the energy here more than anything else.

"See you in a few," and Sandra goes off to explore on another market floor.

"That, how much is that?" I point and stare for a while at the object of my desire. This is a science, an art. You can't be in a hurry because that's offensive. It means you just want to throw your paper down, grab what they have that means so much more to you than the person selling it, and run off somewhere very possibly without even having looked them in the eye. I never touch it although I stand right next to it. It is a beautiful, round, hand-carved game board that has marbles fitted snuggly into thirty-six carved-out, round grooves. All of the balls are a bright, granite green. Do I want to actually play or buy just for display?

"15 mille," he says after a quick look at the game piece and looks away. That number 15,000 again. This is a sure sign it's cheaper than he quotes. The burgundy chocolate, Ivoirien, Muslim merchant says no more than that, no more conversation, and no eye contact. He is trying to keep me from seeing the truth behind his eyes, but I have grown to love this part.

"Five thousand francs?" I play.

"No, 15,000 francs," he spells it out making sure to enunciate each and every vowel he can create, existent or non, in each of his words.

"Ummm," I make a face and shake my head slowly to show that I want it but am not about to pay this amount. I spin on my right toe to walk away.

"Non, merci," I remember to add a polite 'no, thank you' as I leave.

"Wait. I can do 13,000 francs." I keep walking, another step and another. At the third step he says, "Wait. Well, I can go to 11,000 francs."

"I don't have the money." Then, I seal it with a smile spinning on my right toe again. I never carry a purse, fanny pack, or any of that. I want to look the part when necessary. Our stipend is a little less than a lot. Just enough. He smiles back.

"How much do you want to pay?" Inside, I smile at this, but outside I frown and act as if I'm about to ask for something disagreeable.

"Five thousand," I ask. He doesn't flinch.

"No, you can't get that for five thousand anywhere." That's an interesting response. Sounds like he almost doesn't know what it's worth or maybe simply a good marketing trick. I sit down. I am fatigued, but I decidedly like him. He is a nice older man. He wears a white boo boo and black leather sandals with a button also wrapped in leather that sits in between his big toe and the next. Then come his flat, cylindrical, Muslim hat and his honest hands that he gesticulates with as he smiles.

He doesn't grip on to anything in tension or put his hands behind his back. Does he really need this sale? We talk instead about the weather, about what food I plan on eating when I get home today. I speak some Jula to him and he loves this the most. I tell him I'm American and leave it at that. No James Bond this time. He volleys everything I say, either with a laugh or a funny comment back.

I sit here for over an hour enjoying myself and forgetting Sandra, as I'm sure she has forgotten me. I watch customers go by and come in where I am, then walk away uninterested to the next stall. He never presses me to buy anything. I feel welcome, comfortable, at home, relaxed, and happy. Great to be able to talk and laugh with someone or be in their space without them wondering why or finding a way to rush you out or get something from you—no, none of that. If this is all part of the merchant game, it can't be too lucrative. I smell friendship.

I've all but forgotten about the light, granite, green marbles and get up to leave. There is nothing that I really, really have to have right in this moment except air. It's hot. I spin on my right toe into the aisle when Sandra comes flopping down the stairs—perfect timing is not needing to watch the time.

"Wait," I hear the familiar voice and word once more, except this time it is warmer and more heartfelt. "Take it for 2,000 francs." If he only knew how much 2,000 francs is to me. He probably knows, but in the last hour I must have made up for the other 13,000. I don't even want the game. I get what I need, even if we do not understand each other all of the time. Hah! I am so honored to get a bargain from him and you know it is an honor when you watch other tourists bargain until their hearts fall out, only to end up paying exactly what they do not want to pay while you end up paying very little.

"Tiens cadeau," he adds. I get a gift, too? A little extra something that is in his shop. It is a thank you for the time, not for the business. Money does not get us the things that we want or need, people do.

Back in the taxi, we completely relax again. Sandra and I zone out our respective windows. Particular things occupy someone else's mind, not ours. We wind through the city to the highway for the Abidjan Volunteer House. Out the window ahead is a man walking on the divider in the middle of the highway. He performs the balancing act for free. He can place both feet together side by side on the divider without either foot going over the side, but this is still a divider and this is still the highway.

No shoes protect his feet. His pants are shredded from waist to bottom. Holes have taken over his pants. He has no doubt been wearing these clothes every day for the last year at least. His short-sleeved shirt is decorated with black stains. Dirt cakes him. His hair is cut relatively short so this couldn't have been going on for too long. His hands are out to the side and as he walks he gingerly places one foot in front of the other. His shoulders swivel and his legs sway, too. His hands splay out and down, imaginary bags on each wrist.

'Homosexuality is something that the Europeans created,' is the opinion Céline offers as the one many Ivoiriens, formally educated or not, seem to share. I have never met a homosexual or homeless person in Cote d'Ivoire before. Here, where homelessness doesn't exist. Where if you find yourself out of the village and alone in the city, it means you either ran away or were kicked out.

Here, if no one speaks to you or asks you for anything, if no one even takes the time to size you up or insult you for good measure, if you find yourself out in the city alone and you can't help but talk to yourself, as he is, because no one has talked to him in longer than he can remember, it is because you do not exist in the minds of others.

Speaking up to nudge Sandra out of her dream becomes impossible. Tears squeeze out after being stuck under my bottom eyelashes for several seconds. I imagine myself inside his body and allow him to show me how it feels—to be in pain, confusion, and hopelessness everyday from being an outcast.

Saying that homosexuality is not an Ivoirien thing may not necessarily be a form of resistance to homosexuals but rather the result of never having seen it that way before. Not every culture has labels for sexual acts. For many, sex is just sex and does not always reflect who can love whom. The book HIV & AIDS in Africa: Beyond Epidemiology (edited by Ezekiel Kalipeni, Susan Craddock, Joseph R. Oppong, and Jayati Ghosh) notes that behavior can be separated from sexual identity in the minds of many, and therefore A.I.D.S. tendencies for the sake of statistics are hard to pinpoint in places that don't see sexuality as a form of identity. The book explains that for many people sex is simply an act and that " . . . humanity is not inevitably and definitively framed by the homo/heterosexual binary, but that the reality may be more fluid, with people transgressing that neat binary in a variety of ways."

Therefore, my ways of seeing sexuality which I as an American may unknowingly impose on the people of Zragbi during my A.I.D.S. awareness outreach may actually be damaging in that I place stigmas on acts that did not originally have those stigmas. Connecting homosexuality to a high incidence of A.I.D.S. cases solely based on statistical evidence from the States, without knowing all the ways that people "get down to James Brown" in Cote d'Ivoire, is highly inappropriate.

When Céline makes this statement she just so happens to be

completely naked in my house and oiling up her skin in front of me on my bedroom floor. I don't have much furniture. One minute she is clothed and the next butt naked. There is not much more I can say about this scene because I do not respond to her sudden nakedness verbally or physically—I just say 'oh,' let her oil her skin, and get dressed—too shocked for words.

Maybe she hopes something happens, so her statement is merely a defense mechanism in case I reject her. Who knows? I do doubt, however, that there was ever a time when Ivoiriens were unaware of homosexual acts, whether they had a label for them or not. And, I doubt this man balancing so carelessly on the divider wants to be out here alone like this. Maybe he hopes he will fall off. It's a very strange thing to see a homeless person in Cote d'Ivoire. How he is, must be who he is. I'm sure he would change if he could. Why would anyone be something that gets them ostracized unless they couldn't change it?

"Maurice is looking for you."

"Me? Why?"

"I don't know. He just says that he wants to talk to you," Céline recalls as she gathers up clothes on the porch next to the water basin to wash.

"Jijina! Take this money and get me some soap." The change is a little more than Jijina needs for soap so Jijina pauses at the money now in her outstretched hand and looks back at Céline. "Get something for yourself, too," Céline adds with a blank face disguising her generosity.

"Thank you, Tantie!" Jijina and Eliane call her 'Tantie' in French for Auntie, but Céline is more of a mother to the two. Their real mother is not around.

Maurice is the bigwig in Grézouou who owns the two big mansions. Hmm, maybe he has some projects he wants to work with me on! I put on my new Teva sandals I find in the Peace Corps Office on my last trip to Abidjan, sent from my real mother. Thanks, mom. I walk over to Grézuou alone. My pagne stays wrapped tightly around me. I switch into a longer-sleeved shirt and don a shawl around my head to protect me from the red dust sure to swirl up from walking or any passing bicycles or baidjans along the road.

"Mamaren?" A group of teenagers ask in Bètè. Where am I going? Everyone in Zragbi always asks me this. Maybe because they think I, the American come from so far away, might really be going someplace!

"I'm going to Grézuou."

"Aaaah," they let out and nod their heads all over the place. You'd think I gave them a piece of information that would help them cross a river in a boat without a paddle.

I love the weather here. Hot! I don't know how this came to be. It takes me much longer to break a sweat now. My skin has built layer upon layer of suntan. Even the sand always mixed between my toes feels good. To be able to wear sandals every single day throughout the year! My toes are free and breathing. My eyes eat color, fed with real green grass, the tall trees with misty gray bark shooting up high into little green afro puffs, and the red ant hills piling up high trying to compete with the trees. Small random bodies of water and miniature ponds meet me along the road's edge to Grézuou.

A twenty-foot-wide, small clearing on one side of the road opens up, and I stop to catch a glimpse of some strange movement in sight. In the clearing a little ways away from where another ant dune stands is a hole big enough to see from the road. Movement comes from the hole. Let me get closer. Oooooo. Out streams black on top of sharply black ant, beautifully contrasting the red earth beneath them. They don't climb out one by one but in tens all packed together, moving out so quickly that some are invariably pulled up onto the backs of others for not moving fast enough.

"Mamaren?" 'Where are you going?' I get to ask the ants this time. Are you army ants? The line determinedly streams up and out perfectly to a destination twenty feet away on the other side of the clearing and down into an opposite hole. No breaks in speed and the thickness of the line remains the same for all the minutes I stand here. They move as fast as my eye across a page, endlessly down into the opposite hole. This has got to stop at some point. Tens of ants coming out of a hole every second!? There are hundreds out in the open at any given moment and I've surely seen thousands in the last five minutes and what about before I get here? I want to stay and watch them, possibly try to break up the line to test their persistence but no more ant play. I can't imagine how these ants will act all together if I do something crazy like that.

Why don't humans work together this way? Is it because we are too big and our food needs are too great for us to do so? Maybe because we would curse someone out and get into a fight for moving too slow or too fast? Too competitive? Too different? Too many competing objectives?

All these ants look exactly the same except for a few bigheaded ones. Still, they get along. Perhaps humans used to be as uniform as these ants and then someone said, 'Hey, get off my back! Carry your own weight!' So we separated and started looking differently because we were in different environments and living different lives. Is it human nature to eventually not get along? I am a single ant moving in a less clear direction, but am I searching for my pack or for who I am?

The eight-foot, black, steel fence is open. I enter the gate in full view of the two mansions to the left and right, facing each other from the rear on two ends of a large courtyard. Behind the mansion to the left is a 500-foot water tower off in the distance but still within their compound. The grounds are sporadically tended after. The water tower shows rust but is no doubt working since there is a water pipe coming up from the side of one house, dripping water into the basin beneath it.

Inside the fence contrasts the outside. A broken-down well stands directly across from the black gate in a neighboring yard. It is not even as good as the well Céline and I use on the way to the fields, but a vast, concrete courtyard stretches around every part of the two mansions. A tree is alone in the middle of the court surrounded by neatly laid brick. Oblong, green leaves flow down from a tree in a purposefully abstract fashion. Maurice wants to speak with me? Well, here I am.

"Helloooo! Oops . . ." Wrong language. " . . . Bonjour! Bonjour! Maurice!"

No one is here. What am I thinking by coming at this time in the morning and most of the early afternoon people are out in the fields?

"Tu es qui?!" booms a loud voice behind me at the gate. This young woman is no doubt younger or at most the same age as I am but reigns down on me tens of feet away as if she owns the entire courtyard including me now in it. She wears an old, barely sparkling, fitted shirt underneath another shirt that flatly sits on her tiny breasts. Her pagne hangs poorly around her waist, a corner almost dragging on the ground as if she just threw it on to rush over here. She has a bed-head, sewn-in weave, and when she speaks she has an Abidjan French accent instead of a Bèté one lingering underneath her French. Her brown skin glows in the sunlight although her face frowns.

"You are who?" she asserts again as I stay quiet while examining her. I have to assert back. I know from my short time here not to show any signs of weakness when not among friends.

"You, you are who?" I demand in a normal, less-stressed-out-than-she-is tone.

"Je suis la mère de la fille de Maurice!" She raises her voice as she rolls her eyes to tell me that she is the mother of the daughter of Maurice. Ooooh! I done walked into some baby's momma drama. Yeh, this probably doesn't look right, but it's not like I can call up and say I'm coming or that Céline warns me. No one calls ahead anywhere here. They simply make plans to be someplace and show up as soon as they can. I can't make plans to see him unless I see him first! I'm gonna' have to switch this around and quick.

"Nice to meet you!" I smile. "I am an American living in Zragbi." Throw out the status lest she beat me down. I should say 'the American.' I'm the only one out here. Her eyes close momentarily as she relaxes back into a smile. "Maurice said that he wants to talk to me so I walked here. Is Maurice in?"

"He is on the field. They are playing football today." Football?
Baby's Momma and I pass through the Grézuou schoolyard with
shorter buildings than ours and a worn-down well in the center.
When we reach the field, 'football' evidently means soccer. Somehow, us Americans got confused about what football is and started
tossing the ball in the air. We should call ours airball, not football.
Soccer is the true 'foot'ball.

"They are practicing for their next game against Zragbi," says
Baby's Momma.

"Zragbi has a place to practice, too?" Baby's Momma eyes me
sideways. How could I miss I bunch of grown men playing soccer in
Zragbi?

"Oui . . . Ah! There Maurice is," she replies 'yes' and her expression quickly changes on spotting Maurice.

"Maurice!" An older gentleman looks up. That's her man? He
has a good twenty years on her at least. He is a little scrawny for a
Bèté.

"I'm making a call," he says, as he disappears behind side spectators. He has a phone?! Can I make a call to New Jersey, please?

Just then, the game heats up and one player is the center of attention. He barrels down the middle, weaving around opponents,
feeding the ball away from himself to others and getting it right
back every time until he gets stuck near the sidelines where I am
with all the spectators. Three people are on him. Compared to his
opponents, he has a calm look on his face, barely needing to move
his upper body to manage his maze of footwork.

Suddenly, he pulls his right leg back and kicks the ball off to the
side. My side! The ball rises higher and, too astonished from the
surprise kick, I don't dodge the ball coming straight toward me.
The people in front of me are either shorter kids or squatters so
they don't have to duck, although all of them do.

Woosh! The ball goes right by my left ear. I watch it whiz by
me the same way I watched Baby Green slither by my feet—in awe.
Once I snap out of it I shoot a glance back at the player. He smiles
at me.

Baby's Momma leans over and chuckles, "He did it on purpose. He likes you."

He smiles some more and looks down muttering to himself in disbelief that he made such a mistake. Still I detect a smile. He is tall and seamlessly dark. He stares right at me and offers a smile so handsome that I feel a shock of energy lift me up from the inside. He looks down then up again as I haven't yet smiled back and politely yells, "Excusez-moi, excusez-moi!" scanning the entire crowd, pretending to be worried that he might have hit them, too. The game is soon over after a few more up and down the fields. A bunch of us—including Baby's Momma, Maurice, and some soccer players—walk back to the mansions.

"What is your real name? Céline tells me everyone calls you Pahdré."

"Raven . . . and La Blanche," I quip.

"They call me that, too. It doesn't mean anything." I look at Maurice at this. He is a cross between Ghandi and W.E.B. Dubois. He is lighter than the Bèté but darker than me.

"Thank you for coming. I used to live in America for several years as a student . . ." he goes on before it hits me. Maurice is speaking to me in English! He has a flat, American sound, but his Abidjan French accent lingers at the end of every word.

"Oh! What did you study? Where did you go to school?" The English flows forth. I haven't spoken to anyone in English in more than a month. Whenever it has been a while, once it comes out it can't be stopped. I certainly speak less of any language while in Cote d'Ivoire, English or otherwise, than when I'm at home in America.

"Boston University. I studied engineering." What is he doing here? He is the only person in Grézuou or likely for miles who has been out of the country and off the continent. He reads my mind but maybe just my facial expression.

"I choose to live in the village in peace. I am Ivoirien. I am Bèté, 100 percent"—he says the last bit with the same urgency that I do when I tell Ivoiriens I'm Black. But, of course, the fact that he has to state that in this all-Bèté setting throws a red flag. I don't ever hear him speak to anyone in Bèté. In spite of my doubts, however, I accept it. Otherwise, I'd be forcing my view on him the way others force their view on me. I mean, what am I gonna' do, think of everything I've ever known and try to fit him into that? Or, am I going to allow him to create his own identity in spite of whatever someone elsewhere chose to do with theirs? Identity is the one thing that is yours to do with as you wish. If a tomato can be a fruit then anything is possible.

"Why are you here?" he continues. "You are a Peace Corps Volunteer?"

"Yes, a Health Volunteer for A.I.D.S. and . . ."

"A.I.D.S.?" he scoffs. "Malaria kills more people here than A.I.D.S." Yes, that does make more sense, seeing as mosquitoes are everywhere here and bite daily.

A young man goes inside to bring chairs at Maurice's direction. Five chairs are set up in the courtyard while another man enters the gate carrying a lamb.

Maurice's neighbors live in houses with roofs that leak in the sunlight and the rain without screens or windows to protect themselves from the malaria-infested mosquitoes at night. He has running water, but his neighbors have barely potable, run-down wells. His house is built by a professional architect. The gates rest wide open, but Maurice lives in a bubble.

"I'm ready," Maurice springs up and disappears. I am left with the boy who brings chairs, none of which he sits on. A few soccer players who are spent from playing but interested in whatever spectacle is to occur with me here, sit together talking around the courtyard still in their blue and white uniforms and spikes.

I look up to the mansion in front of us and see Baby's Momma breast-feeding her infant in the window, talking with a girlfriend and having a good laugh. It's getting dark. I've gotta' get back and close my windows. Time passes when you walk everywhere.

Baby's Momma told me his name. Maxime is showered and wears khakis with a blue-and-white-striped Tommy Hilfiger shirt. Clean and new. His clothes are not worn down hand-me-downs from the Salvation Army but clothes he bought in a store somewhere. He sits right next to me.

"Ça va?" he asks me, and I respond in the affirmative with a smile. Yes, I feel fine now. Thank you for asking. Darkness? What darkness? I can stay up all night just at the smell of his cologne.

Maurice returns after a short while with a bunch of plastic plates. Baby's Momma follows him with more plates, baby nowhere to be seen. About eight of us eat—some sitting, some standing, some crouch around the plate in front of a person sitting in a chair. Maurice hands me my plate with a smile on his face and no more.

No rice. No sauce. Just a bunch of dark, very visibly seasoned meat. This is a lot of meat to eat all at once, especially now that I'm used to eating only bits and pieces of meat carefully parceled so that everyone eating has just enough.

"What is it?" I ask.

"It's lamb. It's good," Maxime assures in French. I haven't eaten lamb in a while, years in fact. If I had fond memories of it, I would have eaten it more often.

"Il faut manger," Maxime prompts without having touched his yet. Eat, I do. I have no napkin or fork. I pick a piece off the two thick slabs of meat on my plate and it starts to fall off the bone. Everyone is quiet watching me draw the piece nearer to my mouth.

My body lights up. An explosion of flavors perfectly combined. It's magic. I hear satisfied grunts at my expressions and everyone else dives into their plates. The more I chew, the more I love it. It is the best piece of meat I have ever eaten in my life, and I now understand why nothing comes with it. Poor lamb. I finish it, want more, and without asking another whole slab appears. No European seafarer in the Atlantic slave trade knows about these spices. C'est doux, dey. It's good.

"I made that," Maurice says smiling away, up, and off in the distance with sheer pride. I want to come to Grézuou everyday to eat this lamb. I can live off of this lamb. Maxime simply smiles at me. He has less meat than I do. Everyone does, in fact. I am the honored guest. To get even a morsel is a big deal. To have a full plate of it is opulent.

Out of the corner of my eye I see the young boy who brought

the chairs. Having learned to share at any moment possible in this country, I offer him the third slab I cannot finish. Fearing rejection, I hold the plate out to him without saying a word. He jumps at the chance, bows his head quickly, and says a merci. He doesn't eat right away. He looks around with his head barely raised as if waiting for permission. No one says anything so he sits down and slowly begins to eat. Soon, two more little visitors sit down next to him and they all split it between them—legs in a happy jitter, smiles on their faces, and eyes darting for fear it will be snatched away at any minute.

"Maurice? Do you have a phone?"

"No." I guess I hadn't understood on the field earlier.

"Oh. How do you communicate with your family then? Is your family here in the village?" He seems alone here except for Baby's Momma.

"These are my father's houses. I watch them for him because he knows I prefer to be here in the village." So, there are more houses then? "He travels a lot. He has been all over the world." Maurice has no siblings. I discover that Maurice is Maxime's nephew although Maurice is much older. Maurice freely shares a lot of information. He is, by virtue of his father, a Grand Type and so I guess Maxime is, too.

Maurice does mass farming with a team of villagers over more land than the land he owns at his house. He has a truck to haul crops and other loads back and forth but for the most part does little work with his hands except cook lamb.

"Let me introduce you to Alexi," Maurice says as the man who tried to force a bottle of soda down my throat appears.

"Bonsoir," Alexi greets, now nervously. I watch him. We all move to the second mansion, which has more lighting outside of it. Alexi and Maurice then go inside the house and come back out with a full karaoke system. Alexi flips on the mic and Michael Jackson starts blasting through the speakers posted beside me.

'Beat it! Beat it!' Michael wails, and more people gather in the courtyard. Michael Jackson, again? As I take it in, I don't know whether to scream in laughter, stand there with my mouth wide open, or fall out on the ground. So, I do all three. Here we all are. All ages. All different levels of education. All different world experiences. All different work ethics and necessities to work. All different skin colors. All different heights and shapes. Some speak in Bètè because they haven't gone to school long enough to pick up French. Some only speak in French because they grew up in the city. Everyone takes a turn at the mic and everyone knows most of the words to every single song that comes out of the speakers. Here. In Cote d'Ivoire. In West Africa. Next to a huge functioning water tower to my right and a broken down well to my left.

I can only sit and stare. Maxime stares too—at me. It isn't menacing or creepy. With the music blasting and everyone distracted, singing and dancing moves they've seen Michael do, Maxime finally engages me.

"You from America?" he speaks French with a Frenchy French accent.

"Oui. Je suis americaine noire." 'Black American,' I make sure to clarify as per usual. His French is impeccable or it must be because my strain meter is on high.

"Oui," he responds. "American Black," he adds in English but then returns to French. "I know. We learn about you in school."

I'm in a textbook? You certainly aren't in ours. The only time we learn about Africa in my high school days is in reference to slavery. We can only look down at our skin to remember ourselves. Africa exists for American Blacks about as much as American Blacks exist for Africans. Our knowledge is restricted to one or two eras in history. That's it.

"I live in Abidjan," Maxime goes on without the presence of a question. "But, Zragbi is my village. Do you live there?" He already knows that. He doesn't have to ask, but then I guess he is only trying to make conversation as I can do very little on my end with his accent firing at me.

"Are you Bètè?" I make a small effort also already knowing the answer.

"Yes, but I don't speak much Bètè." I figure that. Every time someone asks him something in Bètè, he responds in French. An

Ivoirien whose main language is French. That's like me. A Black American whose main language is English. I wonder if he thinks that irony is as strange as I do. Well, even more strange for him since he is in his country of origin and still can't speak an Ivoirien language. That lamb alone would have had me speaking Bèté by now. I don't know what his problem is.

"What do you do?" He pauses a bit long at my question. Red flag.

"I'm a student in Abidjan, but I'm taking a break now. I'm going to finish my terminal exam next year." The same baccalaureate that Céline never got because she got pregnant. Long before Bogo.

"What do you do?" Maxime returns.

"I am a volunteer for the Peace Corps in Zragbi. I am here to do community projects." But, ugh, I haven't done anything yet. Hope that isn't the next question.

"Aaah, Le Peace Corps!" interjects Maurice fondly out of the blue as if I hadn't just mentioned Peace Corps to him earlier. Addressing Maxime, Maurice explains in French.

"Peace Corps is an organization that brings Americans to different countries for a few years to help the villagers. In Cote d'Ivoire, I believe you guys do something like teach us about malaria and A.I.D.S. and do a little waste management and water purification training. Make potable water and do little business projects," he addresses the last couple of sentences to me, but I blink a surprise that I am now being spoken to. He seeks confirmation but loses me in French after malaria and A.I.D.S. So, he translates to me in English what he says.

"Oh, yes. That's true," I finally confirm.

"She has at least one degree," Maurice adds in French in a lower voice without looking at anyone in particular.

"Do you want to see the house?" Maurice returns to an audible voice.

"Yes, please," I smile. I am curious. Maurice springs up and Maxime follows. We go inside the mansion closest to us. There is a stately dining room with fine glassware behind the glass doors of tall furniture pieces. There are mirrors with wood majestically carved for frames. We go upstairs to Maurice's room which has an humungous king-sized bed and another room which has all of his toys—Play Stations, Nintendo cartridges, lots of other games, a big-screen TV that is not so shabby, and plush couches to sit on while he plays for the hours I can imagine he does. All of this? Here? In the middle of nowhere? While everyone around his compound is disparately at great economic disadvantage?

I can't be so surprised. After all, the White House has, less than a half mile behind it, one of the poorest, A.I.D.S.-stricken neighborhoods in the entire United States of America—the Southeast of Washington, D.C. The 19th century writer Henry George explains these kinds of ironies the best with his opinion that progress, necessarily, goes hand in hand with poverty—someone somehow somewhere suffering as a result of someone else's quest for infinite, isolated wealth.

We then head to the second mansion because the other fifteen rooms are off limits. The phone rings as we exit back out the rear.

"I thought you said you didn't have a telephone?"

"I lied . . . Hello . . ." he smirks without looking at me and continues on with his conversation with his rich, in the middle of the woods, delicious lamb-slammin' punk ass. Why does Maurice call me here? In his telephone conversation this time, I have not one inkling, can catch not one word of what he says in French. Now that, that's French from France—not that the French spoken here is inferior. It is just different. It is the same as how American English is no Queen's English. British English, too, is a different version of some older language. So, who cares? Languages change, merge, evolve, and/or die. As long as you get your point across, you're good.

Maxime and I stand there waiting. We are forgotten and after a few minutes Maurice turns to Maxime and directs him to show me the other mansion with a wave of his hand and nod of his head in that direction. It is the same mansion where Baby's Momma stays up on the second floor. Hmph. So, Baby's Momma is not only in a different room but a different house. No wonder she gets huffy when she first sees me.

I have maybe another hour before the sky turns to a complete blackout. There is no way I'm gonna' walk back to Zragbi after that. Céline might be worried.

"I want to see the house, but I have to go," I say pointing to the sky still lacking confidence that my French words are enough.

"I will show you very quickly then we will go," Maxime says without hesitation.

"With me?" Just want to make sure I have my pronouns right. He smiles a yes. Smile on, you triple-chocolate layer cake. Damn, you fine. Should I be having these thoughts? I'm a volunteer and only here a little while. I'm an ambassador to my country. I have to represent. I have to stay focused. I must remember the three Peace Corps tenets of why we are here: to learn about their cultures and ways of life and share that knowledge back home, to exchange a bit about our own with them, and to do some sustainable projects that have a permanent and positive effect.

"Come," he beckons me, allowing me to enter the second house first. I walk slowly up the stairs. Don't know where I'm going. Maxime shoots up the stairs past me the way a kid just home from school would.

I dig him, but I'm determined not to let him know it. He takes me down to the end of the hall where Baby's Momma is getting baby ready for bed. She greets me, much more joyously this time. Her smile is beautiful. As a matter of fact, there are few people I've met in all of Cote d'Ivoire who don't have perfectly white, strong, straight teeth—and my American diet is supposed to be better?

"This room is where I sleep when I visit from Abidjan." We are now at the middle of the hall where he opens the door to a guest room. The style of furniture and furnishings throughout the room are of a different time. The wallpaper is old and peeling at some corners and there is a faint moldy smell, but the design is intricate with gold embroidery raised up from the wallpaper in swirls throughout the pattern. The king-sized bed frame is deep mahogany, sturdily framed. There are night tables at both sides of the bed and bright orange, old school, simple-yet-sophisticated chairs.

I have time-warped back to the 1960s and 1970s. Even the curtains are intricately designed, thick, and of expensive taste. These houses must have been fully inhabited some time long ago when they were first built, but now it's as if they all up and ran out. Maybe Maurice's father has a big family that grew up here. Maybe the kids are all grown up now, each with their own houses someplace, these two left to Maurice alone.

"Thank you. I have to go home now."

"Let's go."

The walk is quiet except for a few smiles and comments piercing the impending night. We reach the ants. By help of the intense moonlight, I see that the ants not only keep it movin' but are now traveling in the opposite direction. Same speed. Same visible number. I learn that insects help spread nutrients throughout the land and keep it fertile. Villagers in Zragbi plant manure in only one section of the field to fertilize it, then continue farming because they know the insects will spread the manure around to the other sections by default of always being on the go—eating and leaving a bit of themselves here and there as they move throughout the soil. Sorry I killed two of you.

We reach Zragbi and Maxime drops me off at Bogo's since Céline is there. Everyone must know Céline is my caregiver by now. She laughs at him.

"I see you found Pahdré," she smiles at Maxime and he drops his head bashfully. "You have fun together?" She loves to tease. Is she asking me or Maxime? He must not know either because neither one of us answer. Céline just laughs in her hearty way, bright whites beaming. "Well, take her to her house then."

"It is nice to see you, Céline. Everything okay with the family here?" Maxime asks. He and Céline are distant cousins.

"Uuuun," Céline responds to him affirmatively.

"Bon nuit," I chirp in. She looks at me with lips puckered to the side and a sideways glance. Then, she snickers on into the house.

He walks me to my door. Dare I? What will happen next? An outward display of interest? A kiss?

"Are you walking back to Grézuou now?"

"No. My mother lives in the Chief's courtyard," so I will sleep below. His mother is one of the descendants of La Vielle, the 120-plus-year-old woman that died recently.

"Thank you for walking me," but he hesitates at my words.

"Good night. Sleep well," he finally speaks up.

"You too."

13

ELEPHANTS, ROMAN NUMERALS, AND ME

"Do you think I can find an Arabic teacher in Zragbi?" I chat up my electrician as he fixes my light switch. "There is a teacher. He lives on the other side of the market. There is a school there. I will show you. Come by my house and I will take you there."

I come to his house for three days straight at the time he says to be there, but he is never there although I meet his wife and kids. The wife is very surprised to see me knocking at her invisible courtyard door, as Baby's Momma was, pleasant nonetheless.

"He will be right back in fifteen minutes," she says the fourth time I come and giggles. I hope so. I'm not coming here again.

I sit on a stool and watch her tend to sheep and arrange mounds of corn. She makes dinner, washes clothes, and sifts through a crop she has just taken in all at once. Clothes soak while she tends to another duty and then pauses to feed her baby who is old enough to walk but not talk. The baby walks around the court-yard happy and free until she sees me. She doesn't scream. She doesn't even stop to figure out what she sees. She simply turns around and goes the other way.

"Allons-y!" he says, finally arriving. Okay. But, where are we going? "Let's go to the mosque." The mosque? I do not want to go to a mosque. I said I want to learn Arabic. Am I going to learn Arabic in the mosque?

"We are going to pray," the electrician finally explains.

"They teach Arabic there?"

"No, but I am going to pray now. You don't want to come with me?"

Is it cultural and customary to partake in the religion of the person you are visiting? I can just say 'no,' but it is an opportunity to be introduced into a portion of the Zragbi community, which I otherwise do not know how to enter. I do love the sound of the Muslim call to prayer. What other religion has something like that? In Zragbi sometimes and in Daloa especially I hear it, crisp and sharp at five in the morning if I'm up.

'Allaaaaaaaaaaahuakba!' is the beginning of the call to prayer that resonates so deeply that I wonder if my ancestors were Muslim. 5 a.m. is the first prayer of five prayers every day, no matter where a Muslim finds herself. Muslims will pull to the side of the road, even public transportation drivers, to pray. It gives you the weight of their religion's importance to them. It is timeless, dimensionless, and unashamed. Christians have to ask things of others such as 'do you pray?' or 'do you believe in God?' but with Muslims there is no need to ask. It is always right in your face. Other cars whiz dangerously by them as they lay out prayer mats at the edge of snake-infested, tall, roadside grass to pray come what may.

"But, I do not have anything to cover my head," I try to get out of it because I don't really know what I am getting into or how I will be received. The electrician quickly looks at his wife, exchanges a few words in Jula, and she comes back with her own headscarf for me to wear.

"Oh, merci," I stammer out in surprise at how quickly he shuts my ploy down. The electrician lives on the Bèté-side of the market as a few Muslims do and the long walk I expect takes us just across the street. Before entering, we stop at a vendor outside the mosque selling books. I have never seen this kind of set-up before. I don't know when to expect a big market day, but when it happens there is always something being sold that was not there before.

He exchanges words again that I don't understand and the vendor warmly presents me with a book for free that has Arabic written with a French explanation on every page. I see what is involved with each prayer, how many times different parts of the head, hands, and feet must be washed before prayer, what need be said, how you need to move at each part of each prayer, and to pray in the direction of Mecca.

A perfectly right way to pray? I gravitate toward the spirit of Islam, not the structure. However, I guess it's the structure that creates its unique spirit. There are parts to all religions that I like, and I don't think that any one religion is better than another. Just as differences amongst languages and cultures are manifestations of your environment, so, too, is religion. As Steve Jobs puts it in his posthumously published autobiography, 'religions are all doors to the same house.'

One's connection to God is absolute and does not fall apart simply because a religious framework or building is not present. God is the good that you create in your life. God is having an awareness of your power to choose.

I enter the mosque, my head now wrapped in a white headscarf. I am still pretty conspicuous, however, as when I enter, every female has on a black or brown scarf. The electrician leaves me here. I do not see any men praying so where is the electrician going to pray?

Walking in further than where I step when I enter the door is impossible. The women fill the entire room from the front, row to row, side by side, all the way to this entrance. I turn around for consultation forgetting that the electrician is gone and realize there will be no instruction. As usual, when clueless I imitate. I kneel down in prayer. The women stir a little, sensing my entrance, and for a moment I am nervous to be found out. All these women. What will they say when they turn around and see me sitting here?

To my surprise no one looks up. There is one and only one fo-

cus—Allah—God. All heads stay bowed and the only sound is that
of the melodious voice of the religious leader, the Imam. He sings
the prayer and the women chant along or remain silent. An invisible mist of peace descends on us. I cry. Well, not gobs of it but two
tears at least. It is the first time in a crowd of Ivoiriens that could
give two shits I'm here. The veneration for God is main. What a
relief. Church in the States can be a show with concerns over who
has on the best, biggest hat or who can wail the loudest. I keep my
head bowed until the end and am glad to be able to jump up, right
out the door. As soon as I get outside, I snatch the white scarf off
my head.

"Did you pray?" I confront the electrician outside. He is con-
versing with other fellow Muslims and continues a while before
smiling back at me.

"I prayed."

"Where?" I disbelieve.

"Back over there," he points to an area at the end of the
mosque, but I see no large group of men as there are women. Maybe because these men have so many wives.

"Come. I am going to introduce you to the Imam of the
mosque." The Imam? Isn't that the holy one? The one who knows
every part of the Koran? The one responsible for the call to prayer?

"Now?"

"Yes." Not too far from the mosque, in an area I often pass un-
awares on the way to the fields, another world appears. We step
into a courtyard. It is not made of the red earth that the houses in
my courtyard and most of the houses on the non-Muslim side of the
market are. Clean, tall, absolutely white walls with stucco texture
stand up around me. The grounds are swept smooth in long rainbow shapes. Many kids run in and out of the house and several
older teenagers sit at the front door in chairs. The electrician walks
up to one and requests the Imam. The boy goes in and calls his
father.

The Imam is not what I expect and contrary to the response I
anticipate, he shakes my hand. I thought Muslims did not shake the
hands of women with whom they are not married or who are not in

their family. He is as divinely chocolate as the walls to his house are divinely white and shorter in stature and rounder in features than most Muslim ethnicities I meet in Daloa. His speech is premeditated and his movements peaceful. The electrician exchanges a few words with the Imam and leaves. That's it? The electrician is kind and always wears some fraction of a smile on his face, but when he has to go he is gone.

Why am I here? What am I doing? I don't even want to be a Muslim. I just want to learn Arabic so that I can go back home and say I know one more of the six official United Nations languages, like the superficial moron I fight not to be. What high-paying job back home am I going to get speaking Bèté? I don't know what I want to do after these two years, but I do want to be able to claim some accomplishment that people back home can relate to since this Peace Corps experience is turning out to be something so unique, I may not be able to translate it into a skill that gets me a job once I'm done! Perhaps this trying to make myself marketable after Peace Corps while I'm still in Peace Corps is the wrong focus?

"Mohammed says that you want to learn Arabic."

"Who is Mohammed?" I ask with wrinkled brows.

"Your friend." Seconds of silence. "You know, the one who brought you here? Mohammed."

"Oh, the electrician."

"Yes," he pauses a moment to look in my eyes then goes on. "I have a school here. You can come and I will teach you Arabic. Come." We walk to the school only a few paces from where we sit. No conspicuous entrance greets us, just a side wooden door. Welcome to the world of Koranic school.

"This is where we will practice." Wow, my very own Arabic teacher. The Imam. How cool is this?! "Be here tomorrow morning at 11:00?"

"Yes. Thank you."

The next morning, there are many kids hustled about the door not making too much noise although standing quite alert. The Imam is talking and gives me a hearty greeting as soon as he looks up.

"Good Morning. Assalam Alaikum."

"Alaikum Assalam," I return in reverse as I know how to give the common Muslim exchange but not its meaning. My new teacher is pleasantly surprised. He guides me into the classroom where there are even more kids on the inside. Children are everywhere, in every corner, filling up every space there is to fill. Long school tables cram with kids on every inch of them and one-person desks have two children each. All ages are there learning different subjects on different levels all at the same time, from middle school and younger to tall teenagers. All are in some degree of white clothing and all are reciting. It is a loud, forceful, and droning chorus of sound.

The classroom is split into about ten sections and each section recites for memorization; from what paper, what book, or what nothing they have in front of them, something that they are to commit to memory. Some have hands raised and opened out as if holding an invisible book while offering up prayer to God. Some keep their eyes closed while they recite. Some recitations are short and brief, repeated over and over again. Some I have to listen to for a while to hear the beginning again. All is in Arabic.

My teacher in his white robe and white hat pulls a very huge chair to the absolute front and center of the room among all the what-goings-on and tells me to take a seat. I'm gonna' sit in that big 'ole seat? Doesn't that seem odd? But, he doesn't hesitate or show any lack of confidence in his decisions. He has total respect from the children. Whatever he tells them to do—done. The kids might peer up at me but don't skip one beat in their rhythm of study given with so much heart. I have never seen any of these children before in all of the months I've been here. Many of them have smaller, thinner features, but all are different variations of brown. Many of the children are tall. All of the females cover their heads in headscarves.

I slowly climb up into the great big chair. The chair is taller than me. I'm a clown up here, up high off of the ground looking down at these kids. This has got to be the teacher's chair. He grabs a book and has me practice number writing in Arabic while he paces the room. Man, these numbers look like messed up regular numbers. What is this? And, that's when the answer hits me. I heard this before but it never made sense until now, seeing it with my own eyes. Westerners and most people everywhere around the world are using what kind of numbers on a day-to-day, minute-to-minute, and second-to-second basis? Arabic numbers!

We don't use Roman numbers. We don't use any other number system except the Arabic number system the Western one is derived from. All . . . around . . . the . . . world. Everyone. Google 'images for Arabic numbers' to compare.

I start to practice writing the numbers. The more I focus on my own repetitive work, the more the noise becomes a welcomed clatter. After an hour or so, my first Arabic lesson is done. I pay him and he is quite grateful. I wish I could help with the school somehow. My first project? Ummm, but then again maybe it is fine the way it is. The kids are learning how to concentrate in spite of cacophony everywhere around them and in limited space. This is the way it has been so what is wrong with it? The Imam has likely grown up in such an educational environment and he is quite a nice guy.

I walk back home from my first day of practice, invigorated and ready for more. I've gotta' put this Arabic numbers book away before anyone sees it. But, Céline eyes it as I briskly pass by the house at the same time she exits it.

"You learn Arabic now?" she catches me. I simply smile. She doesn't pass judgment, but she doesn't say much either. My effort to learn Bèté is all but forgotten at this point. I continue on back toward my house, bucket-bathe myself, and put all the day's sweat to rest down the shower hole.

Céline's daughter Laudine is tall, dark-skinned, and lanky unlike Céline who is short, reddish-brown, and athletically thick. Laudine, in features, is more of a Jula than a Bèté. I don't know if her father

is living or dead. The only time he ever comes up in conversation is
when Céline says, 'Laudine is not my color. She is blaaaack like her
father,' with a snarl. This she inconsiderately says right in front of
Laudine and another cousin standing nearby who is the darkest
person in Zragbi.

"Momma?" Laudine squeaks in her high-pitched voice. "Me and
Clara were over by the soccer field collecting wood and we found
something."

"What did you find?"

"A cobra."

"Did you tell your uncles?"

"No. We came to tell you first."

"Go. Tell your uncles and they will go see," she is firm with
them and off they go running back down toward the Chief's courtyard.

"Céline? What is a cobra?" I check to makes sure my ears hear
right.

"It's a snake." A snake? A cobra?! Aw, hellllll no!

"Here?" I twist back and forth looking on every inch of the
ground.

"Far from here." But, not really. "Down by the soccer field behind us." So, that's where the soccer field is, in a clearing just beyond the Chief's courtyard? I am none too anxious to know any
more information. So, I stop asking. Céline notices that I am catching on to the gravity of the situation and adds one of her characteristic 'uuuuuuuh' short for 'uh-hum we in trouble' or 'uh-hum sure
'nuf. A little while later, her daughter returns out of breath with a
report in Bèté that Céline reports to me.

"It is a cobra. The Laudines . . ." which means Laudine and all
of her friends " . . . were gathering fire wood when they noticed the
cobra sleeping under a pile of leaves just beneath them. They almost stepped on it! The uncles went down and shot it.

"When a cobra is sleeping, don't bother it." Of course. "They
have just eaten if you find them like that. They can eat a whole
person. They say they seen a cobra eat a whole person once."
Who's they? "It rises up taller than you and spits out this white,

sticky stuff to paralyze you. Wherever it bites, you freeze up. If it bites your chest then you can't move your chest. If it bites your arm then you can't move your arm. If it bites your legs, then you can't run anywhere because you get paralyzed." I get the picture. "Then, it rises up even higher and taps you on the head like that, boap! And, you can't move at all because it breaks your neck like that. Then it starts to eat you," her eyes charge in my direction. She is preparing a pretty complex meal effortlessly but stops to fully delve her spirit into the explanation.

"Then they wrap their body around you, squeeze, and break all of your bones so that they can devour your body whole. They eat you. Part by part. Swallow you whole, all the way down to the head. Then, they go searching for a spot to sleep. They look for a spot where there are no ants because they are going to sleep for a long time while they digest the food, so they don't want to be bothered."

"How long do they sleep for?" My eyes search for her answer. She doesn't blink.

"Months. They sleep there for so long that when they move, where they slept is the shape of their body. You know that a cobra has been sleeping there because nothing is growing in that spot. They digest the food for that time they are sleeping, like how the Laudines found that one sleeping, and when they are finished they go down by the water and shit out all the bones!" Well, that was not actually exclaimed, but it sounded so. Shit out bones? What?! Peace Corps didn't tell me all of this!

"They like the rain. My uncles say they seen a cobra rise up in the rain and open its mouth wide like that . . ." and she takes her hands and spreads her arms out as wide as they can go " . . . to let the water come in. The trucks that you see go through here . . . they say that at night when it was raining one time a cobra was out in the middle of the road with its mouth wide open taking in the rain. The truck had to stop there because the cobra was too big to pass. It closed its mouth and looked at the truck, rose up, and started to pound its head into the front of the truck. Whomp! Whomp! Whomp! Like that. And, it put a dent in the front of the truck then went away after hitting the truck for a while."

"I'm going to go take a shower," even though I had already taken one.

"Come back for dinner."

"What are we having?"

"Cobra," she smiles and then adds, "C'est doux, dey!" It's good? Umh, umh, umh. That 'Fear Factor' TV show ain't got nothin' on this.

"We clean out all of the poison and cook it." Poison? Come on. Really? I understand that I am here to have a cultural experience, but this is much like the choice to eat the poisonous fish delicacy Fugu, served in Japan, that a few people die every year from eating. I didn't eat that when I was there and I don't think I'll eat cobra here.

I walk down toward Le Chef's courtyard after nearly an hour of deciding whether or not to eat cobra. I have eaten the strange, pig-fish tasting agouti, frogs' everything, wood-tasting termites, and who knows what else. It is rude not to at least try.

"Pahdré, you had the cobra yet?" a neighbor asks as I pass by her house.

"No. You too?"

"Yeah! C'est doux, dey! It's enough for the entire quartier! They eatin' it over there, over there, over there, and over back there, too," she points in every direction. Oh, my. Is it that long?

I continue on down and walk up on Céline who has a little pot all prepared for me to take back to my house. I eat each piece of snake slowly, waiting a good minute after the first few bites. Being here, I've learned that if something I eat isn't right, my body will let me know it within the first minutes and often within the first ten seconds. Nothing happens however. The meat itself is more rubbery than meaty or fishy. What keeps me eating it, nonetheless, is the sauce. It is a pimanty, tomatoey seasoning mixture of perfect, spicy delight. I am so hungry I eat it all and clock out.

The next morning when I wake up, it's not so easy. I'm tired and sluggish this morning even though I sleep for a good, solid nine hours. As the day goes on, the usual things happen, a few newtowners call me La Blanche, the kids ask me in a thousand different ways to play with them, and I hear some language I don't know exists. The same men try to hit on me and after calling me Pahdré and offering betrothals but being ignored, of course, then call me La Blanche.

I lose track of time and senses. The only thing I can feel is the immense headache going on. Pound for sledgehammer pound of blood pumps to my head. Poom, poom, boom, bang, clop! Uh, enough already with the headache. I should get on over to the hospital. Fever strikes as I walk. Head is hot. Keeping my body straight and moving forward is an exercise. Did I get some of that poison in the meal last night? It would definitely be uncool to die right now. Transportation is unpredictable and a phone is two hours away unless Maurice happens to be around.

My symptoms are malaria-esque. My throat dries up so I go to the market and buy two sachets of ngyamakuji, ginger juice. The juice squirts down my throat as I break open the first plastic bubble of juice from the bottom tip. Miraculously, my fever breaks and I start to sweat. I clobber my way up Bogo's one-step porch. Céline is nowhere to be found. I struggle over to the hospital hall, but no doors are open and no sunlight floods the hall from the rooms as it usually does.

What time is it? I sit down on a patient bench in the waiting hall. Light creeps into the hall from the two side entrances, but I'm not in the sunlight. Aaah, the light hurts even as indirect as it is, collecting in the back of my brain and stinging me every time I open just my right eye. The left eye stays closed. I close both eyes and think to pray. Sip more ginger. If this is from the snake, I would be dead already, right? Maybe all I need to do is relax and cool off.

The heat rises up off of my scorched body. Boy, it's hot outside. Or, hot inside me. I can't open my eyes wide to grasp back into my reality. I'm alone fighting this by myself. I don't have enough grip to alert someone. Could they help me if I do? My head slowly falls back against the aqua-colored wall. Whatever it is, I will get over this.

I am on the second sachet of ngyamakuji. May this ginger do what nothing else has. May this ginger juice cool me down, down to my core, in my veins, and up to my brain. Let my calmness restore my sense of reality. But, I feel myself going . . . No. I have to take over mentally. The last several gulps of the second sachet finally put me over and blanket me with coolness.

Maybe it's just malaria. I can't believe I'm saying that now— 'just malaria.' Which one do you want to deal with: malaria or poison from a cobra? I'll take malaria, please. A cobra bite would have me dead in less than an hour.

There must be some connection, however, between the cobra feast, my immediate pass-out thereafter, and this blindsiding, malarial strike. There had to be something in those big chunks of rubbery skin. Just enough to lower my immunity for the ever-building malaria in my veins to strike? Stupid. Why did I eat that? Aaaaand, I threw away my mefloquine. I have to take care of myself. I am not ten years old anymore. I am not Superwoman.

Has the apocalypse happened and left Zragbi with just me in it? I venture from the hospital over to Bogo's house again, hoping someone is there. Jijina and Eliane cool out under the appatam kitchen in the courtyard, scraping the last bit of rice from the huge marmite they remove from the Bricks. The pot is now solid black several times over from being scorched so many years. Jijina sets it down on the jittery, red earth. Where were these two the first time I passed through here? How long have I been sitting at the hospital? Red earth shoots up around the black marmite and engulfs their sandaled brown feet as if they grow from the soil itself.

Jijina eyes me walking toward her during another one of her head throwbacks to delightfully gobble the crunchy rice down.

"Where is Céline?"

"Elle est en bas là bas." Down below? Now I have to walk all the way down there, too. Self-mumblings get me moving, still spent from the fever and fading headache.

"Come pump water with us," Jijina commands me as usual. She bosses me around like an older sister although she is twelve. I love pumping plus Jijina and Eliane are a comedy act. Eliane heads inside.

"Okay. I'll come later." They never let me leave without a display, however.

"Did you clean the bathroom yet?!" Jijina yells at Eliane. Eliane, much shorter in stature, swirls around to look at Jijina, eyelids fully opening for effect every time she blinks her lashes quickly.

"Me?" she pretends to not know she is being addressed.

"Naw! The midget behind you!" Jijina belts back loudly while she continues to stuff the rice in her mouth and some bits purposefully fall back out.

"Je ne sais pas moi, mais, oh!" Eliane flutters and flits and moves her head from left to right as if confused about which direction she should go. Placing her hands gently on her chest she repeats her last phrase, 'But, oh, I don't know, I . . .'

"Ohhh! You there!" Jijina belts again. "Go clean the bathroom! Bogo's coming home!" She never calls Bogo 'Dad.'

Yelling doesn't faze Eliane. She never yells back. She is very calm at eleven and anyone can see she'd rather have a conversation with herself before saying or doing anything else. If she doesn't finally conclude that the situation or conversation she finds herself in is comical, she is somehow able to disappear without being noticed. She is quite reserved and therefore not easy to attack. Her whims are never expected. Jijina makes efforts to frustrate Eliane, but Eliane, in turn, simply blows away with the wind.

This is a vaudeville show and Eliane finishes an act of which no one has seen the beginning. Eliane sticks out her right leg to the side and bows over it, bouncing her right arm up then swinging it down as she does. You would never know how strong she is unless you see her legs. Saying nothing more, she jumps up into a double step and gets to cleaning.

Alert enough to appreciate the silliness, I subtly shake my head, smile at the two with my eyes, and wave as I leave toward Céline's real house. She stays with an eighty-five-year-old aunt and uncle in his forties. They are always smiling at me when I arrive. Whenever I show up, the two of them are on their way in or out of the house from or to the fields. I have never seen either one of them without sweat.

"Tantie? Céline est là?" I call older women 'Tantie' for auntie as others do.

Tantie shakes her head to say 'I don't know, I just got here' and motions me to have a look inside. Céline isn't here.

"What's wrong?" Tantie asks me in Bèté. Not like I understand much Bèté, but I understand the gestures for it. The same 'what's the matter' gesture the older man at the woodshop gives before realizing he has a Green Mamba is what Tantie uses. Even tilting her head to the side with sad and concerned eyes, all the years in the sun still freeze her habitual smile into place.

"I'm sick," I say hoping she understands basic French and Tantie walks right over to me to place the back of her hand on my forehead without hesitation. She reaches up high on her toes as she is much shorter than me. Up close, Tantie's skin is lava-dark chocolate with black cherries mixed in, glistening in the afternoon heat.

"You're okay," she responds surprisingly in French this time, but her Zragbi Bèté accent strongly stilts her French. She turns to walk away, back bent over, and then slowly turns back around forgetting something. "Céline is coming," she comforts. Her body addresses me, but her eyes only give me a quick look before turning back around again. Then, she turns back to me quickly a second time and laughs at me, quickly pressing her left hand down in the air to make me not worry.

"Pahdré!" she yells at me and giggles.

Respecting the culture is one thing. Dying from it is another. No more cobra, for real. The same way Oyo, the other Fille de Salle with Céline, spits out the cheese I offer her from a Daloa French supermarket—that's the same way I'm going to be if someone offers me cobra tartare again.

And, what happened to all the elephants? I have seen not one elephant yet in this land of ivory—the Ivory Coast—La Cote d'Ivoire. They must have really hunted them all down during colonialism. Looks like cobras will soon be on the endangered species list with Ivoirien elephants as well. Many more Ivoiriens than elephants die under colonialism, however, I'm sure.

I walk up the one small hill to my house sure that Tantie will get the word to Céline that I am looking for her. I drink another sachet of ngyamakuji and take a nap. When I wake up, another day has gone by. My body is on strike. I see the different seed packets from America sitting in the corner in a box, which my real sister sends me, and this gives me extra motivation to stay alive at least for the next ten minutes. I chuck the flower seeds. Corn? I'll try that. I don't put much into planting the seeds. I bury them about an inch or less in the ground beneath my bedroom window and that's it.

After three days, the corn and I are still alive and I already see something green poking through the soil. The corn is an experiment. I'm not gonna' eat them. Someone is peeing in this corner and that is really why I plant them here. Every time I lay down in bed at night, I smell it rise up into my bedroom.

Whoever is doing it can't use my bathroom instead because I put a lock on it. Céline tells me it is mine to put a lock on so I do because every time I go in there someone messes it up. I see bird feathers in there on the shower hole side. Someone shits in there and leaves doo doo smudges by the hole. Sometimes, I see pee on the bathing side instead of the latrine side as well. Little kids no doubt.

The corn grows quite independently of me, high up to the level of my window, three feet off the ground. I see the corn husks taking shape. Maybe after a few weeks. The peeing eventually stops and everything is cool until one morning I wake up and notice one of the baby corns torn out.

"What is this? These people just can't stand me, can they?" I look up and just then Désiré exits her house.

"Pahdré, what happened?"

"Someone took a corn. It wasn't even ready yet," my face screws into a raisin. Désiré laughs a little. I know it's not serious but come on. Add insult to injury by ripping out my corn after peeing on my house?

"Someone stole your corn?" she laughs. "Why are you planting corn here? Why don't you plant out in the fields? I don't think that's a good spot."

"If I don't put something here, people will pee on the wall." Now her face wrinkles into a raisin. Désiré's genuine concern shows in the frown that stays on her brow even though a smile cracks through every other second as we stand here looking at each other. "I don't know, Pahdré." A pause passes and then she adds, "Maybe if you let people use the bathroom they wouldn't pee on your walls." That's why her son Dowa was shitting in front of the house that time! It's not until this moment that I discover my lock on the bathroom is anti-community in a really big way.

"If I let people use the bathroom, they don't keep it clean. It stinks. I don't want to smell that every morning," my French stutter returns with a few uncontrolled blinks.

"Ooooooh, Pahdré!" she ends it. "I'm going to make some food," she laughs and walks off around the corner to cook breakfast for her four kids.

I'm hungry, too. I really want some bread and eggs this morning, but I have to stop. Désiré also tells me this is all the first volunteer before me ever ate. She never accepted invitations to eat with anyone else in all of Zragbi unless Céline made the food and when she couldn't eat with Céline she just ate bread.

14

WHO TOLD YOU THIS IS CHICKEN?

I t can certainly suck being a grownup sounding like a child around a bunch of adults because I don't know the language. To be constantly corrected or outright ignored because I'm not making any sense, take too long to get it out, use completely the wrong word, create a nonsense word, or even an inappropriate word by accident because my accent is wrong—it's all a part of the learning process. Keep talking. Find new ways to express yourself. I don't get stuck on that one word I want so badly to show I can use. The goal is to express myself and enjoy a flowing conversation to the best of my ability.

I used to stress about not always understanding, but now I pat myself on the back for any words I can catch that are enough to figure out the general picture. I store these few words and gradually recognize new ones. I don't know what people are talking about sometimes, but umh, 'I got that word and I got that word' is my perspective. One thing at a time.

After about six to nine months of 'huh?' I only miss one or two words in a sentence. If you've got that much, you can guess with pretty good accuracy what the other words mean. Too, I imitate aloud and in front of the person exactly what I hear. This makes my friends laugh, but in putting their words into my mouth, I am able to slowly piece apart what the long string of sounds they say actually are, and realize I understand.

I used to rush back home at the end of the day, wanting to look up all the unknown words I could store, but after a while I learn to listen. I immediately imitate aloud; slow down people's speech repeating pronouncedly right after them with my lips or in my head; use gestures; watch gestures instead of staring in people's mouths hoping they morph into English speakers; watch facial expressions, emotions, eyes; and use what I learn whenever the perfect occasion arises. My dictionary hates me now.

"Good morning Pahdré," comes the voice of an unannounced visitor, as I creak open the door after his knock.

"How do you know my name?" I ask surprised.

"I live down below," he waits as if that response is supposed to do it for me.

"My name is Franc," he continues.

I'm still not letting him in. Is he a creditor? Who shows up at your door like this? Franc stands out here without so much of a signal, smiling away. Is he selling something? His tattered and stained clothing is nothing out of the ordinary, but his demeanor, smile, and even the way he enunciates every single consonant and every single vowel is an above average performance. I open the screen door to fully take him into scope.

"I hear you want to learn Bèté."

"How do you know that?"

"If you want I can tutor you," he skips to the point. "Céline tells me you need to learn."

"Oh, okay."

"I brought you a book." A little yellow book. "You can use this to learn. It was made by a couple that came here to teach us Christianity. This is the Bible that they put into Bèté with French translation."

A Bible written in Bèté? Wow. I know that Christianity makes up a portion of religious people in Cote d'Ivoire but to have a Bible in an Ivoirien language shows that Christians travel as widely as Muslims in the history of religious fervor. At the top of a mountain I climb with Steve, not too far from Daloa, we see engraved 'France 1646' I recall. The French might not have colonized Cote d'Ivoire at this time, but they have certainly been here exchanging for a looooooong time.

I didn't even know there were any Bibles written in any African languages at all—ignorant on my part. Will this really be a language lesson or a church one?

"It has Bèté on one side and French on the other."

"Thank you," I respond. He is disappointed I return it to him so quickly. I'm not trying to go to Sunday School, man. I'm a Peace Corps Volunteer, not a missionary. He comes three days straight to teach me Bèté. On the third day, I cannot take it anymore.

"I want to learn naturally. Do you go to the fields?"

"Yes."

"Then take me with you," I say, but he hesitates. I never forget in context.

"Okay."

The next day, Franc comes and his two sisters are with him. They introduce themselves. They all have Céline's reddish-brown skin and perfect strong smiles only rivaled by their uniquely large and oval eyes. There is a younger boy as well and if he ain't spoken to, he ain't speakin'.

Let's do this! We walk at least three miles. Walking in the woods with people who know how to do so is the freest feeling. Most of the land is farmed but not the usual farm you might think. It is farmed, tropical rainforest. We arrive and sit under palm, banana, and other trees so green and immense as to block out the sunlight. There are so many trees you would be tempted to say, 'how they get all these trees out here?'

Their chill spot on their land is on top of a little mound with a canopy held up by four wooden poles and one thick one in the center. Franc's oldest sister plunks down and busts a move on some food that she shares with me, probably because I stare at her eating it. Then, she proceeds to rip into her brother about something in Bètè, which has everyone laughing but him. I watch him respond with muffled annoyance and intermittent bursts of a smile he cannot suppress. The older sister is certainly the funny one.

Off to work we go. I am bent over planting rice with them, my back in constant arch. The sweat drops are so big on my forehead, I'm sure they are having their own thoughts by now as well. Why am I doing this? Why am I out here planting rice in the sun? This heat is not for human skin. The sweat feels even heavier when I look over at his sisters and see they are now covered up in long-sleeved shirts. The oldest sister, Funny One, has on a turtleneck even. Am I living in a parallel universe? Who wears a turtleneck in 100-degree weather?! It would be nice to know what they are covering up from.

"Pahdré!" Funny One yells. I immediately look up.

"No, Pahdré. I'm talking to my sister," and she turns to continue speaking in Bètè. They laugh. I plant the rice.

Whatever I do I get into it and I am into it. All bent over, I no longer worry about aches and pains. This is someone's food. The more rice I plant, the more food everyone eats. I plant and plant.

"Pahdré! That's good," Funny One yells from farther and farther away. The two sisters finish their section and are now a good twenty yards off from me.

"It's good?" I ask, and they first glance at each other before speaking next.

"Yeh. Keep planting. You're doing very good," Funny One encourages. I am close to a large bush now crouching down underneath it to plant in every square inch of ground possible.

"Should I plant here, too?" I yell over to them.

"Oh, yeah! That's good, Pahdré!" the first Pahdré says. Right then holes appear. Big ones.

"She's not afraid," I hear Funny One say. I don't look up just then. I keep planting away, all the while staring at these holes until I make the connection between their comments, their laughter, and them being way up over on the hill. These are snake holes! Very slowly I back away. I don't want to give them the glory over me, laughing at me while a snake jumps out and bites me on the fore-head. I play it off cool. When the older sister said 'Pahdré! That's good,' maybe she meant 'Pahdré, that's enough—you can stop now!'

Back in their quartier down below my house, we eat together. The four of them throw everything down all at once upon arrival and invite me in. Their house has multiple rooms with beds and dressers and mirrors. All the walls inside are painted a bright green. The walls are mud and concrete-mixed without furnishings except for random, illuminated light bulbs sticking out of the walls near doorways. No art or fancy drapery hangs and it is no Maurice mansion by any means but a feeling of 'have' as opposed to 'have not' is definitely in the air.

Back outside, Pahdré strips right in front of me as I sit on a stool in their courtyard, and out pops her belly from nowhere. She is pregnant. Very pregnant. She washes up right there with her bucket to the side of the house entrance. She does not care about me being here. She grabs a stool and gets all in her business right there. It happens so quickly, all I can do is pretend it does not bother me. I do not want to look like a prude when evidently no one around here cares. I remember my time in Japan being naked around so many women in the hot springs and no one giving a damn, just gettin' down to the business of being clean. Besides, everyone is family here. It would only be odd if I am the one to start bathing myself butt naked on a stool in front of my house.

Pahdré pulls out a turkey baster without the long metal part, just the pump. She fills it with something, lifts underneath the pagne now wrapped around her waist, and shoots it straight up her ass.

"What is that?" I pull back in shock.

"It's pimant." Hot peppers in the ass? Is that an enema?

Further back from the center of the courtyard, I see an appatam blocked from view by the shower area that Pahdré doesn't bother to use. I leave Spicy Butt behind, no pun intended, walk over to Funny One, and pull up a tiny stool. There under the appatam she prepares our meal. Franc is there, too.

"Wow. What is that? That will be good," I notice something black near the peppers she cuts.

"Rat," she replies, smiling up at Franc who walks off.

"Rat!?" I don't have enough time to censure my response.

"C'est bon," she uncovers the black thing fully. The tiny stool falls away as I peer leerily closer.

"Hahaha!" she laughs and picks up the little body to show me up close. Time to practice being objective. Hmmm. It isn't a New York City rat. It isn't that rat you see jumping out of garbage dumps or scurrying into dark corners on the streets. It's a bush rat. All it knows is green, green, and more green. Whatever else it might eat only knows green as well.

I watch the entire cooking process imagining myself eating rat and when the time comes of course you know what happens—it tastes just like chicken. It goes quite well with the piping hot sauce and steaming rice. This will be my only rat, but I'm going to enjoy it.

"Pahdré, do you want to go to church?" The other Pahdré leans in over her freshly cleaned belly.

"Sure," I say immediately out of respect.

"Where is it?" I ask and Franc replies that it is just across the road here in this quartier after which he says more in Bèté to both sisters. The sisters look at each other again then down at the food they continue to eat.

"I'll take you," Funny One finally volunteers as if forced.

Night falls and I'm already back home. The sisters come up to get me to go over to the church. Where is this church? All I see is regular, red-earthed houses everywhere. The sisters are dressed differently than before. Their heads are wrapped in shawls. The church is a regular house as any other house in Zragbi, but when we get inside, there are plenty of chairs lined up with a row going down the middle as would be in a church. No pulpit stands in the front although space is made for people to drum and play other instruments there. An odd red light filters through the darkness. I can't tell who is who unless they are sitting right next to me.

This is no Christianity I know except for the similar display of emotion in Black Baptist churches. The Abé church in Grand Noyaré is a typical, Western style church. It seems out of place in a village of few amenities but way more recognizable than this.

The drums come alive and the music is a low-key carnival. Around the room, people either stand or sit and raise their hands up in the air shouting. No sermon occurs. People simply walk in throughout the service and pray out their needs or silently praise. One woman sticks out the most at 6'2", beautifully brown, and her neck is as thick as my thigh. She wears a dress slightly torn, very old, and stained, but she is breathtakingly beautiful. I wonder what she is so sadly praying for. She has all the strength and beauty of ten women.

I have few comments for them on the church service afterward. I don't go in the States and am certainly not going to keep going to these red light specials. The sisters know I will not go again. They aren't so happy to be going either, standing and staring with random claps to fit in.

I am surprised I've gone to the fields with Franc, his sisters, and the silent young boy so many times. We are all about the same age and I see them as siblings in a way. Sometimes, I am even invited to eat by other people I don't know who live in Franc's courtyard as well. They are all family anyway. If I am accepted by one, I am accepted by all.

"Pahdré, why are you here?" Franc asks me sitting on my porch a couple of weeks later.

"To help the village . . . to do projects."

"What kind of projects?"

The reality of being a Health Volunteer floods back into my brain. I fumble and stumble to produce an answer. Why indeed am I here? To make a mess for sure. To confuse myself on my identity for certain. To boil myself under this aluminum-roofed house without a doubt.

"Anything," I have the notion to say. His baffled face doesn't change, but after saying it I realize it's true.

"Like what?" he asks.

"Anything. Anything that Zragbi wants to do. I have to find out how to make it happen." What is a Peace Corps Volunteer anyway but someone who makes the impossible happen no matter what? Someone who pulls people together and makes good things happen. Hmph, this must certainly be what a real Peace Corps Volunteer is because everyday we are overwhelmingly forced to accept as possible unheard-of events, manners of people, languages, and customs we never knew existed before.

"I'm going to rest a little," I tell Franc, who is still perplexed by my words.

"Pahdré! What are you doing in there?" my neighbor Rouazo comes up rumbling right after Franc disappears out of sight. Rouazo enjoys giving me a hard time.

"Nothing," I appear at the screen door with a genuine smile on my face.

"Pahdré, do you have a boyfriend?" Rouazo questions slyly.

"No, but I've seen you on a bike with your girlfriend and I know you're already married," I whisper loudly. Rouazo is about six feet tall, but his musculature and size 14s make him bigger.

"Pa . . ." he tries to respond as I cut him off seeing a positive opportunity to thwart his intrusion on my brain space.

"You use condoms with your girlfriend?" Upon ascertaining that there is no one in perceptible proximity, he answers.

"Why do you want to know?" He's going to think that I'm flirting with him but whatever.

"Tu connais la SIDA?" An opportunity to sensibilize him about A.I.D.S. arises.

"I know about that. We wear condoms," but I stare at him incredulously. "Pahdré?" he glances quickly over his left shoulder to make sure no one is around again. "I have worn two condoms at once and they still don't work."

"No!" I almost scream out but stifle myself at the last minute. "If the condoms break, it's not because of the condom. It's because she is too dry. If you have sex before she is wet, the condom is likely to break. Two is even worse."

He is now eyeing me as the master of sex instead of someone who is trying to protect him, his wife, and the woman with whom he often cycles off into the sunset.

"Il faut faire deucement," I explain with as serious a face as possible in spite of the fact that this is obviously turning him on. "Take your time with her before you enter. Make her ready. Then, you can use one condom and it won't break," I try not to be too explicit. This is phone sex through a screen door. Two condoms at once? Man, I never heard that one.

"Pahdré," Rouazo pleas to me. "Les capotes sont chers." Condoms are expensive? I'm just wondering where he gets them at all. Do they sell them at the pharmacy? The hospital? Why aren't they giving them away for free? Back in my bedroom, I grab three condoms from our A.I.D.S. demonstration kit and push them through the hole that the kids have over time worn into my screen.

"Use these!" I scold him.

"Pahdré . . ." he smirks, shifting his body weight from side to side after slowly taking my Peace Corps condom samples.

"Bye!" I shut the wooden door in his face, enclosing myself in an oven in the middle of the day, hoping he disappears from my porch soon so that I can open the door back up.

"Have you seen my husband?" she always asks, baffled. His wife is a very tall, strong, thick-necked, thick-armed woman just as tall and strong as he is.

"No," we all have to tell her. He is either in the fields working or 'workin it.' Rouazo's wife ends up leaving him and no one has any idea where she goes.

"Have you seen my wife?" he comes asking one day.

"No."

15 How Do You Say 'Epilepsy' or 'Autism' in Bèté?

"White woman! You're still sleeping? Are you sick? Come on out!" They alternate a phrase per child and the last one is yelled by all of them one by one.

"White woman! White woman! White woman! White woman! White woman!" Boom, boom, boom!!! They bang until I jump up out of bed from fear of heart attack. I throw the door open and flick open the screen door latch with much feigned authority.

"Burubai-ey!" 'Get out of here,' I demand in Bèté. I don't want to deal with this. I haven't even bathed yet. I repeat my lone phrase several times but Bri Bri, the one who loves to grab my arm to kiss my skin, is the ringleader and knows my bark got nothin'.

"Boohba-ey! Boohba-ey!" Bri Bri laughs, imitating me and showing me my horrible American accent. Her followers then imitate her imitating me, and as cute as she is, with her deep-set dimples, her leadership effectiveness in getting what she wants works to my incredible disadvantage. They all want me out the house so I burst out with much-feigned authority again, glaring down at all seven children standing below me then up at the impending hot sun above.

My real father often tells me stories about how his grandmother would have him get a good switch from a tree—to spank him. I walk out with them around me. They giggle in delight, no doubt wanting something to get into. They at least know I'm nice enough to give them 25 CFA francs whenever I have it on hand or when they ask for it. I still, however, hold a hard heart from being taunted with 'White woman.'

I move through the crowd of mini people and take the perfect diagonal path over to a tree with a thin branch that must be bending down just for them. I yank a twig from it as long as my arm, the crowd of mini people still behind me watching.

"Aaaaaaaaaaaaaah! I'm going to get youuuu," I blurt out in English as I raise the twig up in the air for extra effect and run after them. It's fun. They disperse in seven different directions, pushing each other out of the way, sometimes falling like bowling pins from all the pushes and nudges but immediately jumping up again to dart out whichever way they can, red dirt flying up everywhere. Bri Bri is the leader of the pack so I follow her down the path between our two houses. She now runs with another little girlfriend or cousin of hers. Both laugh. All of the kids are laughing, in fact. I'm not going to do anything to them and they know it.

"Aaaaaaahhh!" I scream again. I pass courtyards and houses and elders sitting on porches. Their eyes widen for a moment until they see the smiles on all of our faces and stare back off into space. 'Round and 'round several different courtyards. Few people are in them because they are off in the fields. These kids are either too young to be in the fields or go to school, so they aren't depended on as much. They only go to the fields if an extra hand is needed. They are all strong with little athlete bodies and have more years of water carrying under their belts than me.

I wear out. They don't but leave me alone. Nevertheless, after all is said and done, I can never deny that the children are my lasting salvation. Everything they do is a great contribution to my soul, good or bad, because they do everything full of energy and

life. Malaria, malnutrition, diarrhea, pneumonia, and other potential life-threatening illnesses—I never experienced that growing up.
Still, they smile so happily. They never flinch at work because it's a
part of maintaining their happiness. Kids in Zragbi know what they
need to know to survive. They learn to make the connection between work and survival. I, however, have not.

'Look at my bike,' a boy who makes his own toys often says. It
isn't a real bike but a miniature one the child puts together from
metal pieces he finds here and there. A bottle cap for the seat and
a windmill mechanism that makes the whole thing go. He makes
the batteries. I don't understand with what and how it moves, but
it does and there are no AAA or AA batteries to be seen anywhere
on or in it.

When each one of their playmates speaks a different language,
they simply adapt and learn all of them. No wonder every Ivoirien I
meet knows at least three languages fluently outside of the French
colonial language. In Zragbi, I am often witness to a conversation
between five different adults speaking a total of three different languages and each responding to the other language they hear with
their own language—one language not being mutually intelligible
with the other. Everyone is open enough to allow the other to
speak in the language they are most comfortable.

Bèté is full of z's and ng's, and there are also languages in Cote
d'Ivoire as tonal as a Chinese language. Some languages remain a
mystery to my ear to this day and I find them hard to imitate. All
of the ethnicities in Zragbi make fun of each other, too. The same
way some Americans make fun of Chinese language or make fun of
what Americans perceive to be the one African language everyone
in Africa speaks.

I chuck the twig, bucket, and dress and start over to the hospital. I can't stay away forever. But, after the Mossi girl's death, I am
now afraid of witnessing anything else horrific. The sun is bright,
the courtyard has been swept clean, and no one has left any rice or
other night or morning happenings on or in front of my porch. But,
they've been waiting. Oh, the rage and the fury of it.

"Laaa Blanche! Laaa Blanche! Laaa Blanche! Laaa Blanche!

Laaa Blanche! Laaa Blanche! Laaa Blanche! Laaa Blanche! Laaa Blanche!" This will not die. The same seven kids. From the moment they catch me closing my door, to the moment I reach them sitting along the road, the name-calling never stops. I come up to them and I want to keep going, just pass the kids on by, ignore them, not let them spoil my day, pretend they don't exist, and erase all sounds of 'La Blanche' from memory. What can I say to get them to stop? They don't speak much French yet and my Bèté is near non-existent since most people have the habit of speaking to me in French.

I look at them. All seven of them and through their jeer, all seven are doing the exact same thing - smiling. They brim from ear to ear with smiles. In fact, walking up to them has them the most excited. I read their faces and succeed in blocking out the chants of 'La Blanche' to capture the moment. If I didn't know any better, it appears they really like me. Some kids are even jumping up and down as they chant what they believe to be my name.

That's it! These are kids. They don't understand the significance of what they are saying or if they do, they don't see why I am upset. Relative to them, I do look white. They probably hear their parents saying it in reference to me and think that it is my real name. Pahdré! The meaning of my name returns. Pah Dré! You must reflect! Think!

They quiet down a little. Heads outstretch in expectation, wondering what will come from my mouth. Or, should I just grab a tree branch and chase them again? Some are ready to flee, but every last one of them is smiling.

"My name is not La Blanche. It's Pahdré. When you see me, call me Pahdré. Don't call me La Blanche, La Blanche, La Blanche. Call me Pahdré, Pahdré, Pahdré!" I shout, "Everyone! Paaahdré! Paaahdré! Paaahdré!" A moment passes and I'm not sure they understand my French, but I insist on my chant and with faces of half confusion and leftover smile, they look at each other for confirmation. When no one knows what to do, they look back at me now smiling down at them and the best, most personal miracle of my time here happens.

"Paaahdré! Paaahdré! Paaahdré!" they start to repeat as I slowly walk off. I add a happy booty twist to go along with each syllable as they pronounce my Bèté name. They get more excited from this and chant louder.

"That's good!" I encourage them. A couple of the kids jump out of the circle of friends and start dancing to the tune of "Paaahdré! Paaahdré! Paaahdré!" just as I am. After this day, I never hear 'La Blanche' out of anyone's mouth again unless they are new or visiting the village or I am out on a trip into town to Abidjan, or some other place where I'm not known as Madame Pahdré.

I reach the hospital and the voices of the children finally fade away. The Sage Femme is busy pulling from her repertoire of languages again. I am ready to sit here and do nothing until the hospital closes or the women stop coming, but then the line dies down faster than usual and by 14:00 p.m. we have not seen a patient in a whole hour. La Sage Femme allows Céline to go home, so we do. She and I walk to Bogo's house and Céline cooks a bunch of seasoned rice full of tomatoes, vegetables, and spice—the major ingredient. She then covers the bowl and we head back toward her own house.

"That smells good, Céline." She smiles at this and throws in a little dance-kick to punctuate her smile. Modest but provocative in dress, Céline has obvious confidence in herself, and her posture stays upright with head up and hips a swivelin' whenever and wherever she walks. She is a sexy nurse who maintains her authority. Everyone knows her station and respects her for it.

"Abidjan!" Smiling and buzzing along, she chokes up and laughs when she hears the familiar greeting. Two men salute her aglow from seeing her, especially the one on the left. Hey! That's the guy that helped me find my house.

"Abidjan!" he calls again, waiting for a response, oblivious to me in Céline's glow.

"Abidjan!" Céline shouts after her laugh and giggles die down.

"Abidjan!" echoes in the street again.

"Abidjan!" she shouts joyously yet again. Should I say it, too? I am wrapped up in the happiness but stop myself, as it seems a special code of friendship. They pass us. Nothing else exchanges between them except for 'Abidjan!'

The Sage Femme works for the entire village, too, and trains Céline, but La Sage is Abé. Bogo is Dida. The teachers at the school are of different ethnicities as well. Mostly Abé or Agni. There is less animosity between ethnicities from the southern regions of Cote d'Ivoire and the Bèté than between those of the north and the Bèté.

"You have a lot of style," I compliment Céline again once the two men pass, and this causes her to put an additional beat to her step. She is silly at heart although constantly under pressure from hospital responsibilities, responsibilities that have life and death consequences. The hop-along is infectious. I, too, put a little spring in my step. I feel so normal around Céline, but it is really Céline making the effort to put both of us at ease. I am sorry she has to carry my big yellow ass around the village, cooking for me and taking care of me however she can. But, she never makes me feel bad about it. I need all the help I can get! I'm not used to nor am I strong enough to cook a meal from scratch the way Ivoiriens do. Real scratch. Not just because you went to the market and put the ingredients together yourself but because you grow the ingredients, pluck them, grind them, make the spice after drying it, chop the wood, make the fire, and damn near hold up the pot over the flame! That is a whole two years of training by itself and I am not here for that. Whenever I can, I find an excuse to give Céline money to show how much I appreciate her.

While manifesting a hum for her new happy foot dance song, Céline stumbles. She stumbles right as five little kids come walking from the other direction. It is Bri Bri's crew. In slow motion they watch along with us as the pot of rice that smells so good flies up in the air and falls flat on the soft, muting earth that absorbs the plop. Secret smiles hold at bay. They look from the ground to Céline. Céline looks from the ground to the sky and finally to me, shrugging a 'what are we gonna' do?' Then, she wobbles an 'oh well' from side to side with her head, bending over to pick up the pot so as not to spill any more rice out. She stands up and mourns the unsalvageable rest.

"Let's go," she calls, but man that's my portion soaking up the red dirt there. Hope I don't have to eat termites now to make up the meal deficit as the people in Zragbi sometimes do when food is scarce.

"Gyali!" yells Bri Bri, waving the other four kids dutifully behind her as she charges forward. Ha! I give her credit. Bri Bri is an original and easy pragmatic. She charges after flashing a look at Céline and me, purposefully not making eye contact for too long but long enough to get the green light. From her eyes I catch her thoughts with the little bird's smile on her face. Oh, the joy of stumbling across food. We smile at each other as Céline has already moved on and walked off. 'Come and eat!' is what she has just yelled to her little crew in Bèté. Céline's seasoned rice is great. I'd eat some dirty Céline-rice, too, except I don't have to . . .

The rice doesn't disperse anywhere but piles up perfectly in a mound on the ground. Only a thin layer of rice from the bottom of the pile is touching the ground. All five squat around the rice evenly distanced apart and grab at it as soon as Bri Bri begins and only take after each time Bri Bri takes.

After eating from what's left in the large pot, I am back up at my house. I am so sticky with sweat and red dirt. I need to wash my butt. I peer into my gigantic, plastic, blue water barrel and see the top of the waterway, way down in the barrel. A cool wind blows into my side window and grazes my right cheek as I come back up from putting half my body down into the barrel to cup the remaining water out into my bathing bucket. Rain!

I rush outside and trip onto the porch, focused on placing every bucket and basin I have right below the edge of the aluminum awning that juts out over my porch. My body is motionless except for the cool wind that moves through my blouse and dares to open my pagne wrap. No pumping today!

"Foooooo! Ssssshhhhhhhhaaaaaa!" The sky opens its mouth, blows its breath, then dowses Zragbi in a blurring, vertical stampede of rain. Rain all day never happens, but when rain visits it is enough for three New Jerseyan rainy days in a matter of an hour.

The water doesn't flood. It soaks deep down into the earth into every single empty space that permits travel. I stare out at the water flowing into my waterware now from inside my front window. No one is outside. People are no doubt in the fields taking shelter under a big banana tree, their homemade palm canopy, and kids all huddled together.

Beds do not waste time in calling you at times like these. No one will be coming to my door or peering into my window and the rain sounds drown out every other sound. Ooooom! Buddha has nothing on me. I space out and pass out.

"Pahdré!" croaks the voice. "Paaaahdrrrééé! Come outside!" Bri Bri summons. I roll out of the sunken spot my body wants to stay in, my right foot catches in the mosquito net, I shoot the net up over my head, and run into the kitchen with quick bare feet making sweeps across the smooth concrete. Through the window, what do I see? Butt naked!

Ummmh? Whaaaat? Hahahaaaaaa! A handful of kids have washcloths and one humungous piece of tan soap between them. They are showering and my porch is the perfect community shower because the rippled awning creates fifty natural showerheads, shooting down perfect streams of water from each recess in each ripple. They pause at my face trying to read what I must be thinking.

"Hahaaaa!" I can't hold it in anymore. They laugh, giggle hilariously with white smiles taking over their entire faces, and wiggle out in the cool rain, happy to tease me.

"Hahahaha! Paaahdré!" Bri Bri yells back, proceeding to clumsily wash her naked body in front of my window. They waste no rain as they yell and scream, splashing in the water. They share the biggest cube of soap ever to exist in our solar system. The soap is so big they need both hands and an elbow to pass it every time. Soap spreads all over their heads, all over their bodies, and into their blinking eyes. Shiny, black, brown, fit little bodies jump around—full bellies and flat ones. The curve in all their lower backs is just like mine, making even the flattest of bellies stick out a bit, no matter how straight an Ivoirien stands.

Bath time in the tub with my sister was playtime as well. We danced around in the tub shaking our little booties, triumphantly happy in our skin the same way Bri Bri, her brother Dowa, and all the other children before me do. I shake my head, smile, and turn my head to go the heck back onto sleep!

From the chasing, to the La Blanche name change revolution, to my acceptance of their naked, Black booties in front of my window getting soap in my water, the kids are a constant in my life. When I'm not home, there is always the sign of my screen door hanging wide open, having been released from the bent nail at the top of the door. The kids are my wake up call, my midday company, my alarm when I'm wasting my day away in bed, my afternoon respite, and my evening surprise.

Later, several kids knock at my door just after sunset. Some I know, some I do not recognize.

"Pahdré! Open the door! Open the door!" they all shout at once so I open it. Their eyes brighten as they watch the door miraculously open, stunned by this gesture in the same way they are when I give them a 25 CFA coin after they demand it. Hesitation lasts three seconds and after they glance at each other for confirmation, one brave, young boy creates a queue to enter.

"Pahdré? What do you do in here?" the loquacious boy asks as he takes reconnaissance of my bedroom. The light in my bedroom highlights the beautiful pink that covers every inch of my walls. He is the ambassador for the adults, no doubt—coming to ask what they are afraid to. The kids sit on my bedroom floor excited and ready for Superman to bust through my wall.

"Sometimes I write. Sometimes I read. I sleep. I use the computer. I eat. That's it."

"Where is your computer?" the boy asks never interrupting his eyes from racing around. He is eight. I point to the computer without turning it on or opening it. He nods his head satisfied, and I'm not sure he knows what a computer is or if he is just good at imitating whatever words come out of my mouth. I'm not about to show him the computer either. We'd be here all night. There is not much to look at, but the children are still somehow happily entertained by filling up my space.

Plenty of paper, markers, and pens, for whatever type of demonstration I might need to do in Zragbi, sit in the corner lonely. I have enough for each child. I unroll a huge piece of paper about three feet long and two feet wide over their hands and the kids move from beneath it as I lay it in the center of them. The five of them quickly gather back around its edges.

"Write something." I say handing each child a writing instrument.

"Like what?" the talkative eight-year-old inquires.

"Anything. Something nice. Use your imagination." The last word I take directly from English and add a French accent to it. Boy, I hope 'imagination' is a French word and that it's one frequently used in their French classes. The fabulous five seem to understand because they start doodling away. Some are big circle drawists. Some are actually creative and draw things that don't exist. Some draw familiar things, but all are quiet. Ha! Victory again!

I sit down in the corner visible to the front door and read. I leave the heavy wooden door wide open. I don't want anyone thinking I am in here doing anything other than getting kids to be creative. Curious ones come to my door.

"Bri Bri! Come help with dinner!" Bri Bri's older sister, Margot, charges in yelling after I open the door. "What are you doing?" she lifts her head up around the brightly lit, pink room.

"Drawing in Pahdré's house," Bri Bri responds matter of factly. The kids, man. I love them. Margot nudges Bri Bri again to get up. "I'm coming," Bri Bri protests calmly. Margot gives her one last you-better-be stare and leaves. I never see Margot at rest or play. I maybe see her exhausted and staring off into space, trying to catch semblance of a thought. After a few more doodles, Bri Bri gets up and takes one of her cronies with her.

"Pahdré. I have to go."

"Okay," I smile. Bri Bri smiles back with her dimples and goes crashing into the screen door, expecting it to open voluntarily. Maybe she has no lock on her own. Eventually they all leave, pulled by hunger pains and forgotten responsibilities at dinnertime. That was nice. That I can give them something that has nothing to do with money. That I can be in the group and not be at the center. But, then they return the next night. More than before. This time there are eleven. Do I have enough pens, pencils, and crayons? The eleven await their gigantic piece of paper and tools.

Their colors jump out at me. None are as light as I am, but there are many a coffee splashed with milk, color-complexioned child. Stark chocolate accepts the pink glow of my room as well. They range between coffee with a lot of cream to a bittersweet chocolate color and none of them share the same hue.

It is a perfect spectrum between the two extremities that exist herein. Their features cannot be predicted by skin color alone. Some have sharp features and others round. Tall, lanky girls fill the space while others come nowhere near my height. They share the crayons democratically. Any little squabbles are soon solved among themselves. Not speaking much Bèté, the only thing I can do is kick them out if things get out of hand, but things never do. They still talk to me in Bèté anyway. Bri Bri often translates what little she can for me.

The only child that says nothing is Apolline. I hear one of them say her name to get her attention for a crayon swap. She switches immediately without any expression on her face. That must be the daughter of the forever 'Apolline-ooooo'-calling mother across the yard from me who sweeps our courtyard smooth every morning before anyone else gets the chance. Apolline's mother is often calling her daughter's name out at dusk.

"What are they doing in there?" I hear Bri Bri's father, Didier, outside my door saying to someone else. I jump up to greet him. Tonight, I have two of his kids—Bri Bri and Louie. Louie drawing is quite a feat because no one can get him to concentrate on anything for more than ten seconds. He quietly draws away.

I open the door for Didier to come in, but he stays there to call his children. Two down and nine to go. Not like I'm counting. Not like I don't enjoy their company, but if this is to be every night, will the village start suspecting me of child brainwashing or something crazy like that? I won't teach anything about malaria or A.I.D.S. without their parents' consent. No burning of this witch at the stake.

Another hour passes. I haven't eaten yet so everyone's gonna' have to go home. Plus, we've gone through several sheets of paper and the crayons are turning into stubs. Everyone gets the hint except Apolline. Her head lifts up to watch whenever a child leaves, but she doesn't budge. She draws nothing distinct and is somewhere between a doodler and a big circle drawer. Whatever she is focused on, she is in her own world. At times, her eyes meet directly with mine. I just look back at her and after a few seconds she continues to draw.

The crowd comes for five days straight until all the paper runs out. I am sorry to have to tell them that they can't draw until I get more paper. Nevertheless, Apolline keeps coming.

"Bonsoir," I greet Apolline. Her eyes set on me as they would an inanimate object, but I open the door anyway. Apolline walks in and stands up against the wall, not too far from the door. "Ça va?" No answer again. Is she scared of me but still wants to be here? Don't get it. A few more seconds go by. Her eyes search outside the door, glance around the kitchen, and peer for a second at the bedroom out the corner of her right eye, then back at me and down at the floor.

"Do you want to draw?" Her empty stare does not quit. I go to grab paper from my diary. It is all I have left. This piece of paper will be one less day I dwell on. I pick up a bunch of bright-colored crayons on their last legs.

"Take it."

Apolline's eyes meet mine and then at what I have in my hands. She searches out the door with bright, open eyes then lies down on the kitchen floor to get to work. I'm not certain whether it is the motion of me thrusting paper toward her or the words 'take it' that make her understand. Maybe she's partially deaf.

Is she working on a brief? My, she has concentration. Her eyebrows pull together in thought. She does not look up at me once this time and definitely does not stop drawing. Maybe she is autistic and that's why she doesn't respond to anyone? There seems to be something just beyond the paper, very intricate and needing all of her attention, but I can't make heads or tails of it. Hmmm. Now, my eyebrows are pulling together. Whatever. I'm no doctor. I pick up my book and sit on the one-inch step that leads into my bedroom, always in view of a passerby.

"Pahdré! You said you didn't have any more paper!" The loquacious boy yells when he sees Apolline sprawled flat and drawing through the screen door.

"I found a little more," I unlatch the screen door. There goes another day in the diary that I will not complain about. He is already lying on the ground with chosen crayon in hand eagerly watching me tear out his page.

They draw on and on, and then the talkative one gets up to leave. Apolline maintains her drawing momentum. He tugs on her. She pulls back and double darts him square in the eyes with her own before continuing to draw. 'How dare you interrupt my Picasso masterpiece!' He is taken aback by her absolute glare and in a huff makes one last effort in Bèté to get her to come, but she doesn't look up. Resigned to walk out by himself, he is bothered by either having to leave alone or the fact that she is still drawing when he has to leave. I open the screen door latch and out into the night he goes. It is quite dark now so I flick on the kitchen light.

"Apolline? It's nighttime. You're not going home?" She stares at me with a tiny bit of expression as I seal my question with worry on my face. How much does she understand at four or five years old in any language? The only time a reaction comes from her is when I offer her the paper and crayons, which she can see, or when the boy tugs her, which she can feel. She is not like the other kids at all. Every one else her age bounces off walls.

Apolline sits up. She continues to plaster her eyes to mine and then out of nowhere puts everything away. She plucks each crayon and places them back in the case in perfect color ascension. Then, she pushes the paper, including that of the boy's who left his there, up against the wall and sits the crayon case on top of the two sheets. She stands up facing me so I stand up from the bedroom step as well. Apolline turns to walk toward the door.

Maybe she is autistic. I've heard of autistic kids who cannot or will not talk but are great with numbers and color coordination and who like to make perfect symmetrical order out of whatever lay in front of them. I hope she starts talking soon or else she might get pulled out of school soon after she starts. How do you say autism in French anyway, or more importantly, in Bèté?

Like clockwork, right before sunset Apolline knocks at my door to the point where I'm just a few pages away from needing a new diary. Apolline stays longer each time and eating before she shows up is a mad dash on my part.

"Apolline-ooo! Apolline-ooooooo!" Apolline's mother's voice breaks through the silence. My head shoots up and Apolline now watches me alert. "Apolline-oooooo!" her mom cries in strain. "Boom, boom, boom!" her mother's fists pound on the wobbling screen door. I spring to unlatch it and Apolline's Momma stands there as Apolline scrambles to her feet then stops right before the doorway when she sees who it is. Apolline's mother smiles down at her.

"What are you doing in . . ." she pauses thinking about what to call me as she looks at me for a moment " . . . in Pahdré's house?" Our heads drop back down to Apolline waiting for a response. If anyone can get Apolline to talk it should be her mother. Three, strong, long seconds roll by. Nothing. At least her mother is patient.

"She likes to come here and draw," I answer for Apolline. Her mother lifts her head up to me and then back down to her daughter.

"She likes to come here to hide! She is supposed to take her bath now." Ooooooh. Apolline simply switches back and forth at both of our images, two objects moving their mouths and sound possibly coming out.

"Apolline. Let's go."

But, she doesn't move. Don't look over at me. I'm not in on this scandal, Apolline. You betta' go with your Momma. Hopefully, you can read my mind Apolline. She continues to be hopeful, however, and tries to wait it out. No one can do anything except wish she gets the point with her Momma holding the screen door open on one side of the doorway and Pahdré, the quasi-stranger, on the other. A good twenty seconds go by at least! Oh my, Apolline! Is taking a bath really that bad?

"Apolline-o! Let's go!" Zero to 120 in five seconds, Momma's temper flares up. She tries to remain calm, but the two of us adults standing here not able to say much in the presence of a child turns us into co-conspirators against ourselves.

"Aaaaaaaaaah!" Apolline cries out as her mom throws the screen door back and steps in to grab her child with one hand. Wow! She has a voice! Apolline's arm no longer her own, she just stares at it grabbed up in her mother's hand as if it is possessed and she has no control over it. They hasten across the porch and are off toward the courtyards below. Gee, have I really taken over the courtyard shower? Why are they going all the way down there to bathe her when they live right across from me? I guess it is true, but I am too American to share with what my American self calls strangers but with what my new Ivoirien self knows to be community.

Kids aren't the only ones thrown down stairs. Teachers are thrown down stairs, too. Some teachers are visually scared of the kids— seven-, eight-, and nine-year-olds—we were wrecking havoc because we felt like we ourselves had been wrecked in ways we did not know how to deal with or because we were somehow at a disadvantage. If we weren't fighting, we were getting terrible grades and if we were doing well in school it was because we had a teacher who cared and who would give it to us straight before we started to mess up. Mrs. B was like that and I was so afraid of her that I made sure I did my homework right!

There were all different kinds of teachers—the Mrs. B's who essentially took care of you, the Mrs. C's who inspired you and then left you to your own devices, the Mrs. D's who would let kids walk all over them, and the Mrs. F's who lost it. One particular Mrs. F did not know what to do with her class. She always assumed everybody ought to be on the same page without having even taught anything yet. If you did not know something, rather than teach you what the answer was, Mrs. F got frustrated which frustrated us and, in turn, we lost motivation.

One particular day was just that—frustrating. One boy who I used to call Fonzy because he reminded me of the 'Muppet Babies' was always busy getting himself into a temper tantrum. Fonzy did not like Mrs. F because she always criticized him and then expected him to cooperate with her. Well, this day he most certainly would not. She told him to answer the question and when he did not know she began to berate him severely. I was frightened with my eyes fixed, expecting a spectacle as usual. Fonzy started to cry. It was so sad. I felt sorry for him and, of course, glad it was not me.

He cried until snot came out his nose and spit out the sides of his mouth. His shoulders sagged and his head bowed down. She grabbed at him once to make him stop, but he drooped himself onto the ground in protest. Mrs. F said, 'get up!' Over and over again she did this until finally she grabbed him up, lunging at him with so much scattered force that she scratched him. Well, by that point she finally figured out she had made a faux pas because she saw blood underneath her fingernail and stopped. She tried to continue on with the class, but didn't nobody care. We wanted reconciliation for Fonzy.

The next day, it was reconciliation he did get. I was standing atop the school steps waiting for the school bell to ring so that we could line up and head in. I saw the fury coming from across the street. Fonzy's mother was not having it, and you know she got up bright and early, missing work and all, to give a piece of her mind to the teacher that scratched up her little boy. Screaming 'Oh, no!' and 'Don't you ever let that happen again!' and 'We gon' see about this!' The mother so outraged in disgust, she did more harm to her boy than Mrs. F did—dragging him up the steps, scuffing his sneakers, and bruising his shins—his feet barely touched the ground with his mother yelling, 'Come on!' You know I wanted to look but just then the bell rang and Mrs. Shark Fin came out telling us to get in line. By the time I got in line, I was all the way at the end and mad about it because I was so anxious to get inside.

"What's going on?" I questioned Mrs. Fin, and don't you know that was the first time I heard the saying M.Y.O.B.—Mind Your Own Business.

Today is Saturday. I am sitting in Bogo's yard waiting for Céline to come back from an emergency pregnancy call. Every child in the village is on Bogo's porch this afternoon. Jijina is in and out of the house doing chores. Eliane is back and forth pumping water. Jijina semi-braids her hair and semi does chores. Seeing her walk about with one side of her hair still braided and the other side out with the comb sticking out from it, I could be in Cote d'Ivoire or America.

All these kids, is it vaccination day? No, it's not. This is a hotspot. They are hanging out. The weird thing, however, is that the kids are doing a lot of moving around and gesturing but aren't making any noise. On Bogo's porch, the circle of kids surrounds one tall, long-legged girl in the middle. She is twelve. She thumps her chest and flails her hands in the air. I hear several indistinguishable sounds come out of her mouth. Is this another Ivoirien language I'm not familiar with? The sounds are so patternless, cryptic, and poorly formed that it suddenly dawns on me that she's deaf. Are all of them deaf? I quickly scan the other children for similar behavior. None of them have it. They communicate with one another sporadically but generally, in the deaf girl's presence, all of them are in a new mode.

I do not detect sign language, but there is certainly a style of communication going on. More commotion and heavy gesturing builds up and it's not distinct or of any pattern. The deaf girl holds a lot of eye contact with one boy in particular. He is half her size but only a couple of years younger. How is he doing that? He's not deaf and he seems to understand everything she does and every stunted sound she makes. His rare green eyes are wide open to the tale, whatever it is, and his fierce upper lip stays that way while he communicates with her. He even gives a few grunts and awkward sounds of his own although he communicates normally with the other children.

It is heated. The circle grows bigger as the fight gets more intense. She steps into the middle of the imaginary circle and communicates her best then steps out. Then, the little boy steps in and he communicates more, through the soul in his eyes more than anything else. They continue this way, taking turns stepping in and out of the middle circle. Awkward sounds, quick and abrupt gestures, and stiff upper lips that only each other understand fill up the air. No touching or hitting, but a fight is on. When the deaf girl steps in again this time, she starts to dance and accompanies each movement with a beat from her own voice. The tone is off, but the off is on beat. The spirit of the whole spectacle is a sheer motivator for anyone to want to join and all the other kids unfamiliar with the gestural communication stand transfixed.

The competition between the two of them manifests joyously. I almost want to start in with my New Jersey's finest dance moves. She jumps back again and the boy jumps in yet again and this time crunks it. Body parts fly in outward motions that have no anticipatable purpose but to go to the beat. She adds her beat while he dances then back in the circle she goes to join him. He steps out then back in to join her. She steps out then back in to join him again, except this time she shuts—it—down! Everyone is now adding a syncopated beat to her own rhythmic, tone-deaf beat.

Tears nearly form in my eyes knowing that these two kids have created a language between them in spite of the girl's deafness. Part verbal, part gestural, and all soul. No one wins. It is a friendly competition and they throw their heads back in laughter at the end.

She reads lips and once I realize she is forming French words, I somewhat understand. I do not know, however, if her deafness is for the same reason as Margot's and Louie's. Céline tells me that some Bèté mothers use an herbal potion they make to cure babies when they are sick or to keep them from getting sick. They put it in their ears. Sometimes they overdo it but don't know this until it is too late. In the case of Louie and Margot, they are only partially deaf. This girl's deafness is absolute. I clap behind her, right by her ear, and she does not flinch.

"Paaauuuudrey." She knows my name. She follows me to the market. All of her words sound nasally and she uses her lips without using her tongue to enunciate.

"J'ai faim," she manages the words. I only hear vowels as I watch her lips and try to imagine the missing consonants. The gesture of her rubbing her tummy helps as well. I go to untie the knot in my pagne tucked in my waistline that keeps my change when several other kids passing by in the market see us.

"Pahdré! She steals! Don't give her any money!" I don't think so. She wouldn't make a good burglar. She'd alert the victims before she'd have a chance to steal anything, making noise and not knowing it.

"Don't say that!" I scold.

"Pahdré! It's true! Don't give her money! I've seen her steal before."

"Me too!" Another little kid chimes in. I fail to see what stealing has to do with whether I give her money to get something to eat. Maybe she steals because she is hungry.

"You lie!" One kid yells after lunging to slap her arm. Dang! I close my knot back after paying my fried fish, fried aloko plantains, and cassava achèké and bounce on back home. I leave them all there to duke it out. She, the oldest and tallest, allows herself to be slapped several times more, only defending herself verbally. The kids do not understand her, scrunching their faces whenever she speaks to defend herself.

Maybe, it is true that she steals. She isn't fighting back. Anyway, don't know, don't care. I'm hungry. Will figure it out later. I get as far as my front door when she catches up to me.

"Paaaauuuudrey!" She smiles the most convincing smile and I let her inside. I put down a mat on the floor in the kitchen. My intention is to sit down and try to speak to her in French since she reads lips, try to figure out whether she is a fibber or a stealer. But, she sits down, rolls her eyes around every inch of my house in view, and goes straight to sleep.

I eat my food while she naps. I feel a little guilty but more hungry than guilty. Sharing is the right thing to do, but making that a habit might have her parents come yelling at me the way Désiré did when I used to give her children bread. I'm sure her parents or caregivers give her something at home. Besides, no one is going to let anyone go hungry in a true village. When she wakes up, you would swear she had eight hours of sleep.

"Merci, Paaudrey." A 'thank you?' I wonder why. She pierces deep into my eyes to answer. 'Thank you for being my friend,' I read there in her smile and she leaves.

Somehow, allowing her to rest equals friendship. Equal to peace of mind or just peace considering how the other kids treat her. She is the village freak. Those kids taunt her as I am taunted with 'La Blanche.'

She is not even allowed to go to middle school. Who will marry her? Who will take advantage of her? She is isolated here in Zragbi with her parents who will not be around forever. There is a school for the deaf according to Céline but does not know where it is. Is it expensive? Maybe I can raise funds for her to go there. 'Her parents don't want that,' says Céline.

Two sachets of spicy, sweet ginger juice from earlier catch up to me. I unlock the bathroom door, pull up my pagne, and go to town standing straight up. Quite an accomplishment. I hear giggling by the door.

"Pahdré!" Jijina yells at me in her angry-at-Eliane voice. "Pahdré! What are you doing?! I see you, heh! I see you! Pahdré! Come pump water with us!" All this to pump water with them? I am relieved, however. They help keep my sense of humor. I am a kid to them as well since I have no kids of my own.

I help Jijina with the rest of their water, placing it on her head and next pumping with another basin while Eliane and Jijina alternate taking the basins I fill back to Bogo's house. Sometimes I walk the water back for one of them when my arms are tired from pumping. Not like carrying the water on top of my head is any easier. Eliane takes me through a short cut. Several teachers are on strike and are meeting to discuss their plan of action. I do not know when the strike started or when it will end, but they stop midspeech to greet me. Eliane keeps going.

"Bonjour, Madame!" I never have the opportunity to speak with the teachers either in school or at home so I am excited.

"Bonjour!" I quickly give the enthusiasm back. I keep walking with basin on head and return through here.

"Come and join us! Come talk to us!" one teacher encourages, all the while with a smile on his face. In fact, all of the teachers are smiling at me.

"How are you? We see you pumping water. You don't have a faucet?" A faucet? What faucet? "They are bringing water pipes to the village so we can all have water at our houses.

"I like the pump," I smile. They say nothing to this but continue smiling up at me seated in their circle. There is one empty chair and they direct me to it.

"My name is Antoine. Kouassi Antoine." The last name usually precedes the first. A lot of cultures, African or not, present their names this way.

"My name is Raven, but I have several other names," I want to get it out of anyone's system before they do. "Gomana, Toubabou Muso, La Blanche." They laugh before I finish. All names for 'White woman' in Bèté, Jula, and French, respectively.

"I'm also called Acua and Aishya Koné."

"Aishya Koné?! Aaaaaah!" one teacher belts out.

"Who calls you Acua?" Another teacher's interest is peaked.

"My friends in Grand Noyaré."

"Oh, you have friends in Grand Noyaré?" Antoine repeats with raised eyebrows. "That's nice . . . We always see you around . . . and we want to know what you are doing here? What do you do? You are from America?"

"Yes, I am American. I am a volunteer with Corps de la Paix," I say all in French.

"Oooooh, les Peace Corps," Antoine reaffirms in Franglish, mistakenly sounding the last 's' out. "What kind of volunteer are you?"

"I am a Health Volunteer. I am supposed to teach the villagers how to protect themselves from A.I.D.S. and malaria, but it is difficult to get them to trust me." Everyone gives a knowing look to Antoine at that last part and bows their heads down a little.

"Umph," produces one teacher. A forced cough departs from another.

"These are my principal objectives, but if someone in Zragbi has a project that they want to do, I can help with that also."

"How?" Antoine maintains his focus in spite of sideways looks around him.

"Find the funds to support the project."

"From where?"

"From the Peace Corps. From the U.S. Embassy. From friends in the United States. There are many sources."

"And, they just give it like that?"

"No, usually you must commit around thirty-five percent of the value of the project. It can be in money or in the supplies or the labor that you contribute to complete the project."

"Oh, really? Have you done a project yet?"

"No." Here I am in my water pumping clothes, looking like a lighter version of them, telling them I know where the money is. Yeah, right. They will not believe it. But, Antoine is persistent.

"When volunteers come to their site, they must first get used to their new environment and learn the languages. Then, they try to find someone who wants to do a project and work together to figure out how to get it done," I hope my French is working.

"Have you eaten Ivoirien food?" Another teacher changes the subject. What the hell else am I going to eat?

"Yes."

"Ooooooooooh! What do you like to eat?"

"I like futu banane with chicken and peanut sauce . . ." made by Céline.

"Chicken? Have you tried any margouillat?" Margouillat?! You mean the big ass lizard that crawled up my arm one time when I was closing my shutters? Is he serious? All of the teachers are staring at him, too.

"You don't like it?" he persists with the question, all heads toward me.

"Which part of the margouillat do you like the best?" Antoine asks with a smile to the tall, lanky teacher, legs outstretched in his chair.

"Oooooh, la tête rouge!"

"La tête rouge?" I speak in spite of myself.

"Hahahaha!" Everyone laughs. La tête rouge? La tête rouge? I know each word, but no visual fills my brain. What on earth is he talking about? Long tail. Hard, bumpy scales up along its back. Usually black and red. Red. Ooooh, the red head . . . is the best part, he thinks?! Joker!

"It's delicious!"

"Aaaaaaaah hah, hah, hah . . .!" Everyone laughs more.

"So, there are many other volunteers?" Antoine gets back on topic.

"Oh, yes. There are more than one hundred of us all over Cote d'Ivoire and also hundreds of volunteers in over ninety countries all over the world right now."

"Well, I want to talk to you because I have some ideas for projects." At this, several teachers excuse themselves. Others break out into conversation among themselves. Antoine, however, stays motivated. Above all, I have an immense sense of automatic trust between us. We have a natural rapport and unlike most he is willing to listen through my broken French. He can see that I am not just some American woman pumping water in Zragbi with the kids for fun.

Very few children are left at the pump by the time my conversation with Antoine finishes. My water barrel is near empty again. If Eliane or Jijina are off somewhere, I'm gonna' have to ask a random child to help me lift an unwieldy basin on top of my head, a request I avoid since I never know which child will be frightened at the sight of me and just not respond. I come upon Eliane sprawled out on her bedroom floor exhausted but still pushing herself to finish her schoolwork. Schoolwork while the teachers are on strike? She doesn't mess around. Jijina, however, is still full of energy and ready to pump. She lifts the nail over the screen door effortlessly with her long, pale brown arms every time we return from loading the basin.

"You don't have any homework to do?"

"No, I already did it before we started pumping." Right. I never see you in a book, girl.

After we finish pumping, she steps up into my room. There is nothing to do at my house, but I'm not going to send her away. She is restless and who knows what she will get into with Bogo rarely around and Céline with her own family responsibilities. No one ever knows where she is when she is gone. She surveys the kitchen after the bedroom.

"You have gas," she scrunches her lips up as she nods approvingly. She steps back into my room again. "Oh, you have a mosquitaire," she jokes in an overly Frenchy French accent. She touches the net to see how it feels and the lips scrunch up in approval again.

Jijina then plops down on the floor supporting her back up against the side of my bed and continues to roll her head around in every direction. I look around, too, and spot my A.I.D.S. kit. It has a wooden penis with condoms that Peace Corps Volunteers use for demonstrations. Why not? I hear Bogo sent her to Daloa to get an abortion once. So, someone's not telling her something. I pull out a condom and hold it up in front of her. Her face freezes at the square plastic for a moment and before she can respond in any way I begin.

"Do you know what this is?"

"Yes," she waits.

"Do you know how to use it?"

"Yes."

"Let me see," I drag out the wooden penis and hand it to her. She takes the condom without much hesitation and opens it with care.

Holding the condom in her right hand, Jijina looks at one side and then looks at another. I am so ready to say, 'if you put it on wrong the first time, you have to get rid of it because a man's pre-come can get on the wrong side before you flip it back over to the right side and you can get pregnant that way even if he hasn't come yet . . .' Blah, blah, blah. But, luckily she does the ingenious and I do not have to figure out how to say all of that in French.

Jijina blows on it! She blows on one side of the condom and it does not budge. She blows on the other side, the now obviously correct side, and it pops right out. Perfect way to find out the correct side from which to wear the condom without risking a wasted condom. I take note. This little girl who I am at least ten years older than is schooling me. She holds up her accomplishment and I laugh without forethought. She lets escape a small laugh bubble as well. Barely a teenager at twelve and she already knows how to protect herself. Good. I do not think I learned how to properly wear a condom until I was in college and that was while about to do it.

Rouazo could not have been worried too much about the price of condoms if he was doubling up and Jijina knows more than I did at her age. The problem quite possibly isn't availability or even awareness. The problem may simply be in understanding why it's necessary.

"Why do you wear a condom?"

"To not get pregnant."

"And, what else?"

"To not get sicknesses."

Should I ask her specifically about A.I.D.S.? I do not know how many people actually understand why it is I am here. A.I.D.S. is a taboo topic perhaps. If someone dies before their time in the Bèté world, voodoo is usually considered the culprit, not A.I.D.S. 'Sicknesses' is good enough if Jijina gets the basic point. I will stop here.

"You are very intelligent. Always use one. Where is Céline?" I wrap it up.

"I have not seen her."

We go out to the porch. It is too hot inside. I set out my mat and we chill, watching people go by, greeting this one and that one. Jijina does not say much. She asks me things she already knows like what country I am from and how old I am. I return similar basic questions that I already know about her. What is there to talk about? Life is in Zragbi only and everyone knows what everyone else is doing, save what may happen behind closed doors and even then.

Back to Bogo's we go where I greet a woman standing akimbo with her two-foot-tall child in nothing but diapers and puffy pigtails, both poised on the porch already facing us when we come up to the house. "Bonjour!" One sight of me, and Puff Tails torques her neck away to the right with mouth hanging open. Wait for it— the common gesture of a child getting ready to sound off. Her stomach draws in tight.

"Aaaaaaaaaaa!"

Jijina disappears quickly into the house. The mom picks her baby up to comfort her without a word to me. I force a quick smile. Céline pops out of the house, giving me a reason to rush off past mother and child to the appatam.

"That's Bogo's sister," Umh, I do recognize that mischievous resemblance.

"Really?" I say, but I don't actually give two plantains since the sister returns no 'bonjour.'

"I was sick," I change the subject.

"Are you okay now?"

"Yes." A lighter flare-up of malaria passed after sleep last night, but I can always do with a little attention. None here, however. If I am no longer sick, there is no issue. She is a nurse and everyone is always telling her when they are sick, when they have been sick, and if they think they might get sick.

"She doesn't like me," Céline's face sours.

"Who?"

"Mama de Grace." Mama of Grace? Who's Grace and who's her Momma?

"Bogo's sister," she breathes forth after a couple of seconds of angling her brows into a v-shape.

"She doesn't like me because she knows Bogo has a girlfriend and she thinks I am cheating with him. I've known Bogo longer than that woman." I knew it. Bogo can't get right. Wait a minute. So that means when I asked Céline what she would do if she found out Bogo had another woman, she knew then? She certainly has not taken his television yet.

"How you know Mama de Grace doesn't like you?"

"Because she said so and she doesn't talk to me. We could be in the same room and she says nothing at all. If I ask her something, she doesn't respond."

So, whatchyu' gon' do about it, Céline? Whoever had who first, Bogo ain't tellin' the truth to the both of you. "She thinks that I'm his Deuxième Bureau." Second bureau? . . . Oh. Second job or secondary job as opposed to main.

"She thinks that I am the second woman," she clarifies taking the time to look up at me and then back down again at the meal she prepares.

"Bogo was violent in the past." Céline, I hope this is adding to why you are about to say this is the last straw!

"I didn't want to be with him. So, I refused to talk to him. I didn't come up to his house anymore. I just stayed in my house. I didn't cook his meals or anything. He does stuff like this all the time." Stuff like cheat?

"So, he came down to my house and came in through the window one night while I was sleeping. He dragged me out of my own house with all of my family around and hit me on the head with a long piece of wood."

"Haaaay?" spurts from my mouth in disbelief. A rising 'haaaay' is one of the expressions I hear when something unbelievable is heard.

"Blood streamed down my face. Blood everywhere. He wouldn't leave me alone. I'm not the Deuxième Bureau. She is."

So, the proof in the pudding is the fact that he wanted you so badly, he came down to your house and tried to beat you unconscious with a piece of wood in front of your entire family? I cannot understand this. How can she not see that she is too good for this and could have beat his ass back worse than Tina Turner did to Ike?

Céline's foul mood will understandably last for a while or as long as Mama de Grace is in town. I eat another one of Céline's great meals and head back home. When I return, a young boy is there surrounded by several kids younger than him.

"Pahdré, Pahdré, Pahdré, Pahdré, Pahdré oooooooooooo! Pahdré, Pahdré, Pahdré, Pahdré, Pahdréeeeeeeeeeeee!" He starts and ends with a snort then a chuckle. He stands on one good, strong leg and drags the other, swinging it forward by using his steady, good leg. The fingers on both of his hands curl up together. One hand is always raised up, chest level, and the other down by his waist. He never has his hands relaxed down by his sides. He can't. His first few Pahdrés ring successively louder and the 'oooooo' part is a straight-out howl. His subsequent Pahdrés alternate high and low, with the final long Pahdré being very low. He greets me with a smile every time but in a voice so annoying that by the time I can recover he has already walked off or gotten into someone else's business before I can say 'hello' back.

"Ça va?" I attempt conversation with him whenever he is calm enough. Snort, snort is all I get back.

"Pahdré, give me some money," snort, snort. "Eeeee! Pahdré-ooooo-Pahdré!" This is the point at which I ignore him for want of how to respond. I cannot very well give him money like I do the other kids when he is acting all weird like this. So, I walk on toward my house again.

"Pahdré!" snort, snort. He follows behind me and I know his one leg is dragging. The other young kids, now sitting on Apolline's Momma's front porch across the yard from mine, start to yell at him. I no longer hear the leg hop behind me so I turn around. The talkative boy who likes to draw is here. He is a little shorter and younger than Snorter but very well spoken in any language and harangues him from the porch. Snorter hops over to the porch where all the other kids are, now actually making an effort to express himself in Bètè.

Through his struggle to form every other Bèté word, Snorter manages one obscure insult. He tries another to defend himself but can only stammer every word out. I have never seen him lose confidence this way before. If he wants to win a fight, he usually overpowers his opponents with nonsense noises until they have to walk away from aggravation. "A na na . . ." but he is interrupted by the loquacious, little badger. "A na na . . ." he starts again in Bèté. 'I said!' over and over again he repeats, until his eyes roll to the back of his head. His hands shoot up mouth-level shaking uncontrollably. His good leg shakes, too, and eventually gives way. He falls to the ground and writhes. His eyes roll all the way back until I cannot see anything but white. Saliva spills out the left side of his mouth and some flies up in the air as he flips over to the other side uncontrollably. His entire body shakes. He's having a seizure! His limited gestures, his lack of use of all of his limbs, the obvious tightness throughout his joints and particularly in his hands—he is an epileptic. A shadow of fear looms over me. He might hurt himself here like this. I rush over to hold him until the seizure passes.

"Noooooooooooo, Pahdré!" A passerby pulls me back. "Don't touch him! You can catch it!" Catch it? Catch what? Suddenly afraid, I pause crouched in midair. What does he have that is contagious and causes seizures? Is it some rare, Ivoirien disease? Maybe it's in his skin? He has a lot of scars all over his body. I am afraid but then again, no. Pah-dré! Think! The reason why he has scars all over and is disfigured is because people stand by like they are doing now and watch him seize. They do not understand his illness. He probably crashes into everything around him and gets severely injured in the process of not being able to control himself. That's why parts of his body are missing in different places! I look around him. Nothing is there that may harm him during his seizure. So, I decide not to hold him, but if he moves too close to anything I will make sure he does not hurt himself.

The Bèté know nothing about child disorders and major illnesses. It is a miracle anyone survives out here and then A.I.D.S. is creeping in on top of that?! Autism and epilepsy, these are diseases barely understood anywhere in the world. Snorter has to be fifteen. The hospital might not have been here when he was born. Bogo and the Sage Femme have not been here that long for sure and I do not normally see kids in the hospital unless they are coming for a vaccination. Only immediately life-threatening or obvious conditions can be treated.

I wake up the next morning refreshed. Was yesterday all a mefloquine dream? No, it was real. I have not taken mefloquine in a while now. And, I do remember connecting with a teacher and am possibly on the way to a first project. I bathe and shower, not hungry. I am so ready to get something started. Let's go!

"Kong, kong, kong!" A loud wrap shakes the door. It is Antoine, the teacher, as eager as I am this morning. I did not tell him where I live, but as with all else, this is a community and there are no secrets.

"Bonjour, Pahdré! Ça va? Are you busy?"

"No, no, no," I step outside.

"I came to talk about projects. Let's walk to the school." Teachers are still on strike, but there are a few students in each classroom, studying and using the chalkboards together.

"I am trying to think of a school project. What kind of projects can you help with?"

"We do scholarships for girls." W.I.D., Women in Development, is a source of funding for this through Peace Corps.

"We also do latrines. I hear the students sometimes use that unfinished, end classroom as a bathroom."

"That's unfortunate, but it's very dangerous to go to the bathroom in the woods. They might be bitten by a snake or something else may happen." What is the something else? "If they have latrines at the school, then it will certainly be safer for the children," he adds. We step into one classroom where there are five young middle school girls.

"These are the girls that always come to class and study. We want to make sure that they go to high school." I spot one girl who figures out complex equations in her head then writes down the answers.

"That's Sena. She is very smart, but her family is from Burkina Faso so she will have to pay to go to school." Tuition is free for Ivoiriens but books, clothes, lodging, and meals while all the girls are at high school in Daloa will cost money. It will be doubly expensive for Sena. She might have even been born in Cote d'Ivoire or here most of her life, but citizenship is not extended unless you have been here several generations.

"Girls often set their age back on their IDs when they have to take off a year or more to help their family. Sena is like that. She lives with her father. The mother and other siblings went back to Burkina Faso because life is too hard here. Sena helps around the house and with fieldwork. She is always busy and won't be able to go to high school unless she can get the money to pay for everything and tuition."

Time to get cracking. I should be able to submit my first proposal by this next quarter in September 2000. French and English versions are a requirement. I pack, ready to catch the next baidjan into Daloa to go straight to Abidjan to do latrine proposal research as well. I am persistent and somehow get to Abidjan and type up and submit my first SPA, Small Project Assistance, proposal for school latrines all in one day. I am back and forth to Daloa and Abidjan trying to accumulate information for several projects now.

October 2000 quickly shows up and Laurent Gbagbo is now President. Out with the old and in with the new. Robert Guéï was President of Cote d'Ivoire when us volunteers first arrived in Cote d'Ivoire back in 1999 by popular military coup d'état. But, as all things must go in a government that claims democracy, there are elections. I don't know who all was running, but there only seemed to be two main candidates. Of course Robert Guéï, as he wants to stay where he is and then Laurent Gbagbo.

Gbagbo has swag to say the least. Tall, charming, and Bèté, the predominant ethnicity in Cote d'Ivoire, the Bèté like him and want to make sure they will be represented. Whatever the ethnicity of the President, that is the ethnicity that gets the most attention. Antoine tells me that the reason why Ivoiriens know so much linguistically and culturally about the various Abé, Agni, Baoulé, and other southeastern ethnicities is because the old President Félix Houphouët-Boigny, who served from 1960 to 1993, invested so much money into their research ignoring most other ethnicities. President Boigny never visited the northern region of Cote d'Ivoire all those years because the people there were not of the ethnicities of his native region. He considered the northern region to be another country for which he had no responsibility. I have tried to research the Kru branch of languages to which Bèté belongs and come up with very little for the southwestern region.

After submitting my proposal and doing research on other projects, I hang out at the Abidjan Volunteer Hostel. Back from the Peace Corps office, I step out of the cab and onto the sidewalk. Out of the corners of both eyes, I see children approaching me. A girl walks toward me from my right and a boy walks toward me from my left. There is something so off and I cannot place my finger on it.

She is his height—four-foot-something. He is her age—ten or eleven. She is as dark as he is. They have similar features. Maybe they are from the same ethnicity. I do have sense enough to step out of the way and cross over the sidewalk to the tiny path leading to the door at the hostel, but the sight of these two keeps me from going inside.

He steps to the right and she does too. They pass each other as ships in the night, at eye level and both looking straight ahead. They do not acknowledge each other. They do not even acknowledge me. She has on clean pressed clothes because she has just come from school and wears a plastic, shiny, blue backpack. He on the other hand has not just come from school. He wears clothes that if moved a little to the left or right will fall off of his wiry, strong frame. All of his clothes are that brown and black color that says these have been his only clothes for years. Both have their heads up high and focus on getting wherever they are going. Not a side-glance or a blink. Not a 'how do you do' or a peep of any type of recognition as they pass. The moment is a slip in time. They walk in and out of each other's starkly different realms of existence. What kind of village is this Abidjan where kids walk the same paths and live on the same streets, but acknowledgement or even knowledge of one another is for some other universe? This is not Cote d'Ivoire. Abidjan is someone else's monster. When I say village here, I mean community.

Laurent Gbagbo is the new President to defeat Robert Guéï. But, of course, Guéï isn't having it and demands a re-election. Alassane Ouattara is tryyyyying to participate in the first and second election, but the dominant ethnicities in the lower half of the Ivoirien region say he is not really from Cote d'Ivoire—as he is from the northern region.

This chaos in Cote d'Ivoire must not be interpreted as culture. The current chaos comes from, not a desire to rule over one another but a refusal of ethnicities to be ruled over by any other ethnicity. Ivoirien tradition is to coexist and support each other's independence. Each village has its own chief, its own centralized government. Why would they want to be compartmentalized?

We cannot expect everyone to ascribe to the definition that we have for progress based only on our realm of experience. If you do not speak a people's language, live with them, and therefore understand their way of thinking, you cannot claim to understand or be able to appreciate their way of life. Can you say your life is better than life in Zragbi if you have never lived in Zragbi before, even through me telling you this story? You have to experience it yourself.

16 POLITICALLY INCORRECT

"Robert Guéï has attacked the Presidential Palace . . ."

"So, what does that mean?" I jump into the conversation already at hand that probably restarts every time another volunteer walks through the Abidjan Volunteer Hostel door. The storyteller is visibly exasperated.

"It means that we might get sent home. That's why they called us all down here."

"To the village?" Confused look on my face.

"No," Steve answers for the volunteer sprawled out on the couch. "Back to America." Back to New Jersey? That just doesn't sound like the spice of life to me right now.

Outside of the hostel and the hotel walls we stay at, we can see the army, presumably Gbagbo's army, taking a morning jog on Rue des Jardins. After a week, we are still in luxury but feeling quite stranded. Again, we gather to hear that we are not leaving the country. Oh, and did I forget to mention that March 2001 comes and goes and my SPA proposal is rejected a second time? I have to do a third submission?! Six months later and still no project!

"Gbagbo's regime has gotten rid of Guéï and Guéï has fled, but given that this is the second scare we've had in such a short period of time, we have been given the option to ET," an older third year volunteer relays.

"ET? What's that?"

"It means that you can Early Terminate. Early Terminate your service and even switch to another Peace Corps country if you want. And, it will not be reflected badly on your Peace Corps record. You still receive the same end-of-service benefits."

"Really?" One volunteer perks up.

"Really?" I am confused. Why are we given the option to leave or transfer to another country if it is also safe enough to stay for those who want to? Why aren't they sending us all home?

"Why should I stay? I have no reason to stay here. No reason," Denise shakes her head back and forth. "None."

Denise states 'none' so resolutely. Has she always felt this way? Her 'none' is so empty. Or, is she saying she feels no connection? No reason to be here as in why should she be here? For me, it's not a reason but a 'why not?' Why wouldn't you want to help someone you've just met if you can and they need you? Why do you have to perceive the connection for there to be one? There is a connection whether you realize it or not. No one survives alone. Everyone needs help from someone else at different points in their lives and why can't that someone be you?

June 2001 miraculously comes and the red-yellow mangoes ripen and hang from the trees a second time, full and fleshy. My third SPA submission is rejected yet again. If this ain't the Twilight Zone, I don't know what. Down in Abidjan, I complain to the Water and Sanitation Advisor, Pat, who happens to be in the office today when no one else is.

"Pat, this is the third time the SPA committee has rejected my latrine proposal. I don't understand it. The first time I said 'okay' to their recommended corrections and I made the changes they wrote down, but then I submitted it and they rejected that, too. Every time I submit, they give me something different to change."

"Let me see it," we walk back to her office. Pat looks at all of my submissions.

"What you have here is perfectly fine. Even what you had the second time was sufficient," and I exhale.

"Ugh, thank goodness."

"Raven, you know, the Small Project Assistance Committee is made up of your own volunteer peers. They don't know what they're doing."

That's so comforting to hear with a three-month wait in between submissions. No wonder some people think Peace Corps is a joke. I submitted the first proposal in September 2000. Now it's June 2001! Having to submit a fourth time? That would make it a whole year and then I'd be leaving about seven months from that time! If anyone is waiting to shit in a latrine in Zragbi, they're just gonna' have to wait.

"I can override this," and she does so right then and there. I pick up my money the next day! FINALLY! My first project!

"Antoine, we can start the latrine project!" I find Antoine once back in Zragbi and spurt out immediately.

"Really? You heard?" His eyes are bright.

"Yes. This week. I have the money so we can start."

"Oh, that's good."

"Scholarships for girls is next," I'm ready to do everything.

"He is not Ivoirien!" many non-Muslims cry. Based on undocumented rumors that Alassane Ouattara is not Ivoirien, although he can show Ivoirien citizenship, he gets the boot again from candidacy and the Muslim population is in absolute uproar that he is not allowed to participate in the re-elections after Robert Guëi's unsuccessful new coup. It's the last straw. For over twenty years,

Ouattara has been trying to become the President although he has always been allowed to hold various other positions in government. The Jula, the Senoufo, the Mossi, and on—they work the land and strengthen the Ivoirien economy, but when it's time to go to high school they often have to pay unlike the Bèté or Abé, for example. They are randomly pulled off of transport and harassed or asked to pay bribes along the route. Sena's family would be one of them.

"Sorry, Pahdré. There is not much to eat today. The Julas have shut down the market." Not a seller. Not a vegetable. Not an eater in sight. The market is deserted.

"Why?"

"The Julas and all of them that want Alassane Ouattara to be President are closing the market to prove a point." The Muslim ethnicities run the market, transportation, and just about everything else that keeps this country's economy going. They maintain the most diverse forms of agriculture and avriculture. Cocoa and coffee, they have that in the bag, too. The Bèté do some crops, but the Jula do more. Céline and I pass through the market and come upon a ruckus on the road. A man's arm is bleeding.

"What's going on?" Céline speaks in Bèté, walking up to the man and two others. The man who is hurt speaks a language that Céline does not understand so one of the other two men standing there translates.

"What happened?" I then ask Céline who frowns deeper every moment she hears more of the story.

"Two men out in the fields somewhere got into a fight. This man said another man cut his arm. With a machete. He said the man who did it is Bèté," she doesn't believe him.

If Bètés and other ethnicities are getting into it, I might have to rethink my option to ET. Was this a little fight or a real fight that represented underlying tensions between ethnicities? Are people simply mimicking the tension they hear is going on in Abidjan on the radio?

I stop at Bogo's house to peek my head in and greet him. It's the least I can do not liking him and all. As I look in, news comes on about Guëi, the now fled and whereabouts unknown, ex-

President. Beautiful images of a suburban town appear on screen.
"Where is that?" I ask Bogo anxiously.

"It's here," he says as he gets up scratching his flat ass and
heads toward the bathroom, passing me at the door.
Whaaaat? That is a full town of houses, row after row of them.
Almost mansion-sized houses with manicured lawns one after the
other, except there is no one there. Not a soul.

"Guëi built that. For his family," Bogo remembers to detail as
he steps into the latrine room. Family? Guëi's family is the size of a
small suburban town? How much did that cost and where did everyone go? I return to my house and my next-door neighbor, Didier
the Lifesaver, greets me with a bright smile except this time he
wants to talk.

"Pahdré, Ayooooo!"

"Ayooooo, Didier!"

"Ça va?"

"Oui, ça va."

"Pahdré?"

"Yes?"

"What are you going to do when you leave here?"

"I think I'm going to Japan."

"The Japanese are very strong. They have all the good technology and cars."

"How do you know that?"

"It's on the radio," he replies excitedly. "They are a very rich
country. Did you know that they invented contacts?"

"Really?"

"Yes. They make a lot of things. Almost as strong as the
Whites." Man, why does it always have to end with that? If these
Ivoiriens don't stop saying that . . .

"The reason why the Whites are strong, at least the ones in
America, is because of the slavery of Black people in the States,"
and then I just stare at him waiting for a reply. There comes none.
Standing there, he looks stronger than most men I know. He
changes the subject.

"Pahdré, I'm going to the fields. Do you want to come?"

"Oh, I'm going to the hospital today,"—a bold-faced lie. I have not been to the hospital in the morning in months. He walks back into his house, argues with Désiré, and leaves.

"Pahdré. My husband just said he is going to hit me . . ." Didier's words nerve her and her already prominent veins in her muscular neck stick out more. If Bogo can get away with beating Céline in her family's courtyard with the Chef down the way, then abuse may be common. Désiré is disappointed, resigned, and disgusted. Apolline's mother always manages to appear whenever Désiré and I are alone in the courtyard. Désiré mutters something in Bèté to Apolline's mother and both now have the same disgusted but helpless look off into the distance.

Apolline's Momma is absolutely beautiful and disfigured on the right side of her eye. Smooth brown skin is featured on every part of her face except for there. Melted skin droops slightly over her eye and all around the right side of it. It is darker than the rest of the skin on her face, an old burn. Where is her husband? She is the only woman here I know, besides me, who lives in a house by herself and it is not just a room walled off as a part of a bigger house like Désiré and I have but much bigger. A man shows up periodically, what seems like twice a year. Apolline's Momma is very happy for that day or two and then he is gone.

Three young girls pass by us in our contemplative states and I hear my name, Pahdré. After the girls pass I ask, "Why does everyone always talk about me?"

"Talk about you?"

"The girls that just passed said my name."

"They weren't talking about you," says Désiré as she laughs with Mama.

"No. It's true. I know I heard my name. Those three girls that passed."

"What three girls?" They laugh even harder now.

"Those three that just passed. They turned left there."

"Paaaah-dré!" She laughs. "One of those girls is named Pahdré also!"

"Oh."

"As a matter of fact, at least two Pahdré's live back over there. Your friend Céline, her name is Pahdré, too. Almost every woman in the village is named Pahdré. It's a very popular name." Hmph, so Céline gave me her name? How sweet. The two continue to talk in Bèté now seriously. Désiré turns toward me suddenly.

"Pahdré, let me tell you about the older volunteer."

"There was an older volunteer?"

"You didn't know that?"

"No. I thought I was the first." And, I really did although Désiré had mentioned this before. It never registered. I was told that I was the first Peace Corps Volunteer here. "Was she a Peace Corps Volunteer too?"

"Yes. Do you know that when she was here, no one could pass by here, on this path in between the corner of my house and yours?" My face surely shows how disturbing the comment is and Désiré continues. "She used to lie in the house nude with all the windows wide open, where all the children could see. She would lay on her bed and read books and things in the nude and never come out. We would complain. 'Why can't you put some clothes on,' we would say, but she would yell at us and tell us not to pass by her house if we didn't want to see her nude. Every morning she would get up to get a loaf of bread and wouldn't speak to anyone. She was even scared of us sometimes. Someone would come toward her and she would run the other way or even scream. She was a racist."

"Was she White?"

"Yes."

It makes sense and it doesn't. The whole reason people volunteer in the first place is to do good for someone else. There are some volunteers, however, even in my own incoming group, who speak in ways as if Africa only exists as it does on television sets and that they never really expected to see African people everywhere, all of the time. Allllll of the time. Maybe some volunteers think French colonizers did Ivoiriens the way Pilgrims did Native Americans—killing most of them and putting the rest on reservations.

"We couldn't understand why she would come here to live with us and act like that. It made us mad. So, one day we decided to get rid of her." Désiré pauses.

"Get rid of her?" I interrupt. What kind of story is this? Is she telling the truth? Apolline's Momma listens and asks a few of her own questions not knowing the entire story either.

"She was in the shower, in the latrine washing herself. Someone had a fake gun and threatened to shoot her, then ran away. We wanted to scare her. She was always scared of us anyway for no reason.

"She was supposed to come and help us, but she did nothing. She just lay around in her house naked." Of course, she ET-ed after the fake gun incident and Zragbi did not have a volunteer for years until me. I have been here over a year and I've never heard this story. What a terrible way to enter a village. Maybe Peace Corps thought I would be better received because I am not White?

"So, we thought you would be just like her."

"Why?"

"Because you are White, too," she responds without more than a millisecond's worth of eye contact.

"I am not White."

They can see that at least. Can't they? They can see I'm mixed although I wouldn't refer to myself in that way in the States. That's more so reserved for someone whose mixture is immediate, when one of the parents is actually White. My family has been mixed for at least seven generations and it is documented. I do not have a White identity, did not grow up with White people as a child, and White people in America would define me as Black as well.

A racist Peace Corps Volunteer? That's more shocking to hear than 'La Blanche.' It is hard when someone calls you a racist, especially when people forget to make the distinction between prejudiced and racist. It is one thing to yell 'La Blanche' at someone and quite another to yell that and then block them from living in your neighborhood for it or hang you from a tree. That's not happening to White people. That's happening to Black people, very often, and around the world. But, Désiré ignores my self-proclamation. Laughing at first, she rolls right over my words.

"We didn't like her. She came here and she looked down on us. She was afraid of us. She would only leave the house to get her little bread in the morning and Céline would even bring her a meal later in the day." She took a breath, stressed from simply telling the story.

"We didn't know . . . why she is here?" French words in that order and now in present tense, as she begins to fully relive the tale. "What is she doing here? Why does she come and all the while looks down on us? Pahdré, you know she jumps every time someone walks near her? Like we are going to do something to her. She is in our village, but she is scared."

The two of them exchange in Bèté some more, with Momma giving some surprise umh's and repugnated ah's while Désiré gives a wide-eyed look of can-you-believe-that right back to her.

"I am not like that. I am Black. So, why would I be afraid of you?"

"Pahdré, je vais aux champs. Tu viens?" Wait a minute. Hold up now. I'm not that Black. Being from strong stock may be why my West African ancestors made it across the Middle Passage to the United States in the first place, but it has certainly worn off in me. So, 'no' is the answer to that question—I will not be coming to the fields with you. And, you know this Désiré because your husband just asked me. I guess her question to my rhetorical one is rhetorical as well—if I am what I say I am then I would go.

"Oh, I have to go to the hospital," the same excuse I use with Didier earlier resurfaces.

I stay in the house burning up under the aluminum roof instead. But, what will make me different than the previous volunteer if I don't force myself to interact more? Having started some projects does not mean much if I do not socialize. Peace Corps is not about throwing money at people and not forging friendships.

It's time for me to start running again. Much farther than before Drunkard and I got into it over wearing shorts outside. Much farther than Grand Noyaré. I start early enough that most early-risers are just opening their eyes by the time I hit the road but late

enough that I do not run off down a side road without complete
view of where I step.

It does not take much to wake up as of late. All those years in
high school, university, and even middle school of late nights and
little sleep from studying or going to swim practice at 5 a.m. have
finally been paid up in this last year of sleeping and I am reset and
ready to go. I take advantage of my newfound early bird-ness.

The front door is heavy and creaks. I have to lift the entire door
up for the lock to fit into place before I can unlock it. There is a
loud clap sound each and every time after which it swings right
open because it is hanging off the hinges. Ssshhhhit. I slip through
the crack in the door and continue to hold it so that it does not
swing fully back while I unlatch the screen door after it. The heavy
door creaks again and my heart jumps. I hold it firmly. I lock both
and I am free. Aaaaaaaah.

The air is fresh. A gentle blue seeps through the dark sky. Here
I go. My college spandex from the lone year of track I enjoyed at
Georgetown still maintains. Red basketball shorts on top keep me
modest and a white T-shirt covers me for the first time in a while.

I am light on the red sand beyond the porch, aiming not to
leave footprints. Off to the quiet of a run—one thing I love. I step
onto the main dirt road which splits right at Bogo's house, and
here turn right. In a few hundred yards, the side road disappears
into the tall foliage that blocks the rest of the wide path from view.
I'll be hidden as soon as I get past this point . . . Yes! The courtyard along the side road, across from Bogo's house, is usually full of
life, movement, and children running adventurously but not now.

Fire smokes out from underneath an appatam right before the
foliage seals me onto the disappearing road. Someone is awake. My
heart beats fast. The blue sky lightens by the second. I time the
sunrise perfectly and if I miss waking up at the right time then I do
not go. Being seen, asked a question, judged, called out, said 'good
morning' to, called 'La Blanche,' or any of that—hell no. As far as
I know, nothing but the smoke has seen me.

A slow trot allows my eyes to adjust to the new darkness on the
path that the foliage creates. Ten seconds in and I am a cheetah, or

whichever animal that is with night vision. Yeh, definitely a chee-tah because I can't see shit! What in the world am I doing? Oh my God! I'm going to be attacked by a lion. I'm going to be attacked by a lion! After a few hundred yards more the road opens up wide. My heart breathes. Something yet formless in the dark scurries across in front of me. I do not worry about snakes because our encounters have never been negative. We've got a pact. Anything else that might be out here . . . let's just hope it does not bother me as I will not bother it. I figure any path without grass growing on it is a man-made path, tended to, walked on fairly regularly, and has someone or some village on the other end of it.

Huuu Haaaaa. Huuuuu Haaaaaaaaa. No air in the world like this. My capillaries open, my eyesight sharpens, my limbs loosen and swing. I hear nothing. No babies crying. No Bèté. No Jula. No French. No Senoufo. No Baoulé. No Mossi. The path widens more. The foliage shortens a little. Either that or the darkness shows the true length of the tall grass, as it appears shorter in the emerging light. Aaaaaah. A dip here and there but an adventure. The road moves straight ahead. I run enough to know how far I go just by watching the road. There are slight hills and the biggest hill has a fresh miniature pool of water waiting for me at the bottom that I cabriole over. When did it rain?

The road looks different every day. Something grows where it had not been before. Something disappears.

A man walks in my direction ahead one morning. He's fine, too. He starts to slow down but then picks up the pace. I give him a look to say 'I know what I'm doing here, what about you?' If I'm going to keep running early without anyone and no one knowing, then I've gotta' act like me and my bright red shorts belong. His machete drops from his shoulder, down to his side, and he keeps walking as he watches me pass. It's not a 'you look good girl' watch but a 'this is some weird shit, I'm about to cut you' watch.

I look like a ghost to him at 5 a.m. out here this way with no machete, no bag of seeds, no jug of water, and no one accompany-ing me. Hallucinations must just be someone trying to do something a little different at a strange hour. His morning walks will never be the same. Yes, you have just seen a ghost.

My days sitting inside the house are numbered. I have got to integrate into the village once and for all. Being at the hospital is out, however. I do not want people associating their deaths and the hospital with my conspicuous image. After that woman died in childbirth . . . Crazier connections have been made. That 'Claire doctor who just sits there and watches us, what's that all about?'

Hanging out at the market is a good thing, in-between staying in my house or going to the fields. I come across a group of young twenty-somethings only a little younger than me. We see each other all of the time and say hello. This time we stop to greet each other with the customary handshake. One by one, I shake everyone's right hand and they shake mine—using your left hand in Cote d'Ivoire is a no-no because that is said to be the hand people use to wipe themselves.

One of them is Albino with kinky-curly, blond hair and skin the same color as the White volunteers. He has a wide nose, big lips, and a strong stigmatism which forces him to wear glasses over his unpigmented, crossed, red eyes.

"Pahdré, this is Charles," I am introduced to the albino by another. I reach out to shake his hand and he reaches for mine.

"Oh, the two have finally met!" and "Oh, the two White people are together now!" are the words that come out of his friends' mouths the moment Charles and I clasp hands. I laugh and Charles forces a smile. Hmm, he seems more hurt by the comparison than I ever have. Ain't it a bitch, man? And, you were born here. Your ancestors were born here.

Many Ivoiriens tell me that the places where most albinos are found are in the villages where there is a lot of inbreeding due to isolation. The more isolated the group, the more necessary or maybe unavoidable it is to populate by means of that group alone.

There are quite a few albinos in Zragbi and they do not wander around aimlessly unless they have someplace to go. Pretty much what I do. Passing on the road by the hospital, I meet another albino named Forestain. Forestain is twenty-one. He is more red than white and people call him 'Ryokan' as Céline calls me once when Steve dies my hair on a whim of boredom at the Daloa House. Ryokans come from the mixture of one Albino parent with a non-Albino parent. He has reddish, faded-brown skin with red freckles all over his cheeks and dons wiry, dark red, kinky-curly hair. I salute him as I do anyone who at least gives me eye contact.

"Aiyooo, Forestain!" He greets back, passes me, then slows to match my pace on afterthought.

"Pahdré, I get called 'Le Blanc' all the time, but I'm used to it. It's what I am. They call me it every day to the point where it's my name now. They don't even call me Forestain. No one does. So, I decided that I should accept it and you should accept it, too." He jumps into the controversy on our first conversation.

I am trying to imagine this: allowing people to call me 'La Blanche' without flinching? No, that's not gonna' work. Number one, I have my own name and number two, Forestain and I shouldn't both be treated like aliens with the same status when I'm not even Ivoirien. Once or twice is occasionally funny. All the time is insulting. It's my cultural identity, be it redundant and insufficient in multilingual, multicultural, multi-everything Cote d'Ivoire. The least anyone can do is call you by your proper name.

"But, do you like it?" He looks into my eyes for the first time at this question. "Do you like it when they call you 'Le Blanc'?" He goes to respond but stops himself. The wheels slowly turn so I repeat myself.

"Do you like it when they call you 'Le Blanc'?"

"No," the pain Forestain struggles to deny feeling spills forth in one word.

"If you don't like it, don't let them call you that. What is your name?"

"Forestain," he asserts what I already know.

"Tell them that your name is Forestain, not 'Le Blanc.'"

No two fingerprints of the 7 billion people on the planet are alike. No two people and their sense of perception are either. Someone is always trying to lay claim to the right to define someone else based on their perception. Your perception is your own. That's it. Share it if you're strong enough to meet resistance, and don't expect everyone to agree with you. Even as repetitious as it gets, I explain why I call myself the way I do. After all, I am a Peace Corps Volunteer. This is part of why we are here, ambassadors to our country and responsible for how we are viewed.

"Thank you, Forestain," I have no idea what else to say to him. Good luck, man. I only have to deal with this shit for two years. You have your whole life!

Indeed, volunteering in Cote d'Ivoire gives new perspectives that compete with each other in more ways than I can handle at once. My extremely stressful difficulties with color are a good start, but they in and of themselves cannot reflect the real fight. Why am I here?

It is the non-visibles that I truly grapple with—the things that do not automatically open themselves up to understanding that I have to discover over time to truly know the people I meet. Humans share more than ninety-eight percent of their DNA with chimpanzees, but I do not need to know which chimp is on my family tree. It only takes a quick observation of the human species to see that using physical similarities as proof of relatedness is wholly illusionary. Skin color is only as valuable as its ability to protect individuals in their environments. My eyelashes don't curl up in the sun. My toenails don't fall off either. But, skin changes from second to second even. There could be some great environmental shift in 2020 and the next thing you know, we'll all be purple.

Not surprisingly, Céline is at the hospital. Instead of going in the regular way, I peek my head in through the window as the twins often do.

"Pahdré!" I smile at Céline's surprise. The Sage Femme turns around in her customary chair by the window and quickly smiles as well.

"Bonsoir, Raven," the Sage Femme greets. She along with Bogo and a few others are the only ones to call me by my real name. "Pahdré, go to Bogo's house. I made lunch for you." Whaaaaa. That's what I like to hear. I walk on over to Bogo's and find plenty of young people there in and around the house.

"Aiyooo, Pahdré," greets one young woman my age so I sit right down next to her. She continues watching TV and I, too, become absorbed in spite of not understanding all of what we watch. Then, Will Smith appears. It is a commercial of his famous show.

"Is he African-American?"

"I'm African-American, too," I kill two birds with one stone.

"No," she shakes her head, looks down at me sunken in the couch below her, and might as well have said, 'talk to the hand 'cause this Ivoirien don't understand.'

"I want to know about him. I want to know if he is African-American. Is he African-American?" How is she going to ask me, tell me, then ask me again?

"Yes . . ." She immediately nods her head in sudden understanding after I say yes. " . . . Like me," I continue, and she cringes. She already has her perception of what is what, or what she will allow to be. She knows what she wants to hear. She already has her own definition. There is no point. Plus, Céline is taking too long. Ain't no food over here. A gentleman comes up onto the porch as I leave the house.

"You're that Black American they're talking about," he stands transfixed. "I understand how they took you from here to be slaves. You're a Black American."

"Ain't no Black people in America and she ain't a Black American," interrupts one young girl sitting with her baby on her lap.

"Don't mind her. If it's not something that happened in the last fifty years, these people won't know about it. They themselves had to leave their land to come to Cote d'Ivoire from Liberia. Most people in Cote d'Ivoire come from someplace else so they don't have any history. I know about slavery. I know they took Africans over there."

"Slavery is over. Ain't no slaves over there anymore. I don't know why you keep talking about slavery. That happened a long time ago. They died on the ships didn't they?"

"No. That's the whole point. A lot of us didn't die on those ships. A lot of us made it. There are a lot of Black people in America," but she remains clueless. I'm talking to a teenager with a baby who might not even know how to read, as many of the women in Zragbi do not. Ivan Van Sertima even writes about Africans being in the Americas way before Christopher Columbus. Let's not go into whether or not Black people exist in the States. Maybe when she hears 'slavery is over' she thinks we got sent back home. No. Not all of us.

"Don't worry. They don't get it. I know you come from here."

"He is crazy," Céline appears out of nowhere, slipping these words out the side of her mouth as she passes by and heads toward the appatam. She does not care that he hears her.

Knowledge must be crazy. Like the older man that lives near my house and yells at me when Jijina helps me pump my water and carry it. 'We don't do child slavery here!' Never thought I would see the day when someone would be yelling that my way. He was in the navy for several years, visited all kinds of countries, and when he came back he was a Grand Type. But, as Céline puts it, villagers don't like when someone gets too big for their britches. They put voodoo on them. They make you turn crazy. Still, I question every appellation of 'crazy' I hear since I've heard this former navy officer say the names of Presidents in different countries and events that are very real. He has lots of information; the only thing is he speaks it out of context and not in complete sentences. But, I don't think he's crazy. I think he just gets overwhelmed with all he knows and no one around him to validate it. Maybe this is what would happen to me if I stayed here for a long time.

Only fifty years, he says? Surely Ivoirien knowledge of something so well known would not be so distorted if they had not been ravaged by colonialism and slavery themselves. What are the real characteristics of Ivoirien life, beliefs, and customs unaffected by the colonization of Cote d'Ivoire, just ended four decades before? Do many things still exist?

There are Muslims, Christians, and Animists here. Animists are people who see divinity in nature, animals, and spirits—homage to all life forces and living organisms. It is a belief that energy never dies but takes on a different shape. Simply put, it is the Law of Conservation of Energy. What other ideas have Ivoiriens lost or struggle to hold onto?

"That's butter," I hear someone say in French. Who said that? I turn around. It comes from the hospital so I walk back over, leaving the man and Céline to stare each other down no doubt. A few men are in fierce discussion.

"When you do it like that, then this happens . . ." Butter Man further explains.

Whatever 'this' is, I am trying to figure out if the 'that's butter' I hear before it is being used as a metaphor to describe the 'this' or if someone is really walking around with a stick of butter. I have never even seen butter the entire time in Cote d'Ivoire so it has got to be a metaphor. The French like butter. That's it.

The only complex carb I eat on a daily basis here is rice and if there is bread to be had, I'm not puttin' butter on it. I'm using it to sop up some sauce or wrapping it around a sandwich that I buy on Rue des Jardins in Abidjan. No. There ain't no real butter in this conversation. This man just used the age-old Black American expression I know, 'That's butter!' That's cool, that's fly, that's dope, or that's the shit!

I blink a few times at the thought of a possible transference of a cultural style of communication from one language to another, from whatever languages Black Americans spoke as Africans pre-slavery to the English we have now, a cultural way of using words that transcends or trumps language?! Well, this thought blows my mind. In spite of the fact that Blacks in America no longer know any words from any African language, outside of maybe the 'juke' in juke joint and unknowingly a few others, we have kept our mentality! Our way with words! Our phrases! Our sayings!

"Man, that's nothing!" intervenes Butter Man's opponent.

"Faut dormir!" Butter Man defends himself.

'Faut dormir?' . . . that means go to sleep. What?! Does lightening strike twice? The dissenter just got shut down with a 'go to sleep!' That's another popular Black American expression. Ours, however, is more specifically 'Don't sleep!'

In both instances, the sentiment is 'You're sleeping, fool! It's clearly this or that! You just can't see it because you've got your eyes closed . . .'

Well, Mr. Dissenter does not much like being told that he is unaware and ill-informed about what is cool and what isn't. "Don't tell me go to sleep!" he raises his voice. "You go to sleep! I know what I'm talking about!"

"You don't know what you're talking about! You need to just shut up!"

Now, I don't know what all is going on, but whatever it is, it has gotten serious. The next thing I know, Butter Man is yelling, "You don't know me! You don't even know me!"

I am in New Jersey with this. Several other men jump from the hospital onto the grass where the men are and hold both of them back from getting up in each other's faces. Céline runs out from the appatam to calm the whole thing down.

"That's my slave. Don't be mad at him. He's alright," Céline tells Mr. Dissenter and I nearly have a heart attack. I have not been listening closely enough all these months. One after another after another expression I know so well, here in full force right in Zragbi. 'That's my slave' means 'that's my nigga!' Colonialism in Cote d'Ivoire certainly required slaves to work.

The question however is, is this use as a positive of a negative word . . . is it a cultural communication phenomenon characteristic of only some groups or is this the natural result of any oppressed people—that they inevitably call themselves endearingly what their oppressors used to call them condescendingly? I don't see Jews walking around labeling their residential neighborhoods as 'the ghetto' even though this term first came from Jewish concentration camps. African-Americans use this term instead. How did this word used for Nazi concentration camps become synonymous with poor, Black living?

"Pahdré, I delivered a monster the other day," Céline switches the topic as the dispute is now over and the two are pals again.

"What?"

"A l'hôpital . . . The mother never came to the hospital during her entire pregnancy to be checked or vaccinated," she pulls out a picture that slices the air as she slowly passes it.

"Oh!" A whole half of the back of the head is gone. Just one eye sits in the front of what I assume is the head and this eye only has a partial opening. The other eye and its socket do not exist. The flesh is all different colors, bruised and blistered. I identify one full limb and . . . I have to stop looking at this.

"The husband gave her gonorrhea and it slowly chewed the baby up in the womb."

Damn. Wear a condom. This settles it for me. Why am I here? Not for this. This pic is why I have no business in the hospital . . . this is serious. I'm not trained for this. Sorry to say this, but I am no longer just a Health Volunteer.

"Céline, you don't have to cook for me. I'll go to the market," I say, moving on to lunch after gonorrhea.

17 CHOCOLATE

"Je veux voir . . ." These words float over the wall to me while taking a bath in my shower area in the open-roofed sunlight.

"No!" Didier yells. Who is that? One man wants to see something the other has and Didier screaming back? I keep washing myself, the sun warm on my skin. I can see mango trees in one direction and trees with a sticky, dark purple, apple-shaped fruit in my courtyard. The breeze blankets me sweetly.

"Je veux voir!" and then Bèté words break out loudly. I recognize this voice. This is the drunken guy that tried to hit me. What's he saying he wants to see? A scuffle ensues and something is scraping up the wall on the other side. What the hell? He wants to see . . . me!

"JE VEUX VOIR!"

"No!" Didier to the rescue again. A body scuffle ensues on the other side of the wall. Seeing me naked is not a big deal but purposefully trying to is. I grab my towel draped over the door just as things settle down. Drunkard is alive after all.

"That's not right. Leave her alone," Didier's voice perceptibly follows Drunkard as Drunkard's signature, thumping footsteps walk off.

"Bonjour Pahdré!" Didier reassures me with a morning greeting.

"Bonjour!"

Greeting each other while I am bathing becomes our ritual whenever Didier is around. Thank goodness for Didier. Can't even take a shower good. If it's not cigarettes then it's alcohol slowly stealing the minds of some Zragbi men. I finish up, put the wrap on, go inside, and reach down beside my bed to take out my little, red makeup mirror—the only mirror I have. It is so tiny I don't even remember the shape of my head anymore.

"Pahdré! We're going to the fields!" Désiré stops by and knocks, no doubt encouraged by her husband to ask me to join her.

"Me?" I confirm.

"Let's go!" She raises her voice half-heartedly as if she's been fighting this for a long time and is now giving in. No menace is involved or genuine vigor either.

"Okay!" pops out in English to her. I stuff the rest of my delicious, naturally green-skinned orange in my mouth and untuck my pagne to knot peanuts in the corner of the cloth.

But, it's not just Désiré and Didier going. Everyone in my courtyard comes out of nowhere to join us. Apolline's Momma is here. The Guéré woman who yells at me for not knowing how to sweep the courtyard is here. The wife of the man I slip a condom to is back. When we reach the fields more than twenty people are out under the tall trees with bright rays of light breaking through them, shining on every one of their faces.

"Pahdré!" Désiré amps me up. "Let's do cocoa today!" She sits down with the group of women and men using miniature machetes, lightly hacking at the cocoa shell to break it open. Cocoa fruit sits inside this shell that is the oblong shape of a papaya. This is chocolate in its purest form and Cote d'Ivoire has for decades been the number one cocoa producer. I'm pretty sure you've all had cocoa from Cote d'Ivoire by now.

A machete now magically in hand, I lightly tap away at the

firm, outer casing that holds the cocoa inside. Instead of brown, a very dark purple fills my eyes. But, this purple comes only after removing the stark, bright, absolutely white film of juicy, pulpy skin completely encasing the cocoa seeds inside.

"Pahdré" Désiré emits softly as I enter into their secret society. "We pull the cocoa out the shell and throw it over there."

'Over there' is a handmade bed of wide, green plantain leaves that suspends the cocoa in air to allow the white, juicy substance to drain off and the seeds to dry. Metal cups sit underneath to catch the juice. The seeds aren't really seeds. They are the shape of corn kernels except three times the size.

"Pahdré . . ." Désiré emits more softly this time. "Taste the cocoa." Am I supposed to suck it or bite it? I pluck a big fat piece dripping with white juice and lightly lick it first. Mmmmmmmm. Tastes more sweet and tangy than candy. The taste is as fresh as it looks. I bite into the large seed next. Yuck! Bitter!

The third time I don't even hear so much as a whisper—Désiré taps me and looks around at the others, which makes me look around, too. Everyone is giving everyone else the eye. Am I about to be presented a golden chalice? While tapping open the cocoa in her hand next to me, Désiré nods to the bed of cocoa.

"Take some of that juice," she says.

So, I grab the fullest metal container and sip. Everyone smiles. A few seconds pass and it only takes that long for me to realize what I am sipping on is pure cocoa alcohol, already fermented from being outside or inside the shell, the same way palm wine ferments inside palm trees.

"Wow!" I yell out in English. Every single smile explodes into laughter. Grand Momma, my house rear neighbor, falls off her stool and catches herself by holding on to someone's shoulder. Another woman throws her head back howling and bumps into her husband behind her. No kids are around at all. I should have known something is up.

"C'est doux!" I love it! This is by far the best alcohol I have ever tasted in my life. It tastes like juice and doesn't slap you like alcohol, waiting until it reaches your stomach to do its magic. "This is so good. I could drink a whole lot of this!"

"Pahdré!" Désiré's loud, deep voice returns and she laughs with gorgeous teeth.

"No, Pahdré," Grand Mama interrupts the laughter. "I don't drink that." The energy from her eyes says that cocoa juice is the devil. Temptation and fear show themselves simultaneously in her eyes and as great as this juice tastes, I understand. You could drink a whole lot of it just enjoying the taste and suddenly be dead drunk.

Getting palm wine, on the other hand, is more complex. The arduous and complicated process of getting the wine from a palm tree involves digging a hole at the base of the tree, sticking hollow bamboo in the hole, and firing the bamboo up until all of the rich, white, sweet, frothy goodness is forced to pour out from the pressure built while heating the wine inside of the tree. Sometimes, it is a little sour if it does not come from deep in the tree. Three sips of cocoa wine are enough for me. It goes straight to my head.

"Kee, kee, kee, kee, kee, cra, cra, cra, cra, cra!" Sitting on the bedroom floor worn out after straggling home tipsy, the sound is unidentifiable. Where is this noise coming from? Ugh, I'll just ignore it. I walk toward the door, go to unlock the screen, and it echoes again, "Kee, kee, kee! Cra, cra, cra!" I spin around slowly. My feet push forward unwillingly across the kitchen floor back toward the bedroom. I peek in before stepping up. Nothing. High up into the ceiling corners of the bedroom my eyes travel. I haven't seen any of those ants in a while and they don't make that noise as far as I know.

Maybe, it's just one of those noises, you know? The noises you ignore. Like the kids outside crying when they aren't hurt or all of the noises to be heard out in the fields. Time to bathe. Enough already.

"Cra, cra, cra, cra, cra!!" I crouch down and scan the room in fear. The late notion occurs to check underneath the bed. Miniature off-yellow piles of wood stack up in different spots.

"Kee, cra, cra, keeeee!" Still see nothing. Hmmmm. It's in the bed. Oh, boy. Being cheap has caught up to me. I have wood bugs.

18 COMPLETELY IVOIRIEN

An Ivoirien-tailored, dark pink and brown two-piece with rich Ivoirien tie-dye print and matching top and bottom lay neatly in my trunk. I never put it on, but today I wear it into Daloa on a whim on my way to Abidjan. The top has sleeves that puff-wrap around my shoulders with a white trim that lines the pink ruffles which dip down around my chest from shoulder to shoulder. The skirt is long, fitted, and zips up nicely. Not trying to catch anyone. It's all about the AOL Peace Packs Computer Project for the schoolteachers in Zragbi today, but I want to blend into the crowd of other well-dressed Ivoirien women traveling to Abidjan.

Céline always says, "When you go into town you have to look good. Why you always wearing those same clothes?"

What will be shouted at me this time? Will it be a 'Hey, White woman with that crazy brown and pink dress on! Your dress is too tight! Your sandals don't match!' It's true. The sandals do not match. Luckily, Ivoirien ladies are always practical in this sense but my dress is tight, right, and out of sight.

Same checkpoint again. The same mean Gendarme I know so well. The same demand of my identity card. However, this time he does not say a word to me, hardly looks my way. He quickly scans everyone's identity card and waves the bus through. Maybe, he is not feeling well today.

A woman gets on and sits down next to me and after several minutes of nervousness whereby she stares at me and looks away whenever I look up, asks me point blank without greeting, "Are you a merchant?"

"No," I smile. She smiles back but stays confused.

Another woman boards the van and says something to me in Guéré. I am familiar with the sound of the language enough to know that it's Guéré, but I definitely cannot say anything back. When I do not respond fast enough she passes me her little boy. Okay. So, now I have a two-year-old on my lap. Is he mine? She puts up her luggage and then takes the child back and sits down— smiling and saying in Guéré what must be 'thank you.'

The pleasant ride stays pleasant throughout both Gendarme stops and in picking people up along the road to Daloa. People keep offering me some of their food and I do the same. Some talk to me, too—to tell me they are tired or that it is too hot today. It is the usual but a little more familiar than what I have grown accustomed to while in Cote d'Ivoire.

Once we arrive in Daloa, I wait for the entire van to clear out before I get off. I like to sit in the back to stay the least noticed, number one, and number two, for no one to think that I am getting special front seat treatment as I often do.

"Are you a merchant?" A young man asks me as I weave through people to my famous yogurt.

"No." He smiles at this as well with a confused face.

Once in Abidjan, I catch a taxi easily and the driver says little. He does not look me up and down. I state my destination and we are off. Well, not quite. Getting outside of the gare in Abidjan and through all of the other taxi, bus, walker, bicycle, and small-time vendor traffic is a five-minute ordeal for at least one hundred yards. The cab window is the first to receive my attention for air.

A young boy suddenly appears alongside my cab. He is quiet for a few moments and then starts up in French. "Where are you going? You going to Daloa?" I just came from Daloa, poo poo head. I simply glance at him for a moment then back at the line of cars sitting in front of us.

"I know the way. Get out here. I will take you," he insists.

I say nothing to this again, so he says the same thing in Jula and I just barely manage to figure this out. The French that turns into Jula turns into two more languages before he scratches his head to think of what else he has left in his language repertoire that might fit. He switches from one language to another, holding his head to the side in thought after each one, taking a stab at it and waiting for me to respond.

"Aaaag ooo wa moo waaaaaaaa!" he yells a weird barrage of noises next after thinking I cannot respond to any of the languages he speaks, taps the window with the back of his hand, and dashes off. For sure I know this means, 'I don't know WHAT you speak! Maybe I can speak alien language to you and it will work then!' The driver and I stare at each other and burst out laughing at the young man's comic bewilderment. By miracle, the maze of traffic splits like a parted scalp and we take off.

One hundred and eighty degrees to sudden acceptance. All this time I have been assuming it is just one thing. The pleasant bus ride lacking the usual, unpleasant stares. The questions of me being a merchant. The young man's effort to go through every Ivoirien language he can think of as if I have to be able to speak one of them. How much does my treatment here have to do with skin color? How much more does it truly have to do with how I present myself? The way you carry yourself, the way you present yourself, and language is more important than color. Everyone thinks I'm Ivoirien now. Hot damn!

'It's all about you, isn't it?' one of my favorite volunteers nagged me with this jab at least twice during our three-month training. She would say this in her southern drawl, hips cocked to the side, and an annoyed but jocular look. While I resent the fact that Barbara never allowed me the space to complain about how I feel in my skin here and how I am treated, I see now that everyone will have a critical eye on them for all manner of reasons. Some reasons you won't believe can exist. Like, 'oh, you wake up too early.' Or, 'I don't like the way you wear your beanie. It's bugging me.'

Now, in this Ivoirien outfit, I have the opportunity to see that what Ivoiriens saw in me originally was merely a projection of their situation, their environment, and of how they perceived someone— looking how I looked before— could possibly fit in their world. It is not about how I think I should fit in their world based on my experiences. Ivoiriens are not familiar with my experiences. So, unless I am willing to break it down to every single Ivoirien I meet, I cannot expect too much. I can only smile, be polite, and hope that gets me far enough to receive the gift of even a modicum of open dialogue and discussion before judgment.

It's not all about me. It's about the Ivoiriens and what they go through. That is what I am here for. They didn't come to America. I came to Cote d'Ivoire. When I subtract myself from the equation, no matter how desperately they try to shove me into it, I am able to respond to situations at their core. I'm not always going to be able to bandage my temporarily hurt feelings. Sometimes, I just take it.

In the cab, in the front seat, on my way to the Abidjan Hostel, I see Black men everywhere. As a Black American woman, it is hard for me to separate the Ivoirien man from the Black American man anywhere. Invariably, what I know from my own experience and what I have seen in my lifetime is that both are just trying to compete, survive, and get ahead from the most innate source of motivation possible—family.

I see the markets and the store fronts and the rush of commerce everywhere and the more I see, the more I hope that Ivoiriens are not doomed to inherit all of these empty, rundown mansions that were stranded by rich, old French men in the same way the Fords and other automobile giants abandoned their mansions in downtown Detroit during the riots of the 1950s and 1960s.

Narrow alleyways, fake storefronts in front of real store fronts, garbage with their commerce, female circumcision to prostitution, police that take advantage of prostitutes and threaten taxi drivers for less than a five-dollar bribe. Small table markets competing with supermarkets, barefoot boys selling tissue packets for 100 CFA on sandy suburban commercial streets, and libraries without books. Business clothes worn with Ivoirien sandals, homeless people playing at the lottery box on Rue des Jardins, and the existence of villages with free cell phones but no electricity or running water.

I'm in Abidjan also to check on the U.S. Embassy project submission I made for a women's healthcare NGO idea. It is motivated by one entrepreneurial woman who aims to finance the NGO with a cassava grinder, business project. I meet a doctor, a real doctor (not a Bogo), while in Daloa and he asks me to do a project, so I say why not? Why can't I do projects outside of my site? If they've got the time, I'll find the resources. But, since September 11th, getting funding for anything from any government entity has been taking particularly long, so, for example, funding that is to go to organizations like the Peace Corps around the world has now been redirected to the war effort in Afghanistan to buy weapons and such. I'm doing my best to find money for projects where I can.

No one notices me in my fancy two-piece as I walk through the Abidjan streets. I can be the observer instead of the observed for once. I walk from the Volunteer Hostel to the Peace Corps main office in an Ivoirien, Blaxploitation movie daydream. A turkey husband and wife perched more than two hundred feet up in the air on a telephone pole interrupt the scene. No, not jive turkeys. Real ones. Bats fly around chasing each other in a nearby papaya tree.

"There are a lot of little things like that here in Africa," an Ivoirien man seeing me pauses on the side of the street to explain. You consider that little? I wonder what you consider big?

"What are they?" I face him for a split second to confirm, so transfixed that I only need to know from which direction his voice comes. I've never seen a turkey before. How many other things have I missed from being the center of attention, always being wondered about and never having the space to show wonder myself?

"Those are turkeys."

Ooooh, turkeys. Man, I love eating turkey. Didn't think I was eating something as big and regal as that. The turkey couple is massive. The tail of the male bird hangs down so low and long that you see the tail way before you realize what it is attached to.

I feel present. I feel in the now and aware. Didn't I pass a tailor shop on the way here? I am going to have more of these outfits made. Very nice ones that resemble the ones I see Ivoirien ladies wear and even have them made with the additional pagne that women wrap over the first skirt just in case they need to carry their baby, someone else's baby, or something else period. I like this melting into the background stuff quite a bit. I want to appear as a real Ivoirien woman. So, I turn around and make an order. Then, I skip back toward the Peace Corps office not far from where the turkeys still remain perched.

"Hey Christine! Haven't seen you in a while. How's your village?"

"Girl, it is what it is. I'm getting tired of eating monkeys everyday."

"What?! Who's eating monkeys? They eat monkeys in your village?"

"Yeah. I'm not too happy about it, but my village is out in the serious middle of nowhere. It takes me hours to get into town. We don't have a lot of food in our village. That's what they eat. So, I have to. You know?" No . . . I don't. No volunteer tells me anything like that, not before or hereafter. She is very sad about it. That's a lot of monkeys around for it to be the common, daily cuisine. Some volunteers certainly have it worse than I do.

"What are you doing here in the office? What are all these papers?" Papers are scattered everywhere around her computer. "You must be doing a major project. What they wanna' do? Open up a monkey restaurant?! Ha, ha, ha!" Only a sour face greets my bad joke.

"I'm applying for school. I've got to get this done today before I go back to my village site." The after Peace Corps is always a huge question. What do you do after an experience like this?

"Well, it's early and I have to look up AOL Peace Packs project info. I'll be here with you."

"You might want to go ask the Director's secretary for copies of recent AOL proposals that were accepted so that you know what to do."

The AOL project is simple enough. The most important thing is to communicate the need. It has to be authentic. I have to give those people at AOL a raw sense of the school conditions on top of what is required in the application. Hmmm, what if I have Antoine include a French version of the proposal in his handwriting? It will emphasize the fact that the teachers in Zragbi are using paper for everything, which hampers their efficiency as well as contributes to the recycling problem, which they aren't yet fully aware they have.

I am in Abidjan doing project paperwork for a couple of days. I check in at the U.S. Embassy but no word about my submission. On the way down here, I wear traditional Ivoirien dress. On the way back, I test out some jeans and see if I am hallucinating or if people really are highlighting my appearance over my skin color.

I get up early and board the Abidjan bus without hassle. Slipping out of town without a glitch is always the plan no matter what I'm wearing, but on the way out of Abidjan the Gendarmerie has up a checkpoint they have never used before.

"Identity card!" The Gendarme stomps up the stairs onto the bus. He isn't checking every hand that raises a card into the air. He's checking faces and if their faces say something, he checks their cards.

"Where is your identity card?" he examines a man who responds to him in Senoufo. The man has traditional scars made on his cheeks during childhood, in practice by only a few ethnicities here, to protect him from evil spirits. One scar sits in the middle of each cheek and neither one are working for him today.

The Gendarme rolls his eyes and stares straight at nothing at the back of the bus while making a continual gesture for the Senoufo to get off. What is the Gendarme going to do to him? The Senoufo carries his things in a cloth knotted together in the middle and grabs his things from overhead, moving slowly while keeping his gaze lowered to the Gendarme in a pleading way. Not once does the Gendarme meet his gaze. After the poor man squeezes past him, the Gendarme moves ahead. He gets tired of checking cards and starts to turn around right before reaching the back where I am. God I love the back.

"Carte d'identité?" he spots me out of the corner of his eye and whirls back around. Shit. He doesn't ask me as roughly as he does the Senoufo, but he asks. I provide it right away. Am I in a Hatha yoga class? The others around me in the back go from fear to sighs of relief when he turns to leave, and then deep inhalations of fear and exhales of relief again upon realizing he comes back only for me.

"Do you have a passport?" He wants to see that, too? He checks it then gives it back to me and keeps my identity card. He examines me up and down while standing straight.

"Get off." Get off? Get off for good? I do not hesitate, but I do want to know what's going on. I have been here for two years now, only a few months left, been card-checked not very often, and no one has ever made me get off the bus. I go to grab my things.

"Leave it," he commands softly then heads off the bus. I follow him. Are they gonna' leave me here? Good thing I don't have anything under the bus, but all I have is my passport. The Gendarme has the identity card.

"Stand over there."

I stand next to the unfortunate Senoufo man and now unfortunate me. We stand and we stand. The Gendarme disappears. Five minutes go by. Ten minutes go by. My fear turns to confusion. Then, anger. Young men walk by and stare at me but dare not say anything. I must have anger steam coming off my face. Fifteen minutes. My legs are tired. The sun has no shame and the dry, red earth floats up all around us as I become restless, trudging the earth with my feet.

Twenty minutes. I feel weak. A boy walks by with a styrofoam ice cream box. I want some yaourt so badly, but all my money is on the bus. The young boy spots my gaze and stands there right in front of me, only a few feet away but not saying anything or looking into my eyes. He stares at my feet. He knows I want some, but he doesn't know I have no money on me.

Am I coming to Abidjan or leaving? I almost forget how I ended up out here. This spot right here is now more a part of me than anything before it. Keep your mind alert Raven. What is my list of things to do for projects again? Aw, fuck, my bag is on the bus. All my papers and proposals and plans for the next couple of months are up there.

Thirty minutes. The Gendarme is nowhere in sight and the bus now sits turned off. No one looks out of the window out of respect I suppose. People are out and about in the city.

"Come," the Gendarme's voice lifts my head and the Senoufo follows. I am allowed on the bus, but the bus pulls off without the Senoufo. Dust swirls up around him from the bus taking off and all he can do is watch it leave. He gets smaller and smaller as we pick up speed. Where is he trying to get to? Who is he going to see? Does he have anyone to stay with in Abidjan? Does he have any money to take another bus? He damn sure isn't getting a refund.

Is this racism? No. They are both Black. Ethnicism? Languagism? Maybe if the Senoufo had responded in French? Or, is it just some male ego bullshit? Soon the images of the city are forced out of my mind by the impending green. Trees. Air. There is certainly more oxygen up here. I breathe deeper. Feel safer. But, my identity card is still in my hand. There is a mark on the plastic that encases it from me holding it so tight. I finally put it back in my bag hours later and right before realizing that Daloa's two Gendarme stops are up next. The first one goes fine.

"You look like a bald white man. Where is your hair?" This insult comes at the second stop while a man of arms compares my identity card photo to my reality. I keep it as short as a man would. It hurts to be picked on so much, but he has a gun and is staring at me.

"Leave her alone," an older Ivoirien man in hat and glasses murmurs in French still staring straight ahead with a blank look on his face. The interjection is grandfatherly and it gives me courage. The Gendarme, left boot on the floor of the car and right boot on the ground, leans in to look at the older man to his left two rows back from me. He continues his staring at me thereafter and I continue staring in the direction of his boots.

Do I look like a different person altogether? No. He has seen me before. Today's clothes are either throwing him off or he is making a point.

"In America, when a Black person calls another Black person White, we fight," I finally pick up the courage to respond through the silence in the van to his hurtful comment. Can't believe I just said that. The Gendarme shows a flash of anger in his eyes. He stares down at the picture to steady himself. I'm shaking, but something makes me finally stare him back in his face, albeit lowered head. His own smile breaks him. As he hands me the card back, he laughs and adds one final note.

"White man."

Once we arrive in town, I booty-sprint walk from the NTT gare to the street and jump in a green cab to the Daloa House. Getting home to Zragbi means watching the road to my village go by, crossing the two Gendarme checkpoints, getting out at the Daloa NTT gare, waiting at the Zragbi gare until the baidjan fills up, going back through the same two checkpoints, and riding down the road to Zragbi.

"Straight, please." It's only a short twenty-minute walk from the Zragbi gare to the Daloa House, but I need to take these jeans off ASAP. These damn things are gonna' get a sista' kilt up in here!

I automatically reach up for the seatbelt in the front seat. I don't think I've ever seen an Ivoirien wear one, but I always do sitting in the front—especially when the cab has a crack in the windshield on the passenger side of the seat as this one does. Dang, this seatbelt is the hardest seatbelt to reach. I reach farther and farther back until I have to turn around and look for it. There's no . . . damn . . . seatbelt. Not even a seatbelt holder. Am I supposed to use my invisible one and hope it keeps me from flying through the very visible windshield?

Hmmmm . . . I guess I have just answered my own question. The invisible seatbelt—it's a metaphor for everyday Ivoirien life. You have to protect yourself but don't know how and there is nothing there to give you a sense of safety except your hope that God won't decide to take you out today. People are protected by hope. They have to be. How else would anyone in Cote d'Ivoire get through this miserable experience of death and disease happening all around them on a daily basis? Now, I understand why it is so easy for people to get overly wrapped up in religion when they have nothing else, how missionaries could come sell so many Ivoiriens their versions of hope while snatching resources from underneath them and exploiting them, or why religion has been so strong in Black as well as White, poor, American communities.

Time to get back into character. I scoot-jump out the cab and run inside the Daloa House, change, and get back in the same cab to the Zragbi gare. I take it down a different road this time because the driver says it's better. There are near no people on this road and the cab driver goes faster but not too fast. This is no Abidjan.

"Heeey!" I hear as the driver reaches one road's end. I look to my left just in time to see one of my Zragbi drivers whiz by, throw excited arms out the window, and baidjan come to a screeching halt throwing everyone forward while still happily looking at me. My invisible seatbelt is working today. The baidjan is not even full. It's just the driver, a couple of his apprentis, and two passengers. We breeze through checkpoints. This pink and brown dress has gotta' be magic.

I clean out the cockroaches laying upside down in their death greeting when I open up the door to my house. Christian Franc steps on my porch from the side as I open the windows to let in the light. I'm still in my brown and dark pink Ivoirien smashup.

"Oh, Pahdré! It's been a long time. How have you been?"

"Good. And, you?" He smiles without an answer. Guess not.

"The Chief wants to talk to you."

"The Chief wants to talk to me?" Am I in trouble? Are they going to start making me pay my electricity bill? My hand is still on the window stick.

"Yes. Come on," he pulls me away.

"Sit here," he goes inside the Chief's house after we arrive below, disappearing for only a few seconds. He comes back out with two chairs and the Chief follows. Greetings are exchanged. Franc acts as the Bètè interpreter.

"Le Chef wants to know if you will marry him." Psh! I look at the Chief, whose eyes are never not red from drinking palm wine, whose few teeth permit sight of his tonsils whenever he speaks, whose belly sags down from age, food, and now fieldwork-less days.

"Ha, ha, ha!" I laugh out loud, but no one laughs with me. I only have a moment to fix my affront. I swallow my laughter. Quickly scanning both of them and around me, strangely enough I see that not only is no one laughing, but no one else is here. Come on Chief, you've gotta' be kidding. But, when I meet Le Chef's eyes he meets mine momentarily before looking at Franc and staring at the ground. I still have a few months here and projects to do. What is the most politically correct way to say 'hell no'?

"I'm going back to America."

"She is going back to America," no interpretation is needed, of course. The Chef understands that much at least, but Franc does his duty quickly, interpreting into Bètè all I say in French, not able to hide from me the flash of smirk on his face. 'Good save,' I read in his eyes. He is merely doing as told by his elder and knows the ridiculousness of it.

Does this have anything to do with the latrine project? Now, that I am starting to keep good on my word, the Bètè might think 'well maybe she does have some money and maybe we should treat her like a rich foreigner now. And, well, she is Black after all, right? We watch the Fresh Prince of Bel-Air. She's just like Will Smith! Let's marry her!'

"I can't because I have to go back to America after two years in Zragbi." Francois quickly interprets again and we all get up to leave in our separate directions.

19 MAMMARY GLANDS

There is an old lady breastfeeding on the bus back to Daloa. She boards at the NTT gare in Abidjan. From my seat, I can see the wear in her leathery skin that is a brown gridiron of millions of tiny squares, cracked into existence from the sun on her arms, as she hoists her valuables in the luggage space above the seat right in front of me. Her head is wrapped in a scarf that is tattered because she has probably used it for carrying tubs of water and anything that arms cannot alone. The skin on her face shows at least seventy-five years. Her drooping skin flows down her body to a mysterious lump on her side sticking out from underneath her armpit.

Is that a child slung onto her back, wrapped around her side, suckling on her foot-long, deflated breast that folds back neatly up into the child's mouth? The infant is an infant. A baby. It is a newborn less than a year old that is young enough to not be making more than cries and nonsense words. Now quiet in the mystical magicalness that is the elderly woman's left boob, I'm baffled. No one else is with them. Is this her child? Or, is she taking care of the child in place of a mother who cannot?

Large, old, dilapidating, side street signs of food formula sit up high in the air on billboards along the major roads on the way out of Abidjan and in other major Ivoirien cities as well. Food formula was the rave at one point, but these faded advertisements lack years of refreshment. Not too long ago, French companies promoted formula as the absolute necessity for Ivoirien babies, using the increasing A.I.D.S. mortality rate due to mother-to-infant infections during breastfeeding as a plausible reason for why formula is better. So with that, the most important thing that was helping Ivoirien babies to survive in their already variable environments took a backseat to formula. Mothers were weaning their babies at as young as three and four months old.

But, then as soon as French companies got women used to using formula, they jacked the prices up. Why would France apply supply and demand theory to Ivoiriens as if poor people could miraculously find more money just because companies had cemented a need?

No one could afford the price hike and many babies suddenly died from not having formula because it was no longer affordable and also from not being able to return to their mothers' breasts that had long since dried up after weaning. A wave of sickness among young infants who could not fight off the many diseases swept through the country. They could no longer get their mother's antibodies to help build up their immune systems.

'All of the babies died," Désiré lay emphasis on 'all' in telling the story to me.

Eighty percent of the people who die from malaria are under age five because that's how long it takes to build up the immune system to malaria. You can imagine that combined with the wave of children dying without their mother's antibodies—at least a quarter of an entire age group of infants that should be alive today are dead. French formula companies were forced to shut down in shame and from protest of the great human calamity their business model created.

Breasts are my world. They are everywhere when my comprehension is nowhere. My visual is so important to understand the real sentiment of any situation when I cannot understand whatever language an Ivoirien happens to be speaking in. Understanding body language such as grimaces, smiles, eye shifts and rolls, hand movements, stiff body twists, or no movement at all are all I need to understand what is truly being communicated to me. Likewise, when I see breasts I see mothers, which in turn makes me think of responsibility, which then gives me respect for these women no matter what they say to me.

"Pahdré! Aiyooo!" Désiré yells at me as I get back in from Daloa, getting up from her prostrate, reckless abandon in utter fatigue with one eye still closed. She pushes herself up and smiles. One woman barely glances my way. They are all so tired. Not two, not four, but six bare breasts sit on my porch as I approach my house. At last, my neighbors are comfortable enough with me to do what they normally do. Pagnes wrapped around their waists and breasts free in the sun. It is liberating to see, but the day I start doing that, it is definitely time to go back to America.

"Pahdré, Aiyo," the second woman says with tired enthusiasm but sincerely.

"Pahdré, where are you coming from?" the third woman asks, facing me with a smile and sincere interest. The underlying theme for me, however, is their breasts literally underneath the pleasant conversation. It's not that I don't expect this, but it never happened with me here before. What else are they waiting to show me? I waited and hoped for so long to be invited to the fields with the women in my courtyard or any courtyard. I waited so long to be invited to dinner at any place besides Céline's. I waited to go out on the night walks around Zragbi with other women to their impromptu, community counseling sessions in spite of them happening completely in the Bètè language.

After getting my hair cut in town, I get back to the village same day. I get off of the van at the market as usual and spot Céline sitting on the one big log where people taking the vans into town usually sit and wait.

"Céline? Are you going to Daloa?"

"No," she lifts up a three-foot wide, wooden, round-rimmed net.

I am supposed to know what this is, I guess. "I'm going fishing. I'm waiting for everyone here. You comin'?" she finally explains to my clueless face.

"Yes," I look around just as another van on its way to Daloa pulls up. With my back still to the van, I hear the doors fling wide open hard. The force of it turns me completely around. The apprenti is thrown aside before he can even get the chance to open the door for the passenger.

It's a woman. She is an older woman of my own mother's age, in her sixties. Half bodybuilder, half cross-country runner—I know this because she has no clothes on except for some long-john, cotton, short briefs that resemble the undergarments I see women in Victorian movies wear. No shirt. No shoes. Nothing else except the headscarf she has also slept in.

She jumps out of the baidjan van in a fury screaming with her hands up in the air and takes off through the market. And, let me tell you, the dust immediately flies up in the air several feet and I have never, I repeat never, seen anyone run that fast in my life.

"She has come for a funeral. One of her relatives died in Zragbi. She comes from a village beyond us there." Céline points to the west, away from the main road. "She is a relative. When she heard of the death, she jumped on the next van comin'."

The dust from the woman's speed turns the market that lie behind us into a blur as she takes off down toward my house's quartier area. Céline stands up and yells at the first two young men she sees.

"Go get her before she hurts herself!" Céline smacks her teeth then quickly sits back down while the two young men take off after the older woman to catch her. Their takeoff speed far underperforms the take off of the grieving woman.

"Céline, I have never seen anything like that in my life."

"You'll see a lot more than that at the funeral," she laughs, staring out ahead of her. The part that I always, fortunately, somehow miss. The part where the body is said to rise up out of the casket and walk to the house of the person who killed him or her . . . . Céline also tells me that in the Bèté world, some believe that if you die and you are not of dying age then it's because someone killed you and only someone who is related to you has the power to do so. How can you teach A.I.D.S. to people who believe in that? A team with a Zragbi-tailored approach is needed—not just me.

Precipitously out of the dust walk some twenty women, children, and teenage boys with all manner of nets for fishing. None of the nets are the traditional ones to which I am accustomed.

"Pahdré! Let's go!" all twenty-plus yell at me without stopping on their way toward the road down which the van with the grieving woman recently came. I am tired and just when I am about to ask how much farther, we stop not too far from the market. It is the little path that connects the farthest edge of the market to the fields, near the Zragbi woodshop. The path has a small stream of water to my left and a miniature pond to my right. We stand near the water's edge, staring down at the murky body of water.

"Pahdré?" Céline asks quietly. "Are you going to get in?" All twenty-plus people now stare at me, waiting for me to respond. Was this a part of some plan all along? Are they not going to enter the water unless I go first? I look at the water and the water looks back up at me because I cannot see myself in it.

"Okay," and with that I wade in the water as if a million times before. As soon as I do, everyone else enters along with me, springing to life. All have their nets out and each is busy springing forward in gallops trying to walk through the water and get their fishing spot away from the others.

"Pahdré!" Céline yells my name in her normal fashion now. "Take that end." I take one side of the wooden hoola-hoop-shaped net and together we plunge it down into the water. I am used to a rod with string at the end of it and bait. This is different. There is no bait. The idea is that the fish can't see where they are going and will eventually swim into the net at which point . . .

"Pahdré!" Céline interrupts my thoughts suddenly. "Lift!" She has felt something touch the net before I can realize I should lift. Up in the air we hoist it but nothing. Water flies everywhere in our faces and hair and Céline shakes her head to keep the water from hers. We are waist deep. Well, Céline is chest deep. I'm much taller.

"Oh! My hair is going to get wet!" Céline has a straight perm. It reminds me of Black women back home protecting their perms from anything wet. But, at least she is in the water. Gotta' eat!

Others lift up here and there and all around us. Little kids up to their necks in the water but who know how to swim, have smaller nets. Older women Céline's age have their own triangular-shaped nets or nets of other unique shapes.

"Oooooh!" one teenaged girl yells. She lifts up her net and not one but two fish the size of my hands wriggle around in her net. "There are two!" she yells and her little cousins from the water's edge jump up and down in jubilee. That's enough for their tiny, chiseled stomachs perhaps.

"Pahdré!" Céline's voice breaks the air around me again. "Lift!" I lift again a little more quickly, but the fish I feel in the net gets away by the time the net is clear out of the water.

"Oh!" Céline next yells a third time and looks down in the water and around to the back of her.

"What happened? Another fish?"

"No," she replied. "That was a snake."

"A snake?"

People are jumping up and down catching fish, big and small. Everyone is going to eat tonight! I don't want to spoil it. I assume they fish here often so I'll suck it up. If Céline hasn't gotten out of the water after feeling a snake go by her, then neither will I. Besides, how dangerous can water snakes be?

"Pahdré . . ." and before she can say anything this fourth time I lift so fast and hard that I snatch the net right out of Céline's hand. "Pahdré! Deucement!" Deucement!? We aren't catching anything. This is not the time to be 'gentle.' Either we are going to get it or we aren't and we aren't getting anything.

"Oh!" A fish rushes right by me and flicks my leg with its tail. Huge! I swing around, ignoring Céline completely and try to catch it. As I lift it up in the air, I can feel it in the net. Céline sees me struggling and lunges over, but it's too late. It got away. Ugh! But, then I feel something. It is tube-shaped except firmly soft and squishy here in the water underneath my feet. It is a snake and not

the snake that Céline just felt. There is bound to be many. Step
lively!

"Céline!" I yell over the splashes of water as a young girl dives
between us with her net sensing a ripple in the water. "Over here is
better I think" finding an excuse to move away from my snake.
"AAAAAAh! Oh! Oh! Oooooooh! Look!" Céline and I whirl
around yet again in another direction where just one woman has
been standing for the longest. Her reddish-brown muscular neck
straining is the first thing recognizable. Her teeth bare. Sweat and
water whips around on her glistening forehead as she, not the fish,
gets thrashed about trying to wrestle it from jumping out of her
net. She yanks her humungous net up once and we all see it. Her
net is even larger than Céline's, but it barely contains the fish
which flips, flaps, slaps, writhes, and jerks all around her. It slaps
her in the chest, the chin, and her arms with its thick, long tail.
This fish is well over two and a half feet long, wider than the net
and bent up inside of it trying to flick and flit its way out. Or, trying to breathe!

The woman will not let go. The harder the fish tugs, the more
she beams with pride and strength, her head up in the air smiling
from ear to ear with her eyes tightly closed. Her head is high in
utter pride of capturing a fish so huge, holding it for so long, and
she keeps it to her bosom as if a trophy. It is no longer just something to eat. The fish has transformed into a miracle that she is so
fortunate to receive and she is ever so transparently grateful. That
a woman can be so exquisitely beautiful, supremely strong, and
unequivocally happy all at once is a lesson. This is the kind of
woman I want to be. Strong and beautiful is what a real woman
must be.

The fish is so big and strong, in fact, that two young teenaged
boys fly from out of nowhere, slide-dive into the water, and grab
the fish out of her hands to drag it onto land where they then have
to wrestle with it some more to get a firm grip on it and carry it
off. This woman is surely stronger than the two of them as she does
not struggle nearly as much. She rises up out of the water and
leaves.

After the miracle passes, I feel Céline standing arm-to-arm right next to me, having forgotten where we all are, lost in the glow of the woman's catch. When I finally look down at Céline, she jokes in her usual fashion.

"That was our fish." This time, however, she holds back the starting-from-tongue-and-finishing-at-pouty-lip smack that wants to come out, too. We walk back to Bogo's house and she delves into preparing I know not what as we haven't caught anything. I'm sure food will somehow appear before us as it always does. All of the people around my quartier shared the cobra last time. That woman's big fish has gotta' be next.

What a shame for all of this beauty to be ravaged by A.I.D.S., my secondary assignment coming back to me again. All Peace Corps Volunteers in African countries have A.I.D.S. awareness as either a primary or secondary assignment.

"Do you ever teach people about A.I.D.S. here in Zragbi or at the hospital?"

Céline doesn't look up but continues to make her concoction of fishless soup for a late lunch. Just then, Bogo walks through and my unanswered question is deferred to him.

"We should teach people about A.I.D.S. in the village." But, he barely slows his stride at this.

"Can we give them tests?" I chime in. No answer. The dust kicks up behind him and suddenly he swirls around just before entering the house.

"Is the Sage Femme at the hospital?"

"Yeah, but what about tests? You should take one. I'm itching."

Well, shit. That is several leaps beyond persuasive. Get right to the point why don't you? It is, however, a bit confusing that Céline is automatically confusing A.I.D.S. with other venereal diseases that cause itching.

A.I.D.S. is something too obscure even in a more A.I.D.S.-informed environment. It is something that manifests itself with symptoms of regular diseases already prevalent in the environment. One can't really draw a picture of it. There are no set symptoms. It attacks your immune system and whatever your biological weakness is, according to your environment, is what will manifest—diarrhea from well water, pneumonia, and whatever else among the common afflictions here in Cote d'Ivoire.

I doubt Zragbians will go for a whole description of acquired immune deficiency syndrome—or that A.I.D.S. breaks down your natural immune response to whatever is in your environment. The Bèté believe in sorcery for goodness sakes. 'It itches,' as Céline has just proclaimed is a more basic and believable way to get people to at least listen.

A.I.D.S. and other STDs often occur together, so teaching them to avoid something more tangible will kill two birds with one stone. Something is better than nothing. I am not going to presume to be able to cure the A.I.D.S. epidemic in Cote d'Ivoire, or any other A.I.D.S.-stricken country around the world for that matter, in one fell swoop of two years or the few months left that I have here. The little impact I can make, I will make, and if it helps at least one person then it helps a lot. That is why when Jijina says condoms are for avoiding sicknesses, this is good enough for me so long as in her mind that is enough to get her to use them.

Bogo is making Céline itch down there? Umh. Is that why he is always walking around like a man whose penis is falling off? He always holds his legs tight together like a child needing to go to the bathroom. Bogo is the healthcare giver of Zragbi and he himself is no model of health. But then, too, I have to feel sorry for him the way he screws up his face at being reminded of his mother. It makes me think he had no model of a strong woman through which he could learn to treat women better.

The book HIV & AIDS in Africa: Beyond Epidemiology shows that "[s]elf-efficacy (or the degree to which a person feels that she/he has control over important aspects of his or her life) is an important determinant of health-related behavior." Maybe Bogo's childhood was terrible. People who are traumatized or mistreated certainly have difficulty in doing more than being careless with themselves and other people.

20

CÉLINE 1, JIJINA 0

"You make dinner?" Bogo's voice startles me as he walks up to the house from the direction of the hospital out of the darkness, stepping up onto his porch steps. Céline doesn't respond, continuing about checking for her things in and outside of the house, not wanting to leave anything at all behind.

"Céline?" He whips around as she steps down off the porch right past him, picks up a stool, and then walks back into the house to get something else. "I said . . ." and then mid-sentence decides on other words, "Where are you going?" He starts to see that something is wrong. He follows her into the house. I am tempted to leave and run for help. Jijina and Eliane just stand there outside by the porch darting glances at each other.

Facing the front door from up against the side wall of the bathroom, I can see Céline brush past Bogo again as he tries to ask again where she is going to no avail. Finally, he gets the hint.

"Tantie?" Jijina calls out to Céline from blindness to what is going on. Céline is indeed the most consistent caregiver that she has ever had. Bogo is never around unless he has to be for major hospital days and even then he makes himself scarce.

Bogo grabs at Céline as she passes him the next time. She pulls loose without a word. She is not a weak one. Finally, she speaks up as he more firmly grabs at her arm a second time.

"Let me go. I'm leaving," she sputters out as she struggles to free herself. He pulls her back toward the bedroom and her feet glide across the floor in her sandals.

"Let me go," she repeats, and struggles without screaming the words. Jijina's eyes widen. Jijina always seems to be the strongest, telling little Eliane what to do, but it is Eliane who is calm in this moment. The two of them have no dinner to eat. No orders to fetch water. No money to make sure they have lunch the next day, as who knows if Bogo will take off in the morning to Daloa to see the new mother of his child, forgetting the two before they can catch him on his way out.

Just as I am about to lose my mind in frozen powerlessness, one of Céline's plastic shining shoes sliding across the floor catches, lifts up, and allows her stop her forced glide. She grabs onto the back of the couch and turns herself around, wrenching her right arm out of Bogo's inadequate grasp. He tries, but her futu-pounding arms, firewood-balancing neck, and pump-lifting shoulders are all at task to free her loose!

She quickly dashes out of the house, onto the porch, and down to the earth that she spins back around in, letting the dust rise up pronouncedly around her black, shiny sandals.

"Where are you going?" This question from Bogo immediately flashes the characters of Mister and Celie in The Color Purple movie before my mind. I am ready for him to shout out the lines, 'You're Black! You're poor! You're a woman! You're ugly! You're nothin' at all!' next and then raise his hand up and come toward her about to hit her like when Celie finally leaves Mister . . . Hmmm, this gives me an idea.

This is Céline, my homegirl that feeds me and watches out for me—the only one that doesn't call me White woman, at least not to my face. If anyone is going to help her now it has to be me because eerily there isn't another adult soul around and no one passing by. I am strong enough to do something. I am cleaning and jerking I don't know how many pounds of iron bar when I pump my water every week, carrying water basins on my head back and forth to my house for two hours, strong from running now six miles almost every morning, go to the fields with the women from time to time, have worked my way up to one hundred pushups every day, and cycling my bicycle two hours into town every now and again. My body is sufficient enough if it has to be. Goodness knows Bogo's little, skinny behind isn't exercising anything but his hips.

Nonetheless, my body is my last resort. I'm a lover not a fighter. What will stop him the fastest? I figure putting a curse on someone and psyching them out with that is one thing American Black folks and Ivoiriens have in common or at least that's what happens in The Color Purple. Feeling the character Celie's presence, I channel the energy from the last words she ever spoke to Mister.

"Something is going to come and get you."

But, this doesn't get Bogo to take his eyes off of Céline standing in the dirt. He is ready to jump off the porch and take her at any minute. She just stands there with a look in her eyes that I cannot interpret. Is she upset? Is she getting ready to laugh? Is she waiting for him to come charge her so she can break her foot off in his ass? Is she hoping he will say just the right thing to prevent her from leaving? Standing here watching the two of them try to anticipate each other is too much. I've gotta' throw him off. From somewhere superficial and then eventually somewhere real, I make some shit up.

"If you don't leave Céline alone, something is going to happen to you." I am not dealing with so much French vocabulary, but who cares? Unintelligibility plus intensity should work to my advantage. Stiffen up, Raven. Flex your jaws. More obscure.

"It's going to come down on you," I gesture up pointing to the sky and then bring my hand down again. "You must leave her alone." He glances over at me finally and then looks back at Céline just as quickly, annoyed as if a fly just flew by his forehead. I press again.

"Like that," I say strong and stern, making a cork popping noise with my mouth to show how suddenly something is going to come down out of the air and strike him. His attention on Céline is visibly breaking. Time passes. I've forgotten that Jijina still stands there. As usual, Eliane has long since disappeared. When I meet Jijina's eyes, they cast down to the ground at a loss as to comprehend whose side she should be taking, but her body is taut with attentiveness. Should she side with Céline who is her only real caregiver, with Bogo who is her reputed parent, or me who is busy trying to put fake curses on her father?

"If you don't leave her alone . . . it's going to come down on you," I wait for a response. I can see Bogo is thinking about what he should do with Jijina standing there, the American standing over here who will surely report any negative event involving her to the Peace Corps office if she makes it out alive, and with no element of surprise that he can muster as he did the last time he snuck in on Céline through her window and struck her in the head with a log. He gets frustrated and closes his eyes.

"Toi, tu es qui?!" he spits out. He opens his eyes up again once his head lands in my direction. He is waiting for a response, and if I back down now I will be minus one to him. 'Who do I think I am?' he asks. I'm the mother fucker who's making shit up so good the both of us are starting to believe it and you're standing here asking me just like Mister, 'who you think you are?' Surely Bogo will say next, just like Mister, 'You can't curse nobody!'

"On you . . . like that . . . if you don't stop here," not taking my stare off of him and making my body rigid as I look up into the sky and back over at him. I believe it. I can feel it. Something is going to get him. No one can walk around treating people so carelessly with nothing ever happening to them. The more I speak to him and everyone remains silent, the more I believe my curse is real. I dislike him so much. He never works on a project with me, he never takes the time to have a real conversation with me, he doesn't secure my house in the beginning, he doesn't care that I was going to die the first time I got malaria upon arrival in Zragbi, he treats Céline poorly and has likely given her at least one STD, and he is never around Zragbi to truly help the hospital and pick and train his volunteers well. If this is what all Grand Types are like and how the status quo is, then Cote d'Ivoire is certainly in trouble. The social order here is second-class citizenship of women, which in the face of A.I.D.S. and all else requiring honest relationships is to this country's absolute peril. Who is anyone without mammary glands in their life?

But, Bogo's attitude, in fact, is beyond Ivoirien social order, hovering at alien status. He works here to earn a living, but he is never around. He has the title of Head Nurse for all of Zragbi, but he doesn't really care about these people. He shares his TV and his food with people but mostly when he is not around or does not have to sit or eat with them. Maybe he doesn't even think he is one of these people or even one of his own Dida people. Maybe he thinks he is special. I don't know. I just can't understand how he can take and take because he thinks he is giving so much, but never gives anything of himself from the heart.

Bogo's shoulders drop and he shifts to rest on his left hip. Céline takes this as his retreat, turns, walks away, and I go with her pretending to glance back as if looking for someone else but really making sure he does not follow behind. I want to keep up the witchcraft front so I slowly saunter away. Jijina is there at the house alone, stuck with Bogo and nothing to eat.

This is exactly the way this country has become—the people are stuck with fighting presidential candidates and not much to survive off of while government officials live royally, do as they want to do, and expect everyone else in the country to work for them amidst the chaos. How is Jijina going to survive in all of this?

21

THIS IS WHY I LOVE THE PEACE CORPS

"Hello," the Daloa doctor immediately greets in English. "Bonjour," the U.S. Embassy Lady immediately greets back in French. They smile at each other and sit down at the exact same time, eyeing each other all the while now lovers from another lifetime.

"I don't know a lot of French," she quickly pardons herself.

"I don't know a lot of English," he meets her modesty.

Am I invisible? A dance has begun and two people dancing together are better than three. I sense that more important than the money, it is an opportunity for the both of them to fumble through these languages that they do not know much of, and serendipitously they have willing partners in each other—both with the same, now-enchanting dilemma.

Maybe she isn't so mean. Maybe I just bore her. All my talk about helping the Daloa community and how great this maternal healthcare, not-for-profit business will be. All the money that will be generated. All the lives that will be saved as a result of women finally being able to afford the healthcare resources they so desperately need through a cassava-grinding machine business. Being able to give more women training in maternal healthcare. Yawn. I do apologize for not showcasing you as the star you truly are, Mrs. U.S. Embassy Lady.

I leave. They are adults. The papers, the project details, the amount needed, everything that I am supposed to prepare, I prepared, and she now holds it in her hands. She spreads it out on the table before him for the both of them to dive into, confirm, and sign.

"You two don't need me, right?"

Not that I don't want to be here, but I feel out of place. I have brought these two together and the project will certainly be done with the Daloa doctor's good spirit and fierce conviction. Based on the way he trapped me in Daloa and trusted me to start a project in the first place on hearsay about why I am here, I am not worried about sincerity. I don't even think they notice me leave and as I turn back to check, they are still smiling at each other, trying to figure out who dare speak first and in what language it will be.

I leave back to the Peace Corps office. My AOL Peace Packs Computer project money has come through and I am to pick it up at the nearest Citibank. Ow!

I don't feel comfortable bringing the computers back by myself and I know that Antoine is more skilled at organizing such adventures through his trusty team of teachers. What with the way the luggage is precariously thrown up on top of vans, I don't want to risk it or have everyone know I'm transporting computers by myself.

I do get the cash alone, however. I find the one Citibank in Abidjan. I walk in with my check from AOL for $5,000. The bank clerks call me back into a side room to count out all of the money in front of me. $5,000 in cash is not only a lot to be walking around with in the States but an unbelievable amount in Cote d'Ivoire. Five thousand dollars times the current 600 CFA exchange rate yields 3,000,000 CFA. Céline often speaks about wanting to win the millionaire lottery in Cote d'Ivoire so that she can build houses for her family and buy land and on and on. CFA millions she means, and that's exactly what I have in my backpack. Enough to buy a few houses. I'm not worried, but I do get glances from the cashiers—not so much at the amount but at me stuffing it all in my backpack.

I think this is why I love the Peace Corps. Young people helping regular people in a simplified but impactful way—all based on trust.

"The CFA franc is worthless. It has always been pegged to the French Franc and now to the Euro," commences a conversation I have with an Ivoirien working at an American bank years later.

"What does that mean 'pegged' to the Euro?"

"That means that our currency is not recognized worldwide."

"What?"

"Anytime you go to the BCEAO bank in Cote d'Ivoire and try to exchange CFA for dollars, your CFA must first buy Euro, and then your Euro buys your dollars. Cote d'Ivoire is not allowed to exchange its money on its own. This goes the same for any Francophone countries here who use CFA.

"I can go on for hours showing you how Cote d'Ivoire is not anywhere near independent. France speaks for all former French colonies at United Nations assemblies."

"They don't even let African countries come to the assemblies?"

"Yes, they allow representatives to come from each of France's former colonies, but when it's time to speak on any issue, France does all of the talking at the microphone. This is where we are today. We are not free. We are still giving all we have to France and now all of Europe since the Euro is increasingly becoming the sole means of money exchange there. Cote d'Ivoire's fiscal policy is France's fiscal policy."

"Antoine, we got the money from AOL," I communicate calmly to see if the effect of the information alone will spark a reaction beyond the scream I stifle inside.

"What?"

"Yes," I reply to what I think is a 'what' of disbelief. But, no. He doesn't understand me.

"What did you say? I don't understand."

"AOL. A-O-L . . ." I enunciate slowly and before I can even finish the sentence, Antoine speaks.

"AOL. Ooooh. What did they do?" Ugh. I'm speaking plainly and he still does not get it. He cannot believe it so his mind will not accept the information.

"Antoine!" I finally yell and then quiet down as people look up around us. "The $5,000 for the two school computers, internet access for the school, printer, and other supplies . . . AOL gave us the money."

"They did? How much?"

"Je t'ai dit . . ." I start again loudly and some kids at the school whirl around momentarily until Antoine gives them a look. I continue again, "I told you, $5,000."

"Five thousand dollars? Where is it?"

"At my house." No response except for eyes looking in the direction of where I live.

"Listen, I don't want to get the computers alone so can you come to Abidjan?"

"Okay."

Antoine and I plan to go down to Abidjan next week. I am leaving soon. The U.S. Embassy money has been confirmed and come in as well and the doctor and women in the city are starting their project very happily. Everything is happening all at once.

In these last couple of months ending my stay in Cote d'Ivoire, it feels like I am going to Abidjan at least three times a month. We buy the computers together with two other Zragbi schoolteachers. Antoine is not there, but he meets the computers at the Daloa gare for the last leg of the trip to make sure they get up to their final destination.

Technology is something that I have truly forgotten exists while in Cote d'Ivoire. Not because there is none here but because Peace Corps Volunteers are steered toward independence by any means necessary; be it taking care of ourselves out on site, with transportation, or freedom from technology. This often means resourcefulness without phones, computers, cameras, and so forth. You don't need technology to forge lasting connections with people. You just need a good and tenacious spirit.

I try to use my camera, but that is taboo with the Bèté. The older ones believe taking a picture of them is taking some of their spirit, something that will weaken them. I try to take pictures of the less traditional Bèté in the village, but oddly enough the pictures never come out and that's exactly what they say happens.

"The spirits around us will block it," the Bèté say.

I can never anticipate whether the attention I get will be negative, offensive, or kind so the day I leave, I don't tell anyone. Well, I tell Céline. I don't think anyone else cares. It takes me so long to get money approved to finally get projects actualized, with all of the coup d'état false alarms and 9/11 sapping U.S. funds—I would have the same disbelief of a volunteer's purpose here if I were from this country, too.

No need for me to go parading around announcing that I have done some meaningful projects. I'm just going to sneak out. My name, Pahdré, says it all—I did what I came to do once I figured out what that was—help people. I don't lose sight of the objective in the face of so many cultural differences. I don't ET. I don't go crazy. I don't die from any disease. What little I am able to leave— the scholarships, the latrines, the computers, and the NGO/business funding—will hopefully keep them from second-guessing the next volunteer after me the way I was second-guessed. But, still, it all has made me a stronger person. I produced. I survived. Better late than never. Some Peace Corps volunteers spend two years doing absolutely nothing at their site although the cultural exchange, friendships formed, and languages learned are invaluable. Let the completion of all of my projects be my last positive memory I leave them with.

"Pahdré?!" So many kids and neighbors crowd around my porch. Word that I am leaving has flown around the village. I try to creep out, but I'm surrounded.

"Yes?" I play innocent.

"You're leaving?" my rear neighbor, Grand Momma—who once sent her grandson wobbling around to wake me, the one who warned me in the fields not to drink, the one who has always been nice to me, greets me whenever she sees me, and who looks like an older cousin of mine who used to take care of me when I was little—she stands here smiling at me not allowing me to leave. Tens of kids suddenly gather around her as well.

"Yes," I am so ready to bust out of here. My other volunteer friends have come to pick me up and whisk me away.

"Oh, Paaah-dréééé. Why?" Why? Such a simple question, but responding that I am going home feels like a heavily empty answer. I didn't know why I came here and I don't know how I got here. To this point. Seeing her smiling face as I leave and the questions in all of the children's eyes lets me know that this whole stressful experience is worth it. This is what Peace Corps is all about. Taking chances, not knowing if your work is going to amount to anything but going through it anyway, searching for more than acceptance or gratitude but finding extra satisfaction if you do happen to get either, and developing who you are and who you want to be for yourself. Those things are never easy no matter where you are in the world.

You are either sick, misunderstood because you are still learning the language(s), trying to get a project going that seems like it will never happen, or trying to represent well your country, your culture, your subculture, your family, and yourself at every single moment with every single interaction. They may never meet another American again.

Who you are alone as a Peace Corps Volunteer may end up representing America for all of the people you meet during your service. Yikes. I am ready to finally go, but the sweet conversation lingers as I have not yet answered the question and my Grand Momma still wants to know the answer.

"Why, Pahdré? Stay here with us." This makes me want to stay. A complete turn. No one here has ever spoken so sweetly and sincerely to me in two years. If I had known these projects would take so long, what could I have done differently to prove why I'm here and to gain respect more quickly?

"I have to go back to America," and to prevent any further questioning, I add, "To see my family. It's been a while since I've seen them . . ."

Silence. A sad smile forms on her face and all of the children around her from ages five to fifteen stand there looking at me, confused and with long faces because they will miss me. I feel horrible now. I am just one person and they are many. Regardless of what impression the previous volunteer left before me, how could I expect all of them to love me immediately? How can I feel any resentment for how long it took to get to this point? It has been rough, but these are people just like anywhere else and I am a foreigner to this place. If it had not been this challenge here, it would be another challenge somewhere else.

In the midst of this periodic pleading for me to stay, while I stand here on my porch facing all the confused faces and at a loss for what to say, Antoine walks up and calls me away.

"The Chiefs of the different quartiers have come to see the computers."

"There is a Chief for every quartier?" I had no idea.

"Well, there is only one for the village per say, but there is also one for every ethnicity." We get to the computer room with newly plastered walls and sturdy, new, metal doors that I know AOL didn't pay for.

"Where did these doors come from?"

"The Italians."

"The Italians?" What Italians? Ooooooooh. I've seen Italians come to the Daloa region before. "Where are they? Are they here? How did you apply?"

"When someone tells me to do something, I just do it." Whatever opportunities there are, Antoine seizes and seizes well. No one will be getting in to get these computers. Or, at least not anyone from Zragbi as stealing is so frowned upon here to the extent of expulsion from the village. Stealing a computer? I can't imagine what the punishment would be. Nothing could be worse than being kicked out of your own village, not even death, I think. Plus, the villages are so isolated and unique in each one that it would be hard to find another one that speaks your dialect or your language.

Antoine and I step into the computer room at the same time. There are other teachers already there explaining to all of the Chiefs. Two of them wear long robes with long white beards and small, cylindrical hats.

"These computers have many functions. You can create documents. You can go on the Internet and look for information. You can play media. You can print and fax and even make calls with these computers," the principal goes on, pushing up the bridge of his glasses every ten seconds, recalling every important point.

I kneel down next to one gentleman who Antoine has introduced to me as a Chief on the other side of the village. He is Muslim, but I know not what ethnicity. The amazement he shows at every single syllable the principal speaks—you'd think he found a ten-ton, gold nugget. All the visitors are blown away.

"It can do all that?" Céline says in disbelief as she peeks her head in the door.

"Pahdré," Antoine calls to me. "Don't kneel there. Don't stand next to the computers. They don't like that." Don't stand next to the computers?! But, Pahdré, one I am leaving today, two I am leaving today, and three I am not familiar with all Zragbi Muslim attitudes toward women. I just know that they tend to have multiple wives as opposed to the other ethnicities in Zragbi and tend to prefer their women covered—anything from moderately to extremely.

So, with all of that quickly flashing before my eyes, in what needs to be two seconds as Antoine is urging me to move away from the computers, I get up in my little getup, which does little to distinguish me as American and exempt from such rules, and walk out of the room. I cannot control everything and everyone. I can only control myself.

Besides, stepping outside of the computer room door, what better awaits me? Thirty smiling faces of volunteers and children clamoring to see the computer room and excited to see me emerge just the same.

"Pahdré!" The children yell my name. Yes, I am Pahdré. Antoine resurfaces to take a volunteer picture as the kids jump and shout to be included.

From the moment I leave my house for the last time up until now, this has all turned out to be a stall. Antoine beckons once again. We walk beyond the school right behind it in the area that is Antoine's backyard. Several long tables have been set up and connected in a rectangular shape.

"Pahdré!" the main Chief immediately greets me.

"Pahdré! Aiyoooo!" A Bèté teacher salutes.

"Pahdré, Bonjour!" the Sage Femme is there too.

Everyone is here, in fact. The Chief and his advisers, a few of the oldest teachers, Antoine, people from the hospital, and other Grand Types are all here around the tables. A meal has been made rapid fire for all of us. No one knew I was leaving because I hadn't told anyone. Céline knew that I was leaving this week, but I had not given specifics.

We sit and we sit and we sit. Some of the volunteers sit down to eat as well. Some walk off around the village as if every village where there is another Peace Corps volunteer is their own. I sometimes feel the same.

Finally, I figure out what we are waiting for—Bogo. But, by the time he shows up, we already give in to eating so as not to make the food cold. I do at least.

"Pahdré, you should eat," says the Chief.

"Pahdré, you are leaving today?" Bogo appears suddenly.

"Yes." I look at him blankly and continue to eat.

"But, who is going to take all of your things to Abidjan?" he asks with a smile on his face.

"I already took my things two weeks ago and gave my other things to the kids and neighbors." No expression shows on my face, and I go on to put another hand tip full of futu banane and peanut sauce into my mouth. Got you!

Bogo does not sit down to eat. He actually shows disheartenment. He scratches his head, turns his body this way and that, not making direct eye contact with anyone, and then suddenly speaks to everyone and no one.

"We could have used those computers at the hospital," he gripes. I didn't even know he knew about the computers or cared. Céline is my homologue, not him. At Bogo's temper tantrum, lips smack, grunts are heard, bodies shift in their seats, and then finally the principal speaks.

"Don't be like that."

Bogo is angry because he is left without any devices. Céline is not around although I'm sure her eyes watch the spectacle from somewhere, either that or she has a child standing around to witness it for her. The Sage Femme doesn't even blink at his comment. No one likes Bogo and in this moment it is more than evident. The predominant silence is resistance in fact. No way is the school going to let the hospital get the computers and if they are, the Chief will say something right now. Bogo walks off.

"I'm leaving on a JET plane. Don't know when I'll be back again" are the words I sing as the van pulls off and the children are frozen with nothing to say. J.E.T. Program that is—between the back and forths to Abidjan and even the States, I manage to apply to teach in Japan to freshen up my Japanese and am accepted.

Céline is so pitiful, resigned in fact. I have helped her apply for a passport so that she will at least be able to visit me in America. A day later, she comes to see me off at Socodi Mall in Abidjan, and I give her all the money I have left on me and keep what I need to leave. If I end up needing anything, I know that I can ask another volunteer. What I do not know, however, is that this is the last time I will ever see Céline.

22

I SEE THE SKY IN MUDDY WATER

T he third time I see the mangoes ripen.

"Are you feeling good today?" Dr. Ama begins in cheerful smile mode.

"Yes," happy to say. This is the final medical examination before COS. COS means Close of Service, which will be in Grand Bassam. The lovely Grand Bassam has a hotel, conference rooms, and a nice beach near Abidjan.

"It saved us you know."

"What did?"

"Malaria," Dr. Ama admits in a voice quieter than before. My mouth shapes into an 'o' of surprise, but no sound comes out. I see this is not a subject on which she wishes to speak loudly.

"Malaria is Africa's weapon against the White man. It saved us. It kept West Africa from becoming a South Africa."

Seeing the small numbers left around the table in the conference room, I feel devastation. Very few of us have made it. We go from twenty-three volunteers to eight in two years. One is gored by a bull, one gets E. coli, several people Early Terminate when given the option during the coup d'états by either going home or switching to another Peace Corps country, one hadn't even shown up to the plane in Pennsylvania, one had her house burned down, one had to leave her village due to poor indiscretion, and still others just decide to quit because they can't take it anymore for whatever other reasons there may be.

Maybe everyone who stays, stays for different reasons, but none of us really want to quit. Whether we succeed in doing a lot of projects in our village or barely learning any language at all, we learn a lot about ourselves and at least warn Ivoiriens of Americans. Hah.

The experience calls you whether you respond or not. You know rising to the occasion will make you better. Everything is downhill from here if you never feel challenged this way again—to take a stand for what you believe in and be pulled between the way you are used to living and the new ways to which you are exposed that give you new ideas about how you might now want to shape your life.

You may succeed at staying, but when you leave, even if you achieve twenty projects here, you are still somehow making your life easier by going back to your own country. Ivoiriens will continue to struggle when you're gone. It's not your responsibility to fix the wounds of colonialism, selfish economic policy and politics, and human atrocities toward other humans in general, but you realize that you will always be part of the solution because you are aware of the problems having lived here and seen life through the Ivoirien point of view. Once you are aware, you have to do something. Doing nothing is worse than messing up with good intentions.

Feel sorry for me. A millionaire is not rare, nor is finding people who are suffering. It's finding people who care for others just for the sake of it that is hard to find. There is no evolution in awareness without action. There is no legacy in simply now knowing everything that's going on in the world around you. You are no different than an animal if all you do is survive and don't seek to naturally strengthen everyone and everything you come into contact with.

The old Abidjan airport has disappeared and there is a brand new, bigger one in its place. Magic. It's April 2002 and I'm leaving now. Civil war breaks out soon hereafter and all of the volunteer groups that come after mine have to be evacuated from Cote d'Ivoire and Peace Corps Cote d'Ivoire shuts done indefinitely. I guess it really is a civil war, but my personal experience was only that of petty grievances between one ethnicity and another, feeling powerless, and needing to point blame to understand why life in Cote d'Ivoire is so hard for everyday Ivoiriens. The French way leaves nothing for Ivoiriens but an extreme awareness of Ivoirien ethnic differences and a hunger for a type of power that cannot bring the country together.

Guéï is assassinated September 2002, five months after I leave and two months after I am already long gone in Japan teaching English. President Laurent Gbagbo has been on trial in European courts as of 2013—the first trial of its kind in African presidential history. The international community cannot expect a person growing up in an oppressed society to not then oppress someone else since that is the only nurturing they know in their lifetime. This is especially a twisted expectation when you are part of the international community that is responsible for the oppression.

Loss of lives is heavy in Cote d'Ivoire. Every time I call Cote d'Ivoire or someone in Cote d'Ivoire calls me, I hear news of death. It seems like someone I know from Zragbi is dying every month. If at least one out of one thousand people in your town died every month, what would you do?

During my time in Cote d'Ivoire, it is reported that seventy percent of all A.I.D.S. cases are teachers and that they are infecting their students. The school principal died of unknown causes after I left as well.

"Pahdré, are you okay?"

"Yes, are you okay, too?" Silence over the phone from America to Cote d'Ivoire in 2008. We really have very little to talk about

and very little in common. Our in-person conversations before
sprang out of some immediate need for explanation that I had.
What kind of meat is this? What language is that? What did he
say? Where are you going?

"Are you okay over there? Where are you now?"

"Yes, everything is okay here. I'm in New Jersey. It's in the
northeast of America."

"Uuuuuuh," Céline responds in understanding.

"And, over there in Zragbi?"

"Bogo is dead," replies Céline solemnly and in as plain a manner
as possible.

I feel badly. I had never liked him, but then again I never understood him. More silence follows. I don't know what to say. The
only thing that makes any sense to me is that Bogo died from
A.I.D.S. He had certainly given Céline an STD that 'itches' as she
complained. Céline tells me, too, that the woman he got pregnant
in Daloa eventually dies after Bogo as well.

"It's all sorcery," says Céline. Come on, Céline. You're in the
health profession. You know better than that.

Antoine, the teacher, later writes me with news that Bogo dies
from insuffisance rénale and Céline, mal à la gorge. Yes, Céline
dies, too. I find no point in translating their illnesses because it
doesn't make it any clearer to me. People who were once so full of
life are suddenly dead. These two were young people in their forties
and fifties and they worked every day of their lives and they ate
well every day. They were health professionals for goodness sake.

The only explanation that makes sense to me, given all of the
facts, is that Bogo died of A.I.D.S. and Céline took many more
years because her immune system was stronger. She took care of
herself every day. I often watched her sit and eat whole cloves of
garlic one after the other. Not like that is the cure for A.I.D.S., but
the point is that she never waited even a second to take care of herself when she didn't feel right. Everyone who had sex with Bogo is
now dead. What do you think?

People in Zragbi don't really understand how something as simple as diarrhea, renal failure, or a throat infection killing you can

be indirect symptoms of A.I.D.S., indirect symptoms of their immune system failing because of H.I.V.

I tried to get her a passport, but she never followed through. It cost 20,000 CFA. Two months' work for her. I paid for it but directly to her. She said that she had misspelled her own mother's name and so when she finally went to pick it up she discovered that they had denied her application. Where is the 20,000 CFA then? Gone.

I doubt she ever paid. I doubt she would forget how to spell her own mother's name. She would later ask me whether or not she should start the whole passport application process over again, but I had given up. I didn't feel I could trust her after that. Plus, I couldn't support her on my own. She did not speak English and she had not finished high school and I refused to see her in one of those blue-collar jobs you see non-English speaking people in, in the States. They are treated like second-class citizens.

As tough as her life was with all of the responsibilities she had, it would have definitely been better than being looked down upon in America and me not being able to do much about it because of the reality that I myself, although called White in Cote d'Ivoire, facetiously or seriously, am very much treated as Black in America.

We fell out of contact before she died and now, learning of her death, I feel responsible. If I had persisted on getting her to America, maybe she wouldn't have died from whatever she really died from. I feel sorry for myself because I could have done so much more. Why didn't I do more? I sent money every now and then, but that did not get to the core of the problems she faced.

Being above humanism is being a Peace Corps Volunteer. We have to not be so into material things but find ways to provide resources. We have to be motivated to seek out information through difficulty and get different people from different backgrounds and experiences to work together. We have to support projects that keep the community going without dividing them—making them stronger in who they are and not seeking to emulate anyone else under the guises of development. Self-sustainment is first and then they should have the choice of whether or not and how they want to enter the global world economically, socially, or otherwise.

Peace Corps is the perfect vehicle because individuals, versus larger entities, are the least likely to have motives for giving their support. There is no profit in it for volunteers besides the experience.

The departure from Cote d'Ivoire leaves me with so many images that will never leave my head.

Gas stations, empty paved roads, bowling alleys with 'New Brunswick' insignia at the end of bowling lanes in Abidjan's Hotel Ivoire—these are all remnants of a burgeoning Western copy that dies. But, there was something here before all of that—large African empires covering different border areas, in fact. There is not a need for development but redevelopment. No postcolonial, neocolonialistic farce of a said independent nation but rather a new Cote d'Ivoire, not being controlled by the whims of foreign corporate entities or other large institutions—allowed to finally be what it wants to be, realizing that it has its own resources and it just needs to take them back.

All I can give them are bits and pieces of what I was taught means progress. But, true progress is maintaining your cultural, linguistic, social, and political identity in a way that can be uniquely shared with the world. In a way that people can appreciate your differences instead of complaining about aspects that are not similar to their own. Not throwing away your own culture to imitate the other cultures forced upon you but strong in being yourself without having to force that self on other nations. The same way that an actual family of individuals is able to live together, grow together, and be distinct individuals yet support each other as brothers and sisters.

There are very few countries not currently afflicted by war. With all of the civil and political unrest and coup d'états happening, how can any of it be ascribed to cultural deficiencies when it's everywhere and conflict has been the way of all people for thousands of years?

My struggles with skin color and determination to stay in Cote d'Ivoire through the entire two years and three months of service make me realize that this is also what Cote d'Ivoire must do. Except for an exchange of information and resources, Ivoiriens must resist all outside definitions of who they are. If I had allowed Ivoiriens to define me, where would it have ended? Would I be calling myself White? Would I even be calling myself, based on however I am perceived, in whichever country I choose to go? What does the future hold for Cote d'Ivoire? Will we stop seeing them as tribes in the old sense of the word and start understanding that African countries are made up of numerous distinct and very real ethnicities, which, aside from having different cultures, music, religions, ways of dress, and so on, don't even speak the same languages?

What does all of this so-called advancement mean if we don't survive it? Ten percent of the world's population is doing little more than creating ninety percent of the world's garbage, and over-industrialization is destroying the ozone. What can we really point to, to say that America, for example, is any fundamentally better than Cote d'Ivoire?

In a baidjan from Zragbi one morning, I sit here in the back of the van, all the way in the back, waaaay back there in the farthest left-side corner—the worst seat in the entire vehicle. One leg is pushed up to my chest, my chest slumps up against that leg with my chin drooping over the knee, and my other leg lays down snug between two bags that do not belong to me. The leather on the seat encases my shin making the sweat accumulate there and not leave. I am unavoidably pushed up against the window which is sealed shut and cannot be opened because it has been sewn with the other so that neither one of them fall out of the frame.

I peer through that glass as dull as it is with scratches obscuring the outside. From my cut-off point of view, just eye level with the bottom of the glass, I am barely able to look down through it. But, I do see it. I see it as we pass. An undisturbed puddle of muddy water. And, in that clear reflection, I see the sky in it. I see that the sun is shining beautifully when I look up to confirm it's actually there and not just some vision. It hits me in the eye full blast and in that moment I realize I am finally comfortable, not annoyed at all. I no longer resist what I do not understand. I accept it and it therefore makes me stronger. I do not try to control or ignore the view or the people in the situation but adapt to them. It doesn't always mean that you give in but that you develop appreciation before judgment. That which I do not think is possible always becomes possible when I let go of what I think I know and give in to the unknown. I owe all I am to my experiences—to my knowledge and my lack thereof. I am not made at birth.

In this moment of choosing to appreciate the sun washing down over me, I sense my humanity with my individual identity all at once. That I can only get as far as I am willing to see or experience. I could just look down and see dirty water or curse an uncomfortable traveling situation, but being able to have the simple realization that I am more than what I've been given—that I am my choices—is what helps me know exactly who I am and what my capabilities are. I am what I choose to see.

REVIEW NOW

http://booksbyraven.com/reviews/

CONNECT

Facebook http://www.facebook.com/pageofraven
Pinterest http://www.pinterest.com/booksbyraven
Twitter http://www.twitter.com/Ivoirian2012
Raven's App http://www.booksbyraven.com/app/
Google+   A Happy Raven Moore

CPSIA information can be obtained at www.ICGtesting.com
Printed in the USA
BVOW04s2058050514

352644BV00007B/56/P

9 780989 726603